THE RHETORIC OF OPERATION RESCUE

THE RHETORIC OF OPERATION RESCUE

Projecting the Christian Pro-Life Message

Mark Allan Steiner

T & T Clark
New York London

Copyright © 2006 by Mark Allan Steiner

All rights reserved. No part of this book may be reproduced, stored in a retrieval system, or transmitted in any form or by any means, electronic, mechanical, including photocopying, recording, or otherwise, without the written permission of the publisher, T & T Clark International.

T & T Clark International, 80 Maiden Lane, New York, NY 10038
T & T Clark International, The Tower Building, 11 York Road, London SE1 7NX
T & T Clark International is a Continuum imprint.

Cover design by Wesley Hoke

Library of Congress Cataloging-in-Publication Data

Steiner, Mark Allan.
  The rhetoric of Operation Rescue: projecting the Christian pro-life message / Mark Allan Steiner.
    p. cm.
  Includes index.
  ISBN 0-567-02562-4 (hardcover) — ISBN 0-567-02572-1 (pbk.)
  1. Operation Rescue (Organization) 2. Pro-life movement—United States. 3. Christian conservatism—United States. 4. Rhetoric—Political aspects—United States. 5. Rhetoric—Religious aspects—Christianity. I. Title.
  HQ767.25.S74 2006
  261.8'36—dc22
          2006001130

Printed in the United States of America

06 07 08 09 10   10 9 8 7 6 5 4 3 2 1

Contents

Acknowledgments... ix
Part One: Introduction... 1
   CHAPTER ONE: Operation Rescue and Evangelical Christian Social Protest.. 2
      The Rise and Fall of Operation Rescue......................... 7
      Preview of Chapters.. 14
Part Two: Foundations.. 23
   CHAPTER TWO: Rhetoric as Evangelism.............................. 24
      Traditionally Dominant Conceptions of Rhetoric................ 26
      Beyond Traditionally Dominant Rhetorical Theory............... 28
      A Definition of Rhetoric..................................... 31
         (1) Perspective... 31
         (2) Partisan... 32
         (3) Identify... 32
         (4) Invitation/Temptation................................ 34
         (5) Imposes.. 35
         (6) Audience... 35
      Rhetoric, Theology, and Evangelical Christian Experience...... 36
   CHAPTER THREE: The Rhetorical and Theological Ancestry of
   Operation Rescue: Evangelicalism and Fundamentalism in
   Francis A. Schaeffer's *A Christian Manifesto*.................... 42
      Evangelicalism... 46
      Fundamentalism... 48
         Premillenial Dispensationalism........................... 49
         Reaction against the "Liberal" Turn in American Protestantism.. 50
         The Fundamentalist-Modernist Controversy................ 51
         Separatism... 52
      Problematic Features of Evangelicalism and Fundamentalism...... 53
         Anti-Intellectualism..................................... 53
         The Impulse to Hegemony.................................. 56

    Problematic Features in Schaeffer 59
        Anti-Intellectualism 61
        The Impulse to Hegemony 65
    Conclusion.. 67
Part Three: Representations of the Evangelical Christian Faith.......... 73
    CHAPTER FOUR: Abortion as an Acute Failure of the Christian Community:
    Representations of History in the Rhetoric of Operation Rescue 74
        History as Rhetoric...................................... 77
        The Controversy of Abortion History 78
            Abortion History as Moral: Glessner.................... 78
            Abortion History as Political: Luker.................... 81
        Operation Rescue and Abortion History 84
            Discontinuity of the *Roe v. Wade* Decision 84
            Moral Condition of the United States 86
            Proper Role of the Christian Community 88
        Conclusion.. 92
    CHAPTER FIVE: "A Clear Trumpet Has Been Sounded":
    The Rhetoric of Operation Rescue as Theological.................... 96
        The Theology of Operation Rescue 98
            The Plainness of Scripture............................ 98
            The Primacy of Abortion 104
            Testimony and the Insularity of "Conversion" 107
        Conclusion.. 109
    CHAPTER SIX: The Rhetorical Foundations of Pro-Life Violence:
    (Mis)representation in the Rhetoric of Operation Rescue............ 112
        Rhetoric and Representation............................... 115
        Representative Theme #1: Holy War 117
            Characterization of Scene 119
            Characterization of Those Opposed to Protestors.............. 120
            Characterization of Protestors 121
        Representative Theme #2: Identification with the Unborn 123
            In Obedience...................................... 125
            In Suffering 125
            In Experience of God's Blessing 126
        Calcified Oversimplification: The Rhetoric of Paul Hill........... 128
            Manifestations of the Holy War (Mis)representation 128
            Manifestations of Reductionistic Focus on the Unborn 131
            Manifestations of Calcified Rigidity...................... 132
        Conclusion.. 133

CONTENTS

Part Four: Public Dialogue 139
   CHAPTER SEVEN: Counter-Characterizations of Operation Rescue:
   Oppositional Rhetoric, 1988–91 140
      Rhetoric and Public Vocabulary 143
      Rhetoric and Delegitimizing Discourse 145
      Pro-Choice Delegitimizing Discourse 146
         Dissociation of Operation Rescue and the Civil Rights Movement .. 146
         Operation Rescue Activists as Fanatics 148
         Operation Rescue Activists as Violent 153
      Conclusion 154
   CHAPTER EIGHT: The Limits of Radical Rhetoric: Portraits of the Public
   in the Rhetoric of Operation Rescue 159
      Portraits of the Public 163
         The Public Is Virtuous but Deceived 163
         The Public Is Complicitous in the Evil of Abortion 166
      Public "Passivity" and the Self-Evident Nature of Truth 168
      Operation Rescue and Darseyan "Radical Rhetoric" 172
      Conclusion 176
   CHAPTER NINE: Operation Rescue's Bitter Rhetorical Harvest: Pro-Choice
   Vocabulary as Public Lexicon in the 1993 United States Senate Hearing on
   the Freedom of Access to Clinic Entrances Act 180
      Angling toward the FACE Act: Delegitimizing Images of
      Pro-Life Activists 182
      The May 12, 1993, Senate Hearing 184
      Implications 194

Part Five: Conclusion 199
   CHAPTER TEN: The Lessons of Operation Rescue 200
      Operation Rescue's Representations of the Evangelical Faith 202
      Operation Rescue and Public Dialogue 207
      Evangelical Religion, Politics, and Public Discourse:
      Toward a "Rhetorical" Corrective 210
Index 222

Acknowledgments

In the course of this project, I have accumulated numerous debts both professional and personal. I have greatly appreciated the faculty members throughout my graduate studies who have sharpened my thinking concerning the ideas articulated in this book, particularly (but not limited to) Jim Andrews, Marty Medhurst, Bob Ivie, and Mike Hogan.

This book has benefited more directly from friends and colleagues who read drafts of this manuscript in its various incarnations and offered helpful feedback, particularly Nate Baxter, Mike Farley, Dan Earhart, Barbara Hampton, and Denise Bostdorff.

Henry Carrigan at T & T Clark took interest in this study and patiently guided it through the publication process. Amy Wagner, also at T & T Clark, provided much of the logistical help in the latter phases of this process.

Eilene Wollslager, my research assistant at Regent University, graciously prepared the bulk of the index.

Finally, my profound thanks goes to my wife, Beth, who over the past ten years has been incredibly supportive of my professional life, and has consistently brought levity, sanity, and balance to my personal life.

Part One

Introduction

1

OPERATION RESCUE AND EVANGELICAL CHRISTIAN SOCIAL PROTEST

Only by looking at politics through the lens of faith, rather than faith through the lens of politics, will we be able to comprehend the nature and resilience (and the sensible limits) of the involvement of overtly religious organizations and individuals in our public life.

—Stephen L. Carter[1]

Like Yale law professor Stephen L. Carter's book *God's Name in Vain*, this is a book that addresses the wrongs and rights of religious involvement—specifically evangelical Christian involvement—in American public life, particularly politics. Also like Carter's book, this book falls within a particular line of thinking about the relationship between religion and American public life, a line of thinking notably expressed in Richard John Neuhaus's *The Naked Public Square*, Os Guinness's *The American Hour*, and Cal Thomas and Ed Dobson's somewhat more recent book, *Blinded by Might*.[2]

These authors have striven to offer a balanced, constructive view of this relationship. These authors have in various ways critiqued as counterproductive the overtly political activism of the "Christian Right." On the other hand, these authors recognize and affirm a significant role for the involvement of religious voices in American public dialogue.

Unlike these authors, I am taking a more sharply focused and academic approach. Instead of engaging more generally the issues of evangelical Christian political involvement and the nature of public discourse, I am primarily offering a case study of an important evangelical Christian social protest group. In developing this case study—operating from the scholarly tradition of rhetorical studies—I aim to provide more nuance to the critiques offered by these and other authors. This is important, I believe, because a more sophisticated and multifaceted assessment is a necessary and valuable first step in conceptualizing a meaningful corrective to this important and complicated problem. My hope in writing this book is to use the insights of my own scholarly discipline to add something new to this overall assessment.

The nature and importance of the relationship between religion and public life can be brought into clearer view by asking some questions. Given the likely truth that the vast majority of the social and political activism of the Christian Right has been undertaken in good faith and with desires to honor God and to make the world a better place, how is it that this activism as a whole has been counterproductive at best and violent at worst? How is it that it has been easy—too easy—for academics and cultural elites to dismiss fundamentalist and conservative evangelical Christians (or even religious voices in general) as inherently inimical to civil and productive public dialogue? Why is it that the separation of church and state is so easily seen as a mechanism to protect the state from the church when, as Carter has insightfully pointed out, it is just as reasonably or more reasonably seen as a mechanism to protect the church from the state?[3] How, further, can fundamentalist and conservative evangelical Christians engage in public dialogue in a way that more fully honors the God they worship, and in a way that can make real differences in their various communities?

A more comprehensive answer to these questions presumes not only that there are wrongs as well as rights of religion in politics and culture, but also that much of what passes as religious—particularly fundamentalist and conservative evangelical—activism in our culture likely falls into the former category. Assuming that this is true, why has this happened, and what can (and should) be done?

To be sure, answers to these questions have been put forward. Thomas and Dobson have suggested that politically active conservative Christians, particularly those comprising the Christian Right, have been seduced by the temptations of political power—temptations that inherently arise when standing within the political establishment. Conservative Christians, according to Thomas and Dobson, have forgotten that their primary role is not merely to change laws and public policy, but rather to use the truth they know to engage public consciousness, promoting more fundamental changes in perspective. Conservative Christians have failed in their quest to transform American culture, they note, "not because we were wrong about our critique of culture, or because we lacked conviction, or because there were not enough of us, or because too many were lethargic and uncommitted. We failed because we were unable to redirect a nation from the top down." "Real change," they declare, "must come from the bottom up or, better yet, from the inside out."[4] Forgetting this truth, further, is a major consequence of political co-optation. "Whenever the church cozies up to political power," they observe, "it loses sight of its all-important mission to change the world from the inside-out." Instead, "we try to fill ourselves with power that belongs to the world and seek to usher in a kingdom not of this world by using tools that are of this world."[5]

Carter's critique is quite similar. "If history has taught us anything," he states, "it is that religions that fall too deeply in love with the art of politics lose their souls—very fast." This is so in part because "politics is a dirty business" that "leaves few of its participants unsullied.... When the transcendent language of faith is dragged down into the arena of democracy," therefore, "it usually winds up battered and twisted."[6]

This does not mean that those with deep religious convictions should eschew public and political involvement completely, as did American fundamentalist Christians throughout much of the twentieth century. Rather, Carter's imperative is that "religion, when it engages in the public life of the nation, must do so with some care." In particular, those with deep religious convictions—particularly fundamentalist and conservative evangelical Christians in the United States—need to make sure to maintain their collective role of "prophetic resistance." Rather than merely "gather[ing] enough votes to tell everybody else what to do," according to Carter, public religious activism needs to be consistent with the most significant public role of religion—"stand[ing] apart from politics, apart even from culture, to call us to righteousness without regard to political advantage."[7]

My goal in this book is to help explain why fundamentalist and conservative evangelical Christians have in large part missed this mark. By conducting a sustained examination of the rhetoric of pro-life social protest group Operation Rescue, a group that appealed primarily to fundamentalist and conservative evangelical Christians in the United States, I wish to complement the analyses of Neuhaus, Guinness, Thomas, Dobson, and Carter by offering a somewhat different but related critique of contemporary evangelicalism and fundamentalism.

In a book examining the role of television in contemporary American politics, political communication scholar Roderick Hart claims, "it is how we talk about politics that has let us down."[8] In my view, likewise, it is how fundamentalist and conservative evangelical Christians *talk* about their faith—especially about how that faith is to be brought to bear in public life—that has let them down. In other words, the problems with conservative Christian political activism identified by the above authors can be seen at least in part as a *rhetorical* problem. Such a view affirms that rhetoric—the language and symbols that human beings use to influence others—both is fundamental to the human condition and has considerable power.[9]

Operation Rescue serves as an opportune case study for me to develop this overall claim. The group, prominent between 1988 and 1992, was chiefly responsible for the incorporation of confrontational social protest as an accepted strategy of the general pro-life movement. With its mass blockades of clinics where abortions are performed, Operation Rescue brought the abortion controversy to a new level of contention. Operation Rescue, writes anthropologist Faye Ginsburg, "offered a new vision and strategy to a battle-worn pro-life movement that had achieved few of its specific goals through more moderate methods." The organization, she continues, "had a catalytic effect on a new generation of activists, part of a rising tide of conservative Christian activism."[10] In a relatively recent history of the militant wing of the pro-life movement, journalists James Risen and Judy L. Thomas declare, "Operation Rescue turned what had been a small, ragtag group of easily ignored protesters into a genuine movement, an aggressive national campaign that put the anti-abortion cause back onto America's Page One. . . . Operation Rescue," they continue, "eventually became the biggest social protest movement since the antiwar and civil rights campaigns of the 1960s."[11]

Operation Rescue's historical prominence, as well as its incorporation of confrontational social protest into the pro-life movement, certainly makes the group worthy of study by scholars in a variety of disciplines. My interest in Operation Rescue, however, relates more to how the group's rhetoric was able to shape its activists' motivation and sense of identity. As Risen and Thomas have pointed out, the perspectives of fundamentalist and conservative evangelical Christianity are central to the group's rhetoric. Operation Rescue founder Randall Terry, they write, "succeeded where others failed by following a simple yet powerful strategy. He focused his recruiting efforts almost exclusively on fundamentalist churches, particularly on the pastors of those churches." In order to "transform 'rescue' from a movement that appealed only to handfuls of feverish Catholics . . . into something that would draw thousands of fundamentalists out of their church pews," Terry "chang[ed] the rhetoric in ways that few outsiders ever detected . . .

win[ning] over his fellow Evangelicals by translating anti-abortion protest into their own Bible-based language of judgment and wrath."[12] In this sort of rhetoric can be found not only the key to the group's initial success and later failure, but also an important indicator of what is wrong with the contemporary participation of fundamentalist and conservative evangelical Christians in public dialogue.

In this book, a sustained examination of the rhetoric of Operation Rescue, I claim that this rhetoric most usefully can be seen primarily within the context of larger rhetorical struggles within the evangelical Christian tradition. These historical and contemporary rhetorical struggles relate to both (1) how, as evangelicals, to utilize the symbolic resources of the faith tradition as what noted rhetorician and literary critic Kenneth Burke called "equipment for living,"[13] and (2) how, on the personal and organizational levels, to act upon evangelical faith commitments to engage public culture and to engage in public dialogue.

On both of these counts, I judge the rhetoric of Operation Rescue to be inadequate, even dangerous. Their rhetoric, I will argue in this book, promotes an at best deficient—and at worst dangerous—vision of what the Christian faith does mean and should mean for evangelicals. Further, the rhetoric of Operation Rescue promotes attitudes toward public engagement (political activism, lobbying, public statements, and so on) that are hindering or even inimical to civil and productive public discourse—the type of discourse that would allow for diversity and pluralism in public dialogue, while also minimizing the temptations to incivility, coercion, and violence.

I must add, however, that these rhetorical deficiencies of Operation Rescue should not be judged to be the sole responsibility of the group's rhetors, as similar deficiencies can be observed throughout the history of the evangelical Christian tradition. On the other hand, neither should the blame rest with the evangelical faith tradition itself (nor with religious expression more generally) since, I believe, a meaningful corrective can be drawn from the symbolic resources of that same faith tradition. Indeed, gaining the ability to articulate such a meaningful corrective—for these rhetorical deficiencies and for the larger problems concerning the relationships among religion, politics, and public expression—is an important reason to try to understand better, with a sufficient degree of complexity and nuance, what is wrong.

Such is the plan of this book. First, though, I close this introductory chapter by providing a historical overview of Operation Rescue and a logistical overview of this book's chapters.

The Rise and Fall of Operation Rescue

According to Randall Terry's wife, Cindy, Terry first conceived of Operation Rescue in 1983. During a Wednesday night prayer meeting at their church, he envisioned "being in front of abortion mills across the country and just shutting them down, hundreds of thousands of people just shutting them down all over the country."[14] It was not until 1986, however, that Terry led his first "rescue" at Southern Tier Women's Center in Binghamton, New York. He and six others locked themselves inside the clinic and were arrested for criminal trespass; Terry was then jailed after refusing to pay the fine.[15]

To be sure, the "sit-in" approach to pro-life social protest did not originate with Randall Terry. For this, Risen and Thomas credit Catholic protester John O'Keefe, who staged his first protest in 1975.[16] O'Keefe and others organized a series of "sit-ins" prior to the emergence of Operation Rescue, but these were usually small and failed to attract any sort of sustained attention.[17] "Terry," by contrast, "revolutionized rescue by making it big."[18]

Though done on a significantly larger scale, the style of protest is formally (if not ideologically) similar to the "sit-ins" employed in the 1960s and modeled by O'Keefe. "A rescue mission," writes Terry in describing his group's style of protest, "happens when one or two, or a group of twenty or a hundred or five hundred or more people go to an abortion clinic and either walk inside to the waiting room, offering an alternative to the mothers, or sit around the door of the abortion clinic before it opens to prevent the slaughter of innocent lives."[19]

Operation Rescue advocated the necessity of going beyond conventional legal and political means to end legalized abortion, and embracing a more confrontational approach. "I am convinced," Terry declared, "that the American people will begin to take the pro-life movement seriously when they see good, decent citizens peacefully sitting around abortion mills, risking arrest and prosecution as Martin Luther King Jr. did."[20]

In this respect, the linking of Operation Rescue with past movements involving "civil disobedience" was crucial. "Now, with 70 ministers leading the way," commented Cal Thomas upon the "Pastor's Rescue" that took place during the 1991 "Summer of Mercy" campaign, "whole congregations may be emboldened to follow." "If that happens," he continued, "we've seen the beginning of what could mirror the civil rights movement of the '60s, when ministers sat in and blockaded on behalf of another oppressed minority and participated in a revolution that produced laws protecting blacks against racial discrimination."[21]

Nor was this linkage lost on others who supported Operation Rescue. Other writers (including Terry), in arguing for the legitimacy of Operation Rescue's civil disobedience, labored to establish commonality between Operation Rescue and important, legitimating historical phenomena. Such phenomena include the work of the abolitionists and those who operated the "Underground Railroad" in the nineteenth century,[22] and the work of individuals, such as Corrie Ten Boom and André Trocmé, in hiding Jews from the World War II Nazi government.[23]

In part, as a means of reinforcing this linkage, Operation Rescue emphasized its commitment to nonviolence. Those participating in "rescues" typically were required to sign a pledge card that, in the context of the overall purposes and goals of Operation Rescue, explicitly proscribes violence in any form.[24] On a 1994 CNN talk show, Operation Rescue leader Flip Benham declared that "[o]ut of 75,000 arrests, Operation Rescue has not had one convicted act of violence, which makes it the most peaceful, social revolution in world's history."[25] In his book-length apologia for Operation Rescue, Randy Alcorn asserted that violence is contrary to the basic purpose of Operation Rescue activism. "There are perfectly logical and consistent reasons why we draw lines and do not use violence in rescuing," he writes. "Violence puts human life at risk, and we are to save lives not endanger them. We want to rescue victims, not create victims. . . . [W]e are intervening for the innocent, not doling out punishment on the guilty."[26]

The rhetoric of Operation Rescue frames the group's activism as much more than just nonviolent protest to effect change on an important social issue. The group's rhetoric also casts such activism as "repenting" of the collective inactivity that has left the practice of abortion unchecked, asking God for mercy on the church and on America, and, finally, saving lives. Such deeper motives tie in with tightly held religious convictions, particularly for those espousing the evangelical Christian faith. Terry nicely summed up this deeper level of motivation in an exhortation to the reader of his book. "It is important," he writes, "that you come in a spirit of humility and unity, demonstrating a 'we' mentality and not a 'me' mentality. Remember, our purpose for coming together is to repent for our inactivity on behalf of the unborn. If you're there to get a kick out of getting arrested, your motivation is seriously wrong. Our only reason for doing a rescue is to save children in obedience to God's Word."[27]

Such appeals found broad resonance, and the organization and the size of its protests grew. In 1988 Operation Rescue garnered national attention with its "Siege of Atlanta." Observe Risen and Thomas: "The enduring stereotype of the American abortion war—Evangelical fury crashing against feminist certitude—was fixed into the national consciousness by Operation Rescue's siege of Atlanta." "When Randall Terry and his fundamentalists poured into Atlanta's streets in the summer of 1988," they continue, "America discovered Operation Rescue." This completed "the sudden transformation of anti-abortion activism from a movement of scattered and easily ignored pockets of local protest into a national phenomenon." "[T]he politics of abortion," they conclude, "would never be the same."[28] By the end of the campaign, over 1,200 arrests of protesters had been made.[29]

Operation Rescue's "Summer of Mercy" campaign, held during the summer of 1991 in Wichita, Kansas, was the group's largest and arguably most pivotal. The campaign, which lasted over a month longer than initially expected, began on July 15 as a week-long series of protests designed to "win the hearts and the minds of grass-roots America."[30] By the time the final arrest was made, on August 26, there had been over 2,600 arrests of over 1,700 individuals.[31] But numbers do not tell the whole story. In their case study of the "Summer of Mercy" campaign, communication scholars John W. Bowers, Donovan J. Ochs, and Richard J. Jensen documented the escalation that took place; this included the injunction issued by federal judge Patrick Kelly, the arrests and incapacitation of Operation Rescue leaders, the presence of federal marshals, and the use of mace against protesters.[32]

Concurrent with Operation Rescue's rise to prominence were challenges and setbacks that presaged the eventual collapse of the group. One of these challenges related to vision and recruitment. Terry knew that if Operation Rescue was ultimately to succeed, the group needed to connect with the larger evangelical community nationwide. In this respect, the denunciation of Operation Rescue's tactics by Dr. Charles Stanley, a nationally prominent evangelical and arguably the most influential minister in the South, was pivotal. "The worst blow" in Operation Rescue's 1988 "Siege of Atlanta," declare Risen and Thomas, "came from 'the church.'" "Terry knew," they continue, "that if he could tap into the resources and congregations of mainline churches like the Southern Baptists, Operation Rescue could take thousands, rather than hundreds, into the streets and into the jails." Because of the implications for Operation Rescue's short-term and long-term goals, "Terry and his comrades went to great lengths to cultivate Stanley and win his support."[33]

Stanley's August 1988 leaflet "A Biblical Perspective on Civil Disobedience," distributed at his church and read from the pulpit, was devastating to Operation Rescue. Stanley went beyond a refusal to endorse Operation

Rescue, criticizing their approach to pro-life activism as unbiblical.[34] This denunciation, observed Risen and Thomas, was "a critical turning point in Operation Rescue's fortunes." "Dozens of other Protestant ministers," they continue, "followed Stanley's lead and kept their distance from Operation Rescue, and the organization never won the support of any mainline denomination."[35]

The legal pressure on Operation Rescue, meanwhile, continued to rise. Just the mounting civil judgments against the group forced Operation Rescue to close its national offices in December 1990, after which the group decentralized and re-formed as Operation Rescue National.[36]

Bowers, Ochs, and Jensen have provided an ample description of the federal government's response to the 1991 Wichita "Summer of Mercy" campaign. The federal injunctions issued by Judge Patrick Kelly, the presence of hundreds of federal marshals, and the arrests of movement leaders is summed up nicely in the authors' claim that "[t]he establishment had the power and was willing to use it to gain control of the situation."[37]

The federal government's use of power against Operation Rescue-style protests has figured prominently since the summer of 1991. In January 1994, the United States Supreme Court ruled that owners of abortion clinics can sue "rescuers" under the federal Racketeer Influenced and Corrupt Organizations (RICO) law, thus enabling victorious clinic owners to collect triple damages from protesters.[38] Later that year President Clinton signed into law the Freedom of Access to Clinic Entrances (FACE) Act, which renders a wide variety of violent and nonviolent pro-life protest, including the "rescue" tactics of Operation Rescue, a federal crime punishable by up to one year in jail and a fine of up to $10,000 for first offenses.[39] These types of legal sanctions have raised the stakes dramatically for those who would engage in "rescue" protests of the sort Operation Rescue popularized.

While the organization technically still exists under the new name "Operation Save America,"[40] a good case can be made that Operation Rescue, as an organization of pro-life social protest, is effectively dead. Risen and Thomas characterize Operation Rescue's 1991 "Summer of Mercy" campaign as the organization's "last stand."[41] While the 1991 Wichita protests did "put anti-abortion protest back into the national headlines," according to the authors, Operation Rescue simply failed to capitalize on this media attention. "Buffalo's failed 'Spring of Life' [April 1992]," in their judgment, "was followed by a string of unsuccessful Operation Rescue campaigns in cities like Baton Rouge and Houston.... Unable to keep up the momentum gained from Wichita, Operation Rescue slowly crumbled."[42]

A further measure of Operation Rescue's fall, according to Risen and Thomas, can be seen in the organization's failure to check the increasing slide of the more militant Operation Rescue activists into advocacy of violence. Following the shootings of abortion doctors that had taken place,[43] Operation Rescue leader Keith Tucci called a September 1993 meeting in an attempt "to stave off the final collapse of Operation Rescue, which by then was only a shell of its former organization." Tucci, convinced that the only way to save Operation Rescue "was to make a clean and public break with the new violent fringe," drew a line in the sand with his declaration that "anyone who refused to pledge to condemn violence would have to leave the organization." The meeting, according to Risen and Thomas, "quickly turned into a disaster for Tucci and for what remained of Operation Rescue," as many in Operation Rescue's leadership simply refused to condemn abortion-related violence.[44] In April of the following year, new Operation Rescue leader Flip Benham tried essentially the same thing, but to no avail.[45]

Indications of Operation Rescue's fall can also be seen in the organization's change in protest tactics. In 1996, for instance, it was reported that for an October protest in Indianapolis, Operation Rescue had planned not to block clinic doors, but planned instead to protest at busy street intersections with large posters of "aborted babies."[46] The fact that Operation Rescue's leadership would even consider—let alone carry out—such a fundamental alteration of their defining protest tactic suggests an at least tacit acknowledgment of failure. Further, Operation Rescue's protest tactics have also expanded to issues other than just abortion. In April 1998, Operation Rescue leader Flip Benham announced plans to protest outside Walt Disney World, in response to the theme park's annual Gay Days and Disney's promotion of homosexuality as an "alternative lifestyle."[47]

Randall Terry himself has also given up permanently on the organization and on "rescuing" as an effective pro-life strategy. According to Risen and Thomas, Terry has since acknowledged that Wichita was "Operation Rescue's last chance," and that Operation Rescue activism "was doomed after the movement failed to exploit its brief success in Wichita to win over more churches and church leaders." "We [fundamentalists] lost our nerve," they quote Terry as saying. "And the game was over. The window of opportunity was closed."[48] Terry later formally agreed never again to engage in precisely the sort of protest he championed when founding the organization. While admitting no wrongdoing, Terry agreed to the settlement in order to be dropped from the National Organization for Women class-action lawsuit against Operation Rescue and a variety of other organizations and individuals. "This is simply his way of bowing out gracefully to concentrate on his [1998] congressional campaign," his attorney remarked.[49]

For those splinter groups such as Operation Rescue West,[50] who might have any motive to carry on Operation Rescue's legacy of pro-life "civil disobedience," the legal consequences are as great as ever. Most significant in this regard is the FACE Act, which has been law since 1994. "Once FACE was the law of the land," remark Risen and Thomas, "the potential punishment for conducting a clinic blockade went from a few days in jail to years in a federal prison; 'rescue' quickly ended as a result."[51] Roger Evans, a senior Planned Parenthood official, concurred. "One of our greatest victories was having FACE enacted," he was quoted as saying. "The massive invasions of the early '90s," he added, undoubtedly referring to the "Summer of Mercy" campaign, "have largely gone away."[52] The Supreme Court, furthermore, has refused to strike down the law on constitutional grounds.[53]

In 1998 pro-life activists also suffered another crushing legal defeat. On April 20, a federal jury in Chicago convicted, under the RICO law, prominent pro-life activist Joseph Scheidler, his Chicago-based organization Pro-Life Action League, two of his associates, and Operation Rescue of conspiracy to shut down abortion clinics. As the RICO law applies if "a group is accused of committing just two illegal acts over the course of 10 years," its successful application to social protest groups raises the chilling prospect of silencing both social protest and the exercise of legitimate First Amendment rights.[54]

These events advance the rather compelling suggestion that Operation Rescue, and its particular style of pro-life social protest, is effectively dead. Even so, the group and its rhetorical practices speak to important contemporary scholarly, religious, and community issues. How, then, is the group and its rhetoric to be properly understood?

To be sure, there have been a variety of explanations. One perspective on Operation Rescue emphasizes the group's religious "fundamentalism," with that term understood broadly and quite negatively. Operation Rescue activists, according to this perspective, are best seen as intolerant and incorrigible religious crusaders who pose a significant risk to civil society.[55]

A second perspective emphasizes the political nature of the group's activism, seeing the group essentially as one segment of a virulent "Christian Right." In this view, pro-life activism, such as Operation Rescue's, functions to keep the larger political movement mobilized and galvanized, thus helping to ensure that the Christian Right maintains its influence in the Republican party.[56]

A third perspective views the group through the prisms of power and class. This perspective sees Operation Rescue not just as a manifestation of the Christian Right, but also as a manifestation of the enduring racism and sexism embedded in Western culture. The group is thus linked to white supremacy, the "backlash" against the advancements of feminism, and the resentment of egomaniacal and insecure white males.[57]

To be sure, there is a measure of truth within each of these basic perspectives on Operation Rescue. Yet it seems clear that a corrective is needed to the "progressive" ideological sensibilities that underlie each of these perspectives. Such a corrective should not be merely a matter of political partisanship, though I do believe that engaging, responsible scholarship does not seek to hide the ideological commitments of the scholar behind a veil of "objectivity." For instance, I write this book as a conservative evangelical Christian who desires to ensure that this faith tradition is given its fair due—neither unreflectively maligned, nor celebrated and practiced in an unreflective, uncritical, and/or dangerous way. This of course means that my observations and arguments will reflect certain values, assumptions, and biases. This is also true of everyone, however, including (and especially) scholars—whether or not they make the pretense to objectivity. Indeed, as historian George Marsden has insightfully pointed out, scholarship done from a uniquely Christian perspective serves well to correct for the hidden values, assumptions, and biases that permeate academic culture.[58]

The most telling neglect of the perspectives summarized above is precisely with respect to the religious (specifically fundamentalist and conservative evangelical Christian) motivation underlying Operation Rescue activism. In some cases, it is discounted as only instrumental or pretextual. In other cases, it is acknowledged as significant but is rendered simplistically as a grotesquely distorted caricature.

My hope, by contrast, is to present an account of the rhetoric of Operation Rescue (and of the significant rhetorical practices that have characterized the fundamentalist and conservative evangelical Christian faith traditions) that pushes beyond naturalistic biases and the Enlightenment-based myth of "liberal neutrality,"[59] evaluating these artifacts and traditions on their own terms as much as possible. In so doing, I hope to show how the way fundamentalist and conservative evangelical Christians talk—about who they are, about what the world is like, and about what they need to do, in the words of sociologist James Davison Hunter, "to know and live

Christianity in its authentic and divinely intended manner"[60]—gets them into trouble.

Preview of Chapters

I develop this overall idea in three major parts. In part 2 I lay a theoretical and historical foundation for my analyses of the rhetoric of Operation Rescue. In chapter 2 I set forth the particular conception of rhetoric I am using throughout this book. Building upon some of the major developments in rhetorical theory since the middle of the twentieth century, I conceptualize rhetoric essentially as "evangelism." In so doing, I put forward a conception of rhetoric that is considerably broader than the traditional notions of rhetoric as "argument" and "persuasion." Rhetoric, I suggest, functions more fundamentally and more powerfully in a *generative*, perspective-shaping capacity.

In chapter 3 I explore the evangelical and fundamentalist roots of Operation Rescue from a rhetorical point of view, centering on a rhetorical analysis of Francis Schaeffer's pivotal work, *A Christian Manifesto*. Schaeffer is not only considered to be the seminal philosopher for the Christian Right, but also had a direct impact on Randall Terry himself and provided a significant portion of the rationale for the emergence of Operation Rescue. I argue that Schaeffer's rhetoric exhibits and reinforces two problematic themes in the fundamentalist and conservative evangelical faith traditions: anti-intellectualism and the impulse to hegemony. These are themes that also appear all too strongly in the rhetoric of Operation Rescue.

The analysis of the rhetoric of Operation Rescue begins in part 3. Operation Rescue's locus of appeal is primarily conservative evangelicalism. In plumbing the deep motivational core of this larger group, the rhetoric of Operation Rescue constructs and reflects certain representations of the evangelical Christian faith. In part 3 I explore these particular representations. Chapter 4 focuses on Operation Rescue's particular rendering of abortion history in the United States, particularly as that history connects with Operation Rescue's understanding of the nation's past and present. I argue that in its particular portrayals of *Roe v. Wade*, of the abortion controversy, of the United States as a nation, and of the historical witness of the Christian community, the rhetoric of Operation Rescue encourages its recipients to view the abortion issue as just the sort of severe crisis that encourages sacrificial activism *as Christians*. In so doing, this rhetoric encourages the symbolic forging of strong connections between Operation Rescue activism and authentic expression of Christian faith. By using a particular understanding of the past to make claims on what should be done in the present, the rhetoric of Operation Rescue illustrates the power of representations of history as rhetorical.

The representations of history in the rhetoric of Operation Rescue provide important clues to how the evangelical Christian faith is employed as a persuasive ground for Operation Rescue activism, and how it is shaped symbolically as "equipment for living" for those committed to Operation Rescue. In chapter 5 I pursue these ideas more explicitly by considering how the rhetoric of Operation Rescue functions theologically. I examine not only the key tenets and lines of argument employed by the group, but also the attitudes the rhetoric encourages its audience to adopt: attitudes toward the Bible, attitudes toward abortion, attitudes toward the church, and the like. In particular, I argue that this "theological" rhetoric constructs abortion-related activism as the single touchstone by which Christians can identify with the evangelical Christian faith.

In chapter 6 I focus on the connections between Operation Rescue's rhetorical representations of the evangelical Christian faith and the troubling subject of abortion-related violence. Building thematically upon the analysis of the previous two chapters, I argue for the existence of two representative themes in the rhetoric of Operation Rescue that support a overreductionistic misrepresentation of the evangelical faith. In other words, the rhetoric of Operation Rescue encourages its audience to see their Christian faith as an oversimplified, distorted caricature that strips away from consideration important aspects of that faith. To strengthen my claim of a connection between such rhetorical misrepresentation and the cultivation of an attitude more favorable to violence, I examine a manifesto written by a pro-life activist who advocated and practiced homicide to stop abortions from taking place. In my examination, I show the same rhetorical misrepresentation at work, only in a more completely simplistic and rigid form.

In stressing the powerful role rhetoric plays in shaping perspective, my analyses in part 3 press the point that considerable care must be taken in how evangelical Christians conceptualize their faith. If their view of their faith is oversimplistic and grossly distorted, there will be considerable consequences not only for their own personal experiences with the God whom they serve, but also for how they treat others and how they engage in public life more generally. If their view of the evangelical Christian faith emphasizes spiritual warfare at the expense of all else, for instance, then they are more likely to be unloving, unmerciful, and violent. They are also sure in this case to distort God into an image that is no less than idolatrous. There is more—much more—to God than just the image of an all-powerful warrior that, paradoxically, still is utterly dependent on Christians to fight his battles for him in the temporal realm. There is more—much more—to evangelical Christianity than battling Satan and his minions.

Having examined representations of the evangelical Christian faith in the rhetoric of Operation Rescue, I then turn in part 4 to implications of Operation Rescue's rhetorical practices for public discourse more generally. There has been some concern in recent years over the increasingly deteriorating and fragmented state of public discourse in America. Some have blamed communication media directly.[61] Some have held contemporary journalism responsible.[62] Still others—most notably James Davison Hunter—have combined these factors with the behaviors of participants in public dialogue in explaining the bellicose, fragmented public rhetorical environment that marks the "culture wars."[63] In part 4 of this book, I examine how Operation Rescue has participated in public dialogue. I stress in particular what the consequences have been for the success or failure of Operation Rescue's public rhetorical efforts, as well as for the impact of Operation Rescue's rhetorical approach on the more general state of public discourse in America.

In chapter 7 I explain how the rhetoric of the pro-choice movement sought to characterize Operation Rescue in the public sphere. Rhetorical scholars of political discourse and social protest have recognized the power of terms to shape perceptions of reality and perceptions of what should be done. Black Power activist Stokely Carmichael recognized this power in his declaration, "I believe that people who define are masters."[64] Political scientist Murray Edelman is equally blunt in his claim that "political language *is* political reality."[65] This means that the language—the words, the terms, the verbal characterizations—that carries official sanction in public deliberations is critical in shaping the outcome of those deliberations.

As I will show in chapter 7, the pro-choice movement understood this well. In this chapter I show how the pro-choice movement began to articulate a coherent "vocabulary" of terms to characterize Operation Rescue. This characterization of Operation Rescue—emphasizing (1) dissimilarity with the civil rights movement, (2) fanaticism, and (3) violence—powerfully denies the group public legitimacy. Assuming that this pro-choice "vocabulary" were to become the official one used to deliberate publicly the abortion issue, the results would be singularly disastrous for Operation Rescue. This means, then, that prior to the political and legal battles over the control of public policy, there exists a *rhetorical* battle over the terms to be used officially in characterizing the situation, the nature of the parties, and the motives of the parties.

This rhetorical work of the pro-choice movement, therefore, presented a significant challenge for Operation Rescue. In chapter 8 I argue that the group completely failed to meet this challenge. In examining how the rhetoric of Operation Rescue encourages its audience to conceptualize the public, I argue that the group exhibited naïve views concerning the nature of truth and how to communicate truth convincingly. These naïve views led to Operation Rescue's effective non-engagement in this public rhetorical battle to characterize itself, to characterize its opposition, and to characterize the abortion issue. This enabled the pro-choice movement to have essentially unfettered rein to shape the public vocabulary: the vocabulary officially used in public deliberation.

In chapter 9 I show how this rhetorical maladroitness contributed directly to Operation Rescue's downfall. In my rhetorical analysis of the U.S. Senate Labor and Human Services Committee hearing on the FACE Act, which took place on May 12, 1993, I show not only how the hearing was dominated by a pro-choice "vocabulary" of terms, but also how that vocabulary constructed a characterization of the Act that proved impossible for pro-life representatives—and the Senators sympathetic to them—to argue against. In this hearing, then, we see how Operation Rescue's rhetorical failures led to the group's most pivotal legal defeat: the passage of the FACE Act.

The analyses in part 4 stress two basic points about Operation Rescue's rhetorical maladroitness. First, Operation Rescue's rhetorical appeals were fundamentally misconceived from a pragmatic standpoint, and these misconceptions contributed directly to the group's downfall. Second, the group's rhetorical approach represents a danger to the health of public discourse in America. It is dangerous in that it encourages and reinforces both public passivity and the fragmentation of the American public. It is also dangerous in that it encourages and reinforces a rhetorical climate in American public dialogue that makes it more difficult to handle fundamental moral differences without resorting to coercion and violence. This is, in my view, hardly the sort of public witness that is consistent with the basic values of the evangelical Christian faith tradition.

In examining the rhetoric of Operation Rescue, this book offers a case study of what, by most accounts, is the most significant effort of fundamentalist and conservative evangelical Christians to engage in social protest against the established legal and political order. By attending to this rhetoric, we are able to see more clearly how Operation Rescue was able to appeal to fundamentalists and conservative evangelicals, convincing many not only to set their faces against the status quo in the United States, but also to break the law, confront the police, and risk jail time in so doing. By attending to this rhetoric, we are also able to see how Operation Rescue sought—by words and by acts—to convince public America of the wickedness of its public policy and its need for dramatic change with respect to the abortion issue. By attending to this rhetoric, we can understand better how Operation Rescue succeeded in becoming a genuine protest movement that captivated the nation. By attending to this rhetoric, we can also understand how Operation Rescue ultimately and comprehensively failed in its quest to change American public policy with respect to abortion. These are, to be sure, significant insights into the power of rhetoric to shape individual and community lives.

The more important lessons, though, follow from these insights. What makes the rhetoric of Operation Rescue important to deal with, ultimately, is what it teaches us about how evangelical Christians (particularly conservative evangelicals and fundamentalists) conceptualize their faith, as well as what it teaches us about how evangelicals understand their role in public life. Writers like Carter, Guinness, and Neuhaus have advanced good cases not only for the claim that evangelicals have brought to bear a deficient understanding of their faith in their engagement in political activism and public life more generally, but also for the claim that their engagement has failed to improve (or has even degraded) the quality of American public life. Attending to the rhetoric of Operation Rescue helps us to understand better how this has happened.

By understanding more specifically how powerful rhetoric is in shaping these deficient views of Christian faith and Christian political involvement, I hope that evangelical Christians (myself included) can become more sensitive to the ways in which words can let them (and others) down. By becoming more sensitive to this power of words, I hope that evangelical Christians can use rhetoric in ways that help them to think and act in ways that are more consistent with the values and imperatives of the faith tradition they hold so dear. I also hope that, by doing so, they might also be able not only to provide a more vibrant and accurate public witness to their faith, but also to have a significant role in improving the quality of our nation's public discourse and public life. It is in this spirit that I offer this study of Operation Rescue.

Notes

1. Stephen L. Carter, *God's Name in Vain: The Wrongs and Rights of Religion in Politics* (New York: Basic Books, 2000), 2.
2. Richard John Neuhaus, *The Naked Public Square: Religion and Democracy in America*, 2nd ed. (Grand Rapids, Mich.: Eerdmans, 1986); Os Guinness, *The American Hour: A Time of Reckoning and the Once and Future Role of Faith* (New York: Free Press, 1993); Cal Thomas and Ed Dobson, *Blinded by Might: Can the Religious Right Save America?* (Grand Rapids, Mich.: Zondervan, 1999).
3. Carter, *God's Name in Vain*, 67–81.
4. Thomas and Dobson, *Blinded by Might*, 23.
5. Ibid., 59, 60.
6. Carter, *God's Name in Vain*, 19.
7. Ibid., 20.
8. Roderick P. Hart, *Seducing America: How Television Charms the Modern Voter* (New York: Oxford University Press, 1994), 22.
9. This general view is developed from an explicitly Christian perspective in Quentin J. Schultze, *Communicating for Life: Christian Stewardship in Community and Media* (Grand Rapids, Mich.: Baker, 2000). I also develop my conception of rhetoric more carefully in chapter 2.
10. Faye Ginsburg, "Rescuing the Nation: Operation Rescue and the Rise of Anti-Abortion Militancy," in *Abortion Wars: A Half Century of Struggle, 1950–2000*, ed. Rickie Solinger (Berkeley: University of California Press, 1998), 228.
11. James Risen and Judy L. Thomas, *Wrath of Angels: The American Abortion War* (New York: Basic Books, 1998), 220.
12. Ibid., 221.
13. Kenneth Burke, "Literature as Equipment for Living," in *The Philosophy of Literary Form: Studies in Symbolic Action*, 3rd ed. (Berkeley: University of California Press, 1973), 304.
14. Cindy Terry, quoted in Judy Lundstrom Thomas, "Terry and His Cause Allow No Neutrality," *Wichita Eagle*, August 25, 1991, VUTEXT database, document 238112, 9.
15. Ibid., 3.
16. Risen and Thomas, *Wrath of Angels*, 62.
17. See ibid., 62–74, 132–55.
18. Ibid., 220.
19. Randall A. Terry, *Operation Rescue* (Springdale, Pa.: Whitaker House, 1988), 18.
20. Terry, quoted in John W. Bowers, Donovan J. Ochs, and Richard J. Jensen, *The Rhetoric of Agitation and Control*, 2nd ed. (Prospect Heights, Ill.: Waveland Press, 1993), 127–28.
21. Cal Thomas, "America Fighting the Modern Civil War," *Wichita Eagle*, August 12, 1991, VUTEXT database, document 225090, 3.
22. See, for instance, Terry, *Operation Rescue*, 102–6; Mark Belz, *Suffer the Little Children: Christians, Abortion, and Civil Disobedience* (Westchester, Ill.: Crossway Books, 1989), 85–94; Randy C. Alcorn, *Is Rescuing Right? Breaking the Law to Save the Unborn* (Downers Grove, Ill.: InterVarsity Press, 1990), 107–11.

23. See, for instance, Terry, *Operation Rescue*, 106–10; Belz, *Suffer the Little Children*, 95–104; Alcorn, *Is Rescuing Right?*, 114–16.

24. This pledge is reprinted in Belz, *Suffer the Little Children*, 154–55; Terry, *Operation Rescue*, 228–29.

25. "Abortion and Violence," transcript of *Sonya Live*, narr. Sonya Friedman, Cable News Network, March 8, 1994, 3.

26. Alcorn, *Is Rescuing Right?*, 207–8.

27. Terry, *Operation Rescue*, 229.

28. Risen and Thomas, *Wrath of Angels*, 271.

29. Tom Schaefer and Cristine Crumbo, "Week of Discontent: Abortion Foes from Here and Elsewhere Plan Six Days of Protests," *Wichita Eagle*, July 14, 1991, VUTEXT database, document 196133, 2; Tamar Lewin, "With Thin Staff and Thick Debt, Anti-Abortion Group Faces Struggle," *New York Times*, June 11, 1990, A16.

30. "Impassioned Rally Launches Protest," *Wichita Eagle*, July 16, 1991, VUTEXT database, document 198037, 1.

31. Judy Lundstrom Thomas, "Tiller Rejects Compromise on Protests," *Wichita Eagle*, September 6, 1991, VUTEXT database, document 250100, 2.

32. Bowers, Ochs, and Jensen, *The Rhetoric of Agitation and Control*, 130–35.

33. Risen and Thomas, *Wrath of Angels*, 279.

34. Gayle White, "Rev. Stanley Comes Out against Tactics of Anti-Abortion Group," *Atlanta Journal and Constitution*, August 30, 1988, November 6, 1998, http://stacks.ajc.com.

35. Risen and Thomas, *Wrath of Angels*, 280.

36. "Anti-Abortion Group Will Close Its Offices," *New York Times*, December 17, 1990, B6; Tom Schaefer, "Group Founder Says He Is Responding to a Call from God," *Wichita Eagle*, July 14, 1991, VUTEXT database, document 196177, 2.

37. Bowers, Ochs, and Jensen, *The Rhetoric of Agitation and Control*, 138.

38. William E. Clayton Jr., "Racketeering Law Applied to Clinic Violence," *Houston Chronicle*, January 25, 1994, 1A, 6A.

39. Paul Richter, "Clinton Signs Law Banning Abortion Clinic Blockade," *Los Angeles Times*, May 27, 1994, A20; Steven T. McFarland, "Pro-lifers' New Legal Nightmare," *Christianity Today*, August 15, 1994, 18–19.

40. See Jeff Glasser, "Like a Bad Sequel, the Protest Flopped: A Reprise of Wichita's Abortion Demonstration," *U.S. News and World Report*, July 30, 2001, 22.

41. Risen and Thomas, *Wrath of Angels*, 318.

42. Ibid., 334.

43. In March 1993 pro-life activist Michael Griffin shot and killed Dr. David Gunn immediately outside the Pensacola, Florida, clinic in which he performed abortions. Five months later Dr. George Tiller of Wichita, Kansas, was shot and wounded in his car. See "Let God Judge the Murderer of Abortion Doctor, Minister Says," *Los Angeles Times*, March 14, 1993, A20; "Suspect in Shooting Praised Accused Killer," *Bryan-College Station (Texas) Eagle*, August 22, 1993, A14.

44. Risen and Thomas, *Wrath of Angels*, 357.

45. Ibid., 360.

46. Kevin O'Neal, "Operation Rescue to Stage Visual Anti-Abortion Demonstrations," *Indianapolis Star*, October 9, 1996, 1B.

47. "Anti-Gay Protests to Target Disney," *Chicago Tribune*, April 16, 1998, NewsBank database, document CTR9804160162, 1.

48. Risen and Thomas, *Wrath of Angels*, 373.

49. Matt O'Connor, "Abortion Foe Settles Suit, Ends Protest," *Chicago Tribune*, January 9, 1998, sec. 2, p. 6.

50. Operation Rescue West is a former regional affiliate of Operation Rescue that continues various protest activities, mostly picketing and "sidewalk counseling." The organization maintains a website (www.operationrescue.org) and publishes a quarterly magazine, *Frontline News*. For a list of other such organizations, many of whom still exist, see Dallas A. Blanchard, *The Anti-Abortion Movement and the Rise of the Religious Right: From Polite to Fiery Protest* (New York: Twayne Publishers, 1994), 61–72.

51. Risen and Thomas, *Wrath of Angels*, 373.

52. Jan Crawford Greenburg, "Roe vs. Wade at 25: America's Great Divide," *Chicago Tribune*, April 21, 1998, sec. 1, p. 16.

53. Greenburg, "Roe vs. Wade at 25," 16; Risen and Thomas, *Wrath of Angels*, 373.

54. Abdon M. Pallasch and Judy Peres, "Abortion Foes Suffer Big Setback," *Chicago Tribune*, April 21, 1998, NewsBank database, document CTR 9804210116, 1; Steve Chapman, "Suppressing Violent Protests—or Free Speech?" *Chicago Tribune*, April 23, 1998, NewsBank database, document CTR 9804230047, 1.

55. See, for instance, Blanchard, *The Anti-Abortion Movement and the Rise of the Religious Right*; Ginsburg, "Rescuing the Nation."

56. See, for instance, Sara Diamond, *Spiritual Warfare: The Politics of the Christian Right* (Boston: South End Press, 1989); *Roads to Dominion: Right-Wing Movements and Political Power in the United States* (New York: Guilford Press, 1995); *Not by Politics Alone: The Enduring Influence of the Christian Right* (New York: Guilford Press, 1998).

57. See, for instance, Marian Faux, *Crusaders: Voices from the Abortion Front* (New York: Carol Publishing Group, 1990); Marlene Gerber Fried, ed., *From Abortion to Reproductive Freedom: Transforming a Movement* (Boston: South End Press, 1990); Susan Faludi, *Backlash: The Undeclared War against American Women* (New York: Crown Books, 1991); Linda Kintz, *Between Jesus and the Market: The Emotions that Matter in Right-Wing America* (Durham, N.C.: Duke University Press, 1997).

58. George M. Marsden, *The Outrageous Idea of Christian Scholarship* (New York: Oxford University Press, 1997).

59. These are specifically discussed in ibid., 72–77.

60. James Davison Hunter, *American Evangelicalism: Conservative Religion and the Quandary of Modernity* (New Brunswick, N.J.: Rutgers University Press, 1983), 9.

61. See, for instance, Neil Postman, *Amusing Ourselves to Death: Public Discourse in the Age of Show Business* (New York: Penguin Books, 1985); Kathleen Hall Jamieson, *Eloquence in an Electronic Age: The Transformation of Political Speechmaking* (New York: Oxford University Press, 1988); Hart, *Seducing America*.

62. See, for instance, Thomas Patterson, *Out of Order* (New York: Vintage Books, 1994); David Thelen, *Becoming Citizens in the Age of Television* (Chicago: University of Chicago Press, 1996); Kathleen Hall Jamieson and Paul Waldman, *The Press Effect: Politicians, Journalists, and the Stories that Shape the Political World* (New York: Oxford University Press, 2003); J. Michael Hogan, "Media Nihilism and the Presidential Debates," *Argumentation and Advocacy* 25 (1989): 220–25.

63. See, most notably, James Davison Hunter, *Culture Wars: The Struggle to Define America* (New York: Basic Books, 1991); *Before the Shooting Begins: Searching for Democracy in America's Culture War* (New York: Free Press, 1994).

64. Carmichael, quoted in Bowers, Ochs, and Jensen, *The Rhetoric of Agitation and Control*, 9.

65. Murray Edelman, *Constructing the Political Spectacle* (Chicago: University of Chicago Press, 1988), 104.

PART TWO

Foundations

2

RHETORIC AS EVANGELISM

In both the scientific and the religious doctrine, there is great emphasis placed upon prophecy or foretelling; in both, it is held that certain important aspects of foretelling require a new orientation, a revised system of meanings, an altered conception as to how the world is put together; in both, it is insisted that, if we change our ways of acting to bring them more and more into accord with the new meanings (rejecting old means and selecting new means as a better solution for the problem as now rephrased), we shall bring ourselves and our group nearer to the good life.

—Kenneth Burke[1]

Truly the maker of a definition is more like a god than a human being.

—Andrew King[2]

Rhetoric, it seems, is used only by one's adversaries, and usually as a substitute for reason, truth, and sound argument. In describing the "rhetoric" that its adversaries employ, Operation Rescue certainly did nothing to dispel this idea. In his first book, Operation Rescue founder Randall Terry reiterated the importance of pro-life literature in the group's quest to "defeat the abortion holocaust."[3] Likening such material to "ammunition" in the "war on abortion," Terry declares that "[t]hese graphic pictures and films speak louder than all the lying rhetoric of the pro-abortion movement combined."[4] At an Operation Rescue rally in 1992, Rev. Richard Exley compared a pro-choice editorial in *USA Today* with euthanasia appeals of the World War II Nazi government, inviting continued audience engagement with the appeal, "Listen to her rhetoric."[5] Reflecting upon the 1988 protests in Atlanta, one Operation Rescue activist sought to encourage other activists by writing that "[c]racks are forming in the stronghold of lies the enemy had devised. The rhetoric of the abortionist is becoming more blatantly erroneous. Their words are turning into sand in their mouths, before the higher court of God!"[6]

Such conceptions of rhetoric are consistent with the popular and unflattering dissociation of rhetoric from matters of fact, truth, and reality; instead, the practice of rhetoric is associated with "ornament," or "manipulation," or "trickery." "In political life," explains rhetorician David Zarefsky, "the term 'rhetoric' often is taken to mean only the catchy slogan, the vivid phrase which embellishes a public statement," or worse, a "public pronouncement which is issued as a 'front' to conceal the darker machinations of government."[7]

These conceptions of rhetoric are originally what drove Plato, well over 2,000 years ago, to criticize both the Sophists and their particular brand of rhetoric so vehemently. Plato's particular ideas regarding the nature of reality, the existence of truth, the accessibility of truth, and the negotiation of truth claims all no longer command broad assent. Nonetheless, Plato's negative view of rhetoric has survived with a remarkable tenacity in both popular and academic spheres.

These unflattering views of rhetoric misrepresent not only the proper scope of rhetoric, but also the function and power of discourse to shape human attitudes and action. A broader (and, I think, more accurate) sense of the function and power of rhetoric is important to acknowledge the fullness of the relationship between discourse and the human condition. A broader and more charitable conception of rhetoric, furthermore, is critical to the sort of analysis of Operation Rescue that I undertake in this book. In this chapter I clarify such a view of rhetoric.

Rhetoric is in truth no mere stylistic embellishment that obscures or stands in the place of responsible argument or responsible dialogue. Nor is rhetoric inherently antithetical to responsible discourse, as is so often suggested by the exhortations "reality, not rhetoric" and "reason, not rhetoric." My position throughout this book is that rhetorical practice is an essential component of responsible discourse, and is an essential component of much, if not most, meaningful discourse more generally. Rhetoric, in other words, should be seen more broadly as the language and symbols that we use as human beings to influence ourselves and others.

This position is essentially consistent with the view taken in what I have termed "traditionally dominant rhetorical theory," which I describe more fully below. With its conception of rhetoric primarily as "argument" and "persuasion," however, traditionally dominant rhetorical theory is too narrow. Rhetoric, in my view, does not function merely to debate controversial issues of fact, value, or policy. Rather, it functions as symbolic inducement with respect to the full range of human experience. Rhetoric functions more fundamentally and more powerfully in a *generative*, perspective-shaping capacity. Rhetoric, in other words, does not merely "sugarcoat" or obscure the truth; rather, rhetoric works to build our conception of what the truth is. This broader conception of rhetoric is critical if we are more fully to understand how the rhetoric of Operation Rescue taps into and shapes its activists' senses of what their faith is, what their faith means to them, and how they can live more fully in accordance with that faith. This broader conception of rhetoric is also critical if we are to gain a fuller appreciation for how much of the rhetorical effort of fundamentalist and conservative evangelical Christians is not only inconsistent with the faith they profess, but also damaging to American public discourse and public life.

In this chapter I first mention traditional rhetorical theory, primarily as a means of contrast with my own broader conception of rhetoric's function and scope. Following my discussion of traditional theory, I put forward and explain my own definition of rhetoric, comparing the practice of rhetoric most directly with the practice of *evangelism*. It is a definition that borrows fairly heavily from contemporary rhetorical theory, particularly the ideas of Kenneth Burke. Finally, I close with a brief reflection on the relationships among rhetoric, theology, and evangelical Christian experience. In this way, I connect my conception of rhetoric more explicitly with my overall claims about the rhetoric of Operation Rescue.

Traditionally Dominant Conceptions of Rhetoric

There is no uniform agreement on the origins of rhetorical theory. Nonetheless, the importance of rhetoric as an art can be seen readily in disputes about its practice that took place over 2,300 years ago. In the fifth century BCE, the emergence of democracy in certain Greek city-states, particularly Athens, created a more widespread need to speak publicly and effectively. At least in part as a response to the legitimate needs of the citizenry—to have a voice in public affairs and to defend themselves in the law courts—the Sophists appeared and gained in popularity. "Sophists," states classicist George A. Kennedy, "were self-appointed professors of how to succeed in the civic life of the Greek states," itinerant teachers who "taught primarily by public or private declamation of speeches which presented in striking form their ideas and their techniques of proof."[8] Without eliding the considerable diversity in sophistic rhetorical theory, one can discern a largely speaker-centered model in sophistic rhetoric, a model that highlights "the power of the orator to accomplish whatever he wishes, to make great things small, small things great, and even the worse seem the better cause."[9]

It was this at least implicit devaluation of "truth" in sophistic rhetoric that led the philosophers of the day, particularly Plato, to condemn the Sophists and their brand of rhetoric. Plato's harsh criticism, to be sure, followed from his own philosophical and ideological commitments. He conceptualized truth as absolute and existing in the "Forms." He believed this truth to be at least somewhat accessible by means of Socratic dialectic. He also believed that the discovery and application of this truth was best done in a political system in which "philosopher-kings" rule. These commitments, to be sure, were not shared in the general sophistic worldview. Plato rightly judged sophistic rhetoric—based on human contingency rather than on truth—to be an assault on his conception of how truth should be discovered and employed for the betterment of all.

Nonetheless, the celebrated conflict between Plato and the Sophists rested on a particular conception of the essence of rhetoric: *persuasion*. Especially within the public context of fifth-century BCE Athens, there seemed to be at least common ground on what counted as rhetoric. In that public context, rhetoric meant public speaking or civic discourse practiced in the law courts, in the public legislative assemblies, and on the public squares.

This common ground was also shared by Aristotle, who, in his treatise *On Rhetoric*, staked out a moderating position between Plato and the Sophists. Rhetoric, in Aristotle's conception, is defined as "an ability, in each [particular] case, to see the available means of persuasion."[10] In contrast to both Plato and the Sophists, Aristotle saw this artistic skill as an amoral instrument that could be used for noble or base purposes, much like skill in swordplay or martial arts. Nonetheless, Aristotle believed that widespread skill in rhetoric is the best safeguard against the triumph of falsehood over truth. In Aristotle's view, such widespread skill would help to ensure that no one side has an unfair advantage, enabling truth, which is inherently more persuasive, to carry the day.

"By almost any standard of judgment," declares rhetoric scholar Thomas B. Farrell, "Aristotle wrote *the* book on rhetoric."[11] Considering the longevity of Aristotle's outlook on rhetoric—in terms of both rhetoricians inspired by Aristotle and those not—the claim is justified. The longevity of this basic conception of rhetoric, conceptualized as an art or skill employed in specific instances of persuasion, can be seen in numerous instances. These include the Roman rhetorical tradition (as seen particularly in Cicero and Quintilian), the survival and authoritative use of much of Cicero's writings and the handbook *Rhetorica ad Herrenium* into the Middle Ages, and the unquestioned dominance of *On Rhetoric* as a "master text" for the study of rhetoric throughout much of the twentieth century.

This "traditionally dominant" rhetorical theory I have sketched has been seen not just in terms of this dominance of Aristotle in rhetorical studies, but also in terms of theory that focuses on rhetoric as *argument*. Philosophers Chaim Perelman and Stephen Toulmin are particularly noteworthy examples in this regard.[12] While their specific models differ, both theorists present conceptions of rhetoric that draw upon "informal" argument, starting with premises that the audience accepts and moving that audience to acceptance of a particular conclusion. This artistic, rhetorical conception of argument—based primarily upon the "persuadability" of the audience—is significantly different than conceptions grounded in the rigors of formal logic, which start with "givens" and reason to conclusions that are absolutely certain.

Beyond Traditionally Dominant Rhetorical Theory

While the traditionally dominant conception of rhetoric—as persuasion in specific contexts—is important, it is nonetheless limiting. Specifically, such a conception tends to downplay the significance of discourse—language and symbols—in shaping attitudes, values, and perceptions of reality. Such a conception reinforces the view that language functions in a surrogationalist capacity, providing more-or-less transparent representations of ideas and objects that are non-linguistic.

However, the notion of language as objective, value-free, and merely descriptive has come under scathing attack in a broad array of disciplines. Political scientist Murray Edelman has confidently proclaimed the *generative*, reality-shaping function of language. Observing that "[t]he critical element for political maneuver for advantage is the creation of meaning," Edelman states that "[i]t is language about political events, not the events in any other sense, that people experience; even developments that are close by take their meaning from the language that depicts them." "So," he then declares, "political language *is* political reality."[13]

Such critiques have been increasingly common since the 1960s, especially in the wake of failed attempts to create an expressly value-free "observation" language. Peter L. Berger and Thomas Luckmann made this critique prominent in sociology with their seminal work, *The Social Construction of Reality*.[14] In *The Structure of Scientific Revolutions*, philosopher Thomas S. Kuhn brought the notion of symbolic interpretation a step further by arguing that even in the most "objective" of disciplines—the natural sciences—interpretation of phenomena cannot transcend perspectives; rather, perspectives shape how phenomena are interpreted and given meaning. In other words, meaning is not somehow "given," inherent in acts or phenomena, but rather is attributed to acts or phenomena by the interpretive "equipment" of a perspective.[15]

Nearly thirty years before the appearance of Kuhn's book, Kenneth Burke set forth essentially the same idea, but with a more fundamental emphasis on the roles of language and symbols. In his 1935 work, *Permanence and Change*, Burke advanced the idea that language and perspective are inseparably related. He argued that as symbol-using beings, we can make sense of our world only through the symbolic realm, by means of perspectives or "orientations" that are symbolically constructed.[16] This symbolic construction of perspectives is accomplished along the lines of organizing metaphors or classification schemes, primarily resources of language. As Burke asks:

> Indeed, as the documents of science pile up, are we not coming to see that whole works of scientific research, even entire schools, are hardly more than the patient repetition, in all its ramifications, of a fertile metaphor? ... We have, at different eras in history, considered man as the son of God, as an animal, as a political or economic brick, as a machine, each such metaphor, and a hundred others, serving as the cue for an unending line of data and generalizations.[17]

Such a generative role of symbols is further illuminated in Burke's essay on "Terministic Screens." Burke claimed that the linguistic and symbolic resources we employ to make sense of reality act to filter what we observe and how we make sense of that reality. "[A]ny nomenclature," he explains, "necessarily directs the attention into some channels rather than others"; while serving as a "reflection of reality," the nomenclature must also function as a "selection of reality" and a "deflection of reality."[18]

This partiality of language is also seen clearly in what Burke had earlier called "perspective by incongruity."[19] Perspective by incongruity refers to a process by which language and/or symbols are used to assault taken-for-granted meanings and categorizations that make up our understanding of how the world is put together. In so doing, such "incongruity" provides a reminder of the fact that the relationships of meaning we employ "are not *realities*, they are *interpretations* of reality."[20] Rhetoric scholar Richard B. Gregg has described perspective by incongruity as a symbolic connection of "two phenomena that are not 'logically' connected in order to understand one of them in an entirely new way."[21]

Communication scholar Mark Pollock has illustrated this idea of perspective by incongruity by using newspapers and police as examples. Normally a newspaper is thought of as a means by which information is delivered to a large audience. "But what happens," asks Pollock, "if we think of it somewhat incongruously as a means of delivering large, desirable audiences to advertisers? This incongruous definition may lead us to rethink some of what we take as given about a newspaper, perhaps leading us to reinterpret our relationship to it."[22] A similar effect occurs in thinking of the police as a "gang" and applying terms normally associated with gangs, such as "colors" and "turf," to police. Such an incongruous connection then shapes and alters our understandings of both gangs and police.[23]

Perspective by incongruity can also clearly be seen in the rhetoric of social protest figures like Malcolm X. In his speech "The Black Revolution," Malcolm X made repeated use of this linguistic device to challenge and reorient understandings of history, of the U.S. government, and of the state of race relations. The salutation, for instance, is rendered with the incongruous "Friends and enemies..."[24] The "minorities" of the United States (meaning those who are not white) are reoriented as a "majority."[25] The United States is reoriented as a "colonial power" that "still enslaves 22 million African-Americans... by depriving us of human rights," of "the right to be human beings."[26] The peaceful struggle for civil rights, exemplified by the work of Martin Luther King Jr., is reoriented as "the black man taking his case to the white man's court."[27] The essence of civil rights, traditionally conceived ideologically in terms of "democracy and all those other flowery words," is reoriented materialistically as a "[r]evolution... based on land."[28]

As the example of Malcolm X suggests, the notion of perspective by incongruity—"misusing" language to reveal the "constructed" nature of perspective—has found a forceful application in social protest and social movement studies. Social protest rhetoric was usually condemned in earlier speech and communication studies for failing to conform to traditional standards of rational persuasion. Following the introduction of Kenneth

Burke's ideas to the field of communication, however, rhetoric and communication scholars began to recognize that the discourse of rational persuasion can function profoundly to co-opt social movements. Since the established order controls the *language* used publicly to characterize people and events—in addition to controlling formidable resources and the coercive power of the state—social movement rhetoric must challenge and misuse that language. That means, in part, saying things and behaving in ways that are inconsistent with or even offensive to the cultural sensibilities of society.

As communication scholars Charles J. Stewart, Craig Allen Smith, and Robert E. Denton, Jr., have suggested, then, movements must not only "prescribe and sell courses of action" and "mobilize the disaffected," but, more fundamentally, they must also "transform perceptions of reality."[29] This admonition supports a broader, generative conception of rhetoric, in which rhetoric both challenges and affirms basic elements of perspective. In this sense, then, rhetoric functions as "evangelism" in essence, as I describe below.

A Definition of Rhetoric

I hold to a conception of rhetoric—functioning as symbolic inducement—that is considerably broader than the traditional conceptions I have mentioned. Rhetorical discourse, in my view, works more fundamentally and more powerfully in a generative, perspective-shaping capacity. In certain significant ways, rhetoric has the spirit of "evangelism" as its essence, in that there is always an inherent worldview, a "gospel," at issue in rhetorical discourse.

Corresponding to my vision of rhetoric as evangelism in essence, I offer a definition of rhetoric as *discourse that imposes an invitation/temptation, upon a particular audience, to identify with a partisan perspective*. There are a number of important terms in this definition, and in what immediately follows, I elaborate on these terms in a way that will show clearly how I use the term *rhetoric* in this book.

Perspective

Fundamental to my conception of rhetoric is the term *perspective*, drawn from Kenneth Burke's ideas about rhetoric. In using this term, I clearly have in mind Burke's concept of "orientation," briefly defined as "a bundle of judgments as to how things were, how they are, and how they may be."[30] In keeping with Burke's notion of the human being as the "symbol-using animal,"[31] an orientation might best be seen as a symbolically constructed worldview. This worldview dictates how signs and events are to be interpreted and take on meaning, how actions are to be characterized, and how the good life is to be conceptualized.

Orientations, as schemes for assigning meaning, direct the nature of motives. As Burke explains, "Since we characterize a situation with reference to our general scheme of meanings, it is clear how motives, as shorthand terms for situations, are assigned with reference to our orientation in general."[32] An orientation can also be seen as an implicit "gospel" or "promise," for if we act in accordance with the meanings provided by the orientation, we will surely bring ourselves nearer to the good life. It is this connection in particular that has led me to characterize rhetoric as evangelistic in essence.

Partisan

Any orientation, further, is invariably *partisan*. "A way of seeing," Burke explains, "is also a way of not seeing—a focus on object A involves a neglect of object B."[33] A vision of the good (or desirable) in any perspective requires a contrasting vision of the bad (or undesirable). "The hierarchic principle," Burke was to write later, "is inevitable in systematic thought."[34] No orientation or perspective, therefore, can be completely inclusive. Even overtly ideological critics like Sharon Crowley acknowledge this to be the case. While exclaiming that the primary responsibility of the rhetoric scholar is "showing people . . . how language is deployed as a means of coercion, and how they can resist that coercion," she admits that "[a]ll criticisms are exclusive of someone, somewhere."[35] Whether admitted or not, then, exclusive foundational commitments or worldviews are inescapable.

Identify

By the term *identify*, I have in mind Burke's concept of rhetoric as identification. In *A Rhetoric of Motives*, Burke argued that the domain of rhetoric should be expanded beyond the traditional realm of persuasion to the broader realm of identification, of which traditional persuasion is a part. Functioning as identification, in Burke's view, rhetoric does much more than induce assent to propositions or theses, as Perelman believed. Rather, the symbolic inducement of rhetoric is to "consubstantiality" among different people and different parties, in which the parties share the "dialectic substance" of identity and motives.[36] In a world in which people and groups are at odds with one another, in other words, rhetoric promotes shared understanding, shared identity, shared motives—all of which, according to Burke, constitutes a significant sense of oneness in different individuals and groups. In this way, Burke can claim that rhetoric "is rooted in an essential function of language itself ... the use of language as a symbolic means of inducing cooperation in beings that by nature respond to symbols."[37] To Burke, human beings have this powerful impulse as a response to the world in which they live. "Identification is proclaimed with earnestness," he observes, "precisely because there is division. Identification is compensatory to division."[38] Within this expanded scope, then, rhetoric functions as a way of managing the ambiguity between pure identification and pure division:

> In pure identification there would be no strife. Likewise there would be no strife in absolute separateness, since opponents can join battle only through a mediatory ground that makes their communication possible, thus providing the first condition necessary for their interchange of blows. But put identification and division ambiguously together so that you cannot know for certain just where one ends and the other begins, and you have the characteristic invitation to rhetoric.[39]

Rhetoric scholar Maurice Charland's study of the *peuple québécois* nicely illustrates how rhetoric functions as identification, particularly in creating and sustaining meaningful communities.[40] In his analysis of political discourse urging independence for Quebec, Charland showed how this rhetoric functioned to create and sustain a new social and political identity—the *peuple québécois*—in which people partaking of that identity assumed a shared history, a shared tradition, and a shared set of motives.

The power of the identifier "Aggie" for many Texas A&M University students also illustrates how rhetoric, as identification, functions to build and sustain community. This identity is built up both institutionally and uninstitutionally (in the student culture). It is built up with a unique vocabulary, such as "fish" to refer to freshmen and "fish camp" to refer to new student orientation. This identity is built up with a variety of traditions. Such traditions include the "twelfth man" tradition, observed by standing on the bleachers throughout an entire home football game, and the "bonfire" tradition, which produced national attention and controversy following a November 1999 accident in which twelve students were killed. This identity is also built up with annual observances such as "Silver Taps" and "Aggie Muster," which pay tribute to Aggies who have passed away, and reinforce the uniqueness of the larger Aggie community. All of these things—vocabulary, traditions, and observances—function rhetorically as identification, giving a group of people not only a shared identity but also common beliefs and common motives. This function of rhetoric is considerably more fundamental and powerful than the traditionally understood functions of rhetoric as argument and persuasion.

Invitation/Temptation

I am using the term *invitation/temptation* to account for the continuum between "informative" and "persuasive" discourse, as well as the distinction between "integrative" and "agitative" discourse—both of which categories affirm the central connection between rhetoric and perspective.[41] The qualitative distinction between informative and persuasive discourse is largely spurious; even the most overtly informative of discourses presume a perspective by which the information has meaning, whereas the most overtly persuasive of discourses rest their respective claims upon particular, perspective-bound interpretations of meaning. Thus, while discourse can be seen as existing in a continuum between a nonexistent "purely informative" pole and an equally nonexistent "purely persuasive" pole, all rhetorical discourse is alike in that it implicitly or explicitly proclaims the legitimacy of a partisan perspective.

The term *invitation/temptation* also reflects an acknowledgment that rhetorical discourse, in being fundamentally tied to perspective, encompasses both integrative and agitative dimensions. The term *temptation* might properly apply to agitative rhetorical discourse, which exhibits an "impious" character. With regard to piety and perspective, Burke states, "An attempt to *reorganize* one's orientation from the past would have an *impious* aspect ... *impiety* in something as pious as a new religion. The evangelist is asking us to alter our orientations. He would give us new meanings."[42] The term *temptation* is used to connote this aspect of impiety, which follows the attempt to have one's orientation supplanted by another. The term is not meant to imply "seduction"; rather, in the spirit of evangelism, the new orientation is presented as "good news" and is offered for the audience's benefit.

While agitative rhetorical discourse seeks audience identification with a perspective different from the one it holds, integrative rhetorical discourse works to reinforce a perspective the audience already holds. Unlike agitative rhetoric, integrative rhetoric is *pious* in character. It builds upon, elaborates, and solidifies the perspective in question, corresponding nicely with Augustine's emphasis on the pedagogical function of rhetoric.[43] Therefore, I use the term *invitation* to emphasize the piety of integrative rhetoric. Unlike the proclamation of "Believe!" that characterizes the "good news" of agitative rhetoric, the proclamation of "Put into practice (learn more about) what you believe!" can be seen to characterize the "good news" of integrative rhetoric.

Imposes

I use the term *imposes* because I believe that the making of claims on a particular audience is fundamental to rhetoric. In a well-known essay in feminist rhetorical theory, Sally Miller Gearhart decried this imposition, which she described as "the *intention* to change another," as an "act of violence."[44] Interestingly, though, Gearhart seemed to miss the irony of her own alternative's partisanship. In her assertion that "communication, like the rest of culture, must be womanized," one wonders if she intends that the whole of culture, as well as the institutional practice of rhetoric, be *changed*. But even beyond this, one wonders if Gearhart is actually preaching a particular "gospel" of ecofeminism, which she is implicitly claiming to be true in the ultimately transcendent sense. The concluding paragraph of Gearhart's essay provides some definitive clues. "Feminism," she argues, "is a source, a wellspring, a matrix, an environment for the womanization of communication, for the womanization of Western civilization. It calls for an ancient and deep understanding and ultimately for a fundamental change of attitude and perspective." The final observation of the essay, furthermore, leaves little doubt about the hierarchic principle in Gearhart's thinking. Gearhart declares, "In its challenge to history and to the present social order feminism in this, its second wave, is playing for keeps for all of us—for women, for men, for children, animals and plants and for the earth herself. The stakes are that high."[45]

The irony of Gearhart's position reminds us that rhetoric, like evangelism in the commonly understood sense, cannot avoid making claims. It continually makes claims not only on a particular audience's specific behaviors and beliefs, but also on the basic orientation, perspective, ordering of meaning, "gospel" that underlies behaviors and beliefs.

Audience

Finally, the phrase "upon a particular audience" affirms what I believe to be a central connection between rhetoric and audience. However, we must not think of this relationship as happening in only one particular place and time, as is common in more traditional public address studies. A discourse may operate rhetorically on a different audience, at a different time, and in a different way than the speaker (or source) intended. A discourse may also operate rhetorically even though the speaker/source did not intend it to so function. A discourse might also operate rhetorically in different ways than the speaker/source intended. In the case of Operation Rescue, for instance, a speech or letter that ostensibly seeks to gain volunteers for a near-future "rescue" also works at a much deeper level than simply trying to change short-term behavior. Such a speech or letter also tempts or invites identification with a particular representation of the evangelical Christian faith that underlies Operation Rescue's purposes and practices.

In my view, then, rhetoric can be seen best as evangelism in essence. Rhetoric does function as persuasion in the traditionally understood sense. More fundamentally, though, rhetoric also engages fundamental aspects of worldview and community. It helps to shape what we think reality is. It helps to shape what we think truth is. It helps to shape what we think is good and what we think is worth thinking about. And for Christians more specifically, it helps to shape not only what they think the faith means, but also our vision of how to grow and become more mature in that faith; how, in other words, to be true to the faith that they profess.

Rhetoric, Theology, and Evangelical Christian Experience

Theology, to Kenneth Burke, is concisely defined as "words about God."[46] While I suspect that most theologians—even conservative evangelical theologians—would not take issue with this definition, it is nonetheless a very strategic definition in that it emphasizes the rhetorical dimension in any theological system. Assuming, as evangelicals do, that the Bible is the Word of God and is, therefore, a complete and authoritative source of truth, it certainly does not follow that biblical truth is therefore transparent or "given" in an *a priori* sense. Rather, there is an unavoidable process of interpretation in discovering and applying biblical truth. Evangelical theologians Gordon D. Fee and Douglas Stuart state, "Every so often we meet someone who says with great feeling, 'You don't have to interpret the Bible; just read it and do what it says.'"[47] Although they sympathize with this position in that "Christians should learn to read, believe, and obey the Bible," they also recognize that interpretation is inescapable. "The first reason one needs to learn *how* to interpret," they explain, "is that whether one likes it or not, every reader is at the same time an interpreter." In fact, "[t]he aim of a good interpretation is simple: to get at the 'plain meaning' of the text.'"[48]

My point here is that theology and rhetoric are for all essential purposes inseparable. When one talks about theology, when one talks about how to learn and apply what the Bible teaches, one is engaging in rhetoric. A claim like this assumes that rhetoric has, as discussed above, an essentially generative character.

Such a connection is supported in David Cunningham's award-winning book, *Faithful Persuasion*. "Theology," suggests Cunningham, "cannot rely on descriptions of the absolute and the necessary, for it is not privy to any inside information concerning the ways of God." He insists it "must employ language that takes account of contingency and uncertainty. Composed neither of propositions, nor of directives, nor even primarily of narratives, exhortations, or prophecies, Christian theology is instead—and above all—a form of persuasive argument."[49]

In some of his observations on the relationship between theology and audience, Cunningham hints at the "evangelistic" function of theology, much like the function of rhetoric I have been discussing. "Christian theology," he posits, "is a polemical and partisan activity, and cannot be reduced to a discourse of neutral observation. All theology is controversial theology, for all theology seeks to persuade."[50]

While theology advocates a particular vision of divine truth, it is still nonetheless a rhetorical and limiting construction. "The theological task," observes Cunningham, "is a yearning for truth, a longing for truth; but this side of the beatific vision, theology discovers ultimate truth to be elusive." Because of this, "we ought not seek to declare our meager theological accomplishments to be true. Until we are able to see 'face to face,' all judgments of truth must rest with God alone."[51]

This statement does not sanction an ultimate relativism, nor does it denigrate the importance of theological activity. "Christian theology," Cunningham suggests, "is a religious activity, and those who engage in it do so under the judgment of God."[52] It does imply, though, that theology does not offer us unfettered access to ultimate truth. Theology is rhetorical, not hermetic.

Suggesting that theological work is contingent and rhetorical also does not inherently denigrate theologically conservative conceptions of the evangelical Christian faith. Neither is such a view inconsistent with high views concerning the divine inspiration of Scripture and the authority of Scripture in Christian faith and practice. This view merely insists that rhetoric—understood broadly as evangelism in essence—is inescapably involved in the process of determining what Scripture means, how to apply its truths, and how to revere it as the Word of God. This view merely calls to our attention that rhetoric—understood broadly as evangelism in essence—is inescapably involved when we come to an understanding of what the evangelical Christian faith is, what it means, and how to live it out in an authentic and edifying way. To insist otherwise, in my view, is naïve, dishonest, or both. As we shall see in a later chapter, in fact, such an insistence that the meaning of Scripture is plain and not requiring any interpretation is itself a rhetorical strategy.

Such a view of the role of rhetoric is also critical in answering some of the fundamental questions engaged in this book: How have conservative evangelical and fundamentalist Christians approached the tasks of public expression and political activism, and what has been deficient in these approaches? How does the talk of these Christians lead to beliefs and behavior that are inconsistent with their faith and counterproductive in public dialogue? How does the rhetoric of Operation Rescue provide us with a case study of how these things happen?

This broad conception of rhetoric as evangelism in essence is critical in exploring important connections between the discourse of Operation Rescue and evangelical Christian experience. Throughout the book I am concerned with how the meaning of the Christian faith is symbolically constructed for Operation Rescue activists and for those who identify with Operation Rescue's purpose and vision. I am also primarily interested in how these constructions work to give an implicit and particular coherence that then functions as "equipment for living" for evangelical Christians. Such "equipment for living" offers a particular means by which the evangelical Christian *identifies* with the Christian faith, and offers a particular means, in James Davison Hunter's words, for the evangelical Christian "to know and live Christianity in its authentic and divinely intended manner."[53] It is in this way, I submit, that the problems of Operation Rescue can be connected more fruitfully with the more general blemishes of the evangelical and fundamentalist Christian traditions. It is also in this way that an examination of the rhetoric of Operation Rescue can shed more light on more general problems with respect to public discourse and violence. In so doing, this book provides a keener and more useful diagnosis of some significant "wrongs" of evangelical and fundamentalist Christian religion, both in private practice and in public expression.

Assuming all this to be the case, more specific questions come to bear. What exactly are these blemishes in the historical expression of the evangelical and fundamentalist Christian faith? How are these blemishes—these problematic features—reinforced in rhetoric like Operation Rescue's? These questions are the more general concerns of the chapters that follow.

Notes

1. Kenneth Burke, *Permanence and Change: An Anatomy of Purpose*, 3rd ed. (Berkeley: University of California Press, 1984), 80–81.
2. Andrew King, *Power and Communication* (Prospect Heights, Ill.: Waveland Press, 1987), 60.
3. Randall A. Terry, *Operation Rescue* (Springdale, Pa.: Whitaker House, 1988), 178.
4. Terry, *Operation Rescue*, 185.
5. Richard Exley, address at June 5, 1992 Wichita "Summer of Love" (Operation Rescue) kickoff rally, *Wichita Summer of Love, Part I*, Christian American Family Life Association, 1992, videocassette.
6. "Testimonies from Jailed Rescuers," unpublished collection, Josephine County [Oregon] Right to Life, [1988], 19.
7. David Zarefsky, *President Johnson's War on Poverty: Rhetoric and History* (Tuscaloosa: University of Alabama Press, 1986), 4–5.
8. George A. Kennedy, *Classical Rhetoric and Its Christian and Secular Tradition from Ancient to Modern Times* (Chapel Hill: University of North Carolina Press, 1980), 25.
9. Kennedy, *Classical Rhetoric*, 31.
10. Aristotle, *On Rhetoric: A Theory of Civic Discourse*, trans. George A. Kennedy (New York: Oxford University Press, 1991), 36.
11. Thomas B. Farrell, *Norms of Rhetorical Culture* (New Haven, Conn.: Yale University Press, 1993), 61.
12. Chaim Perelman and L. Olbrechts-Tyteca, *The New Rhetoric: A Treatise on Argumentation*, trans. John Wilkinson and Purcell Weaver (Notre Dame, Ind.: University of Notre Dame Press, 1969); Chaim Perelman, *The Realm of Rhetoric*, trans. William Kluback (Notre Dame, Ind.: University of Notre Dame Press, 1982); Stephen Toulmin, *The Uses of Argument* (Cambridge: Cambridge University Press, 1958).
13. Murray Edelman, *Constructing the Political Spectacle* (Chicago: University of Chicago Press, 1988), 104.
14. Peter L. Berger and Thomas Luckmann, *The Social Construction of Reality: A Treatise in the Sociology of Knowledge* (Garden City, N.Y.: Doubleday Books, 1967).
15. Thomas S. Kuhn, *The Structure of Scientific Revolutions*, 2nd ed. (Chicago: University of Chicago Press, 1970).
16. Burke clearly acknowledged the presence of the non-symbolic world, and he believed that symbolically constructed perspectives are ultimately accountable to the constraints of the non-symbolic world. As symbol-using beings, however, we have no way to engage the non-symbolic world without the mediation of symbols. See, in particular, Burke, *Permanence and Change*, 255–61.
17. Ibid., 95.
18. Kenneth Burke, "Terministic Screens," in *Language as Symbolic Action: Essays on Life, Literature, and Method* (Berkeley: University of California Press, 1966), 45.
19. In *Permanence and Change*, Burke devotes an entire section (69–163) to the systematic development of this idea.
20. Ibid., 35.
21. Richard B. Gregg, "Kenneth Burke's Concept of Rhetorical Negativity," in *Extensions of the Burkeian System*, ed. James W. Chesebro (Tuscaloosa: University of Alabama Press, 1993), 197.

22. Mark A. Pollock, "More on Burke," in *Communication Processes in a Mass-Mediated Age*, ed. Mark A. Pollock (Dubuque, Iowa: Kendall/Hunt Publishing Company, 1998), 87.

23. Mark A. Pollock, "Perspective by Incongruity," in *Communication Processes in a Mass-Mediated Age*, 114.

24. Malcolm X, "The Black Revolution," in *Malcolm X Speaks*, ed. George Breitman (New York: Pathfinder Books, 1989), 45.

25. Ibid., 52.

26. Ibid., 50.

27. Ibid., 53.

28. Ibid., 50, 57.

29. Charles J. Stewart, Craig Allen Smith, and Robert E. Denton, Jr., *Persuasion and Social Movements*, 4th ed. (Prospect Heights, Ill.: Waveland Press, 2001), 18.

30. Burke, *Permanence and Change*, 14.

31. Burke, "Definition of Man," in *Language as Symbolic Action*, 3.

32. Burke, *Permanence and Change*, 31.

33. Ibid., 49.

34. Kenneth Burke, *A Rhetoric of Motives* (1950; reprint, Berkeley: University of California Press, 1969), 141.

35. Sharon Crowley, "Reflections on an Argument that Won't Go Away: Or, a Turn of the Ideological Screw," *Quarterly Journal of Speech* 78 (1992): 464, 463.

36. Burke, *Rhetoric of Motives*, 20–21; *A Grammar of Motives* (1945; reprint, Berkeley: University of California Press, 1969), 33.

37. Burke, *Rhetoric of Motives*, 43.

38. Ibid., 22.

39. Ibid., 25.

40. Maurice Charland, "Constitutive Rhetoric: The Case of the *Peuple Québécois*," *Quarterly Journal of Speech* 73 (1987): 133–50.

41. With regard to propaganda, communication scholars Garth S. Jowett and Victoria O'Donnell have drawn a useful distinction between *integration* and *agitation*. See Jowett and O'Donnell, *Propaganda and Persuasion*, 3rd ed. (Thousand Oaks, Calif.: Sage Publications, 1999), 11–12.

42. Burke, *Permanence and Change*, 80.

43. See Augustine, *On Christian Doctrine*, trans. D. W. Robertson, Jr. (Upper Saddle River, N. J.: Prentice-Hall, 1958), 136–52.

44. Sally Miller Gearhart, "The Womanization of Rhetoric," *Women's Studies International Quarterly* 2 (1979): 196.

45. Ibid., 201.

46. Kenneth Burke, *The Rhetoric of Religion: Studies in Logology* (1961; reprint, Berkeley: University of California Press, 1970), 1.

47. Gordon D. Fee and Douglas Stuart, *How to Read the Bible for All Its Worth: A Guide to Understanding the Bible* (Grand Rapids, Mich.: Zondervan, 1982), 15.

48. Ibid., 16.

49. David S. Cunningham, *Faithful Persuasion: In Aid of a Rhetoric of Christian Theology* (Notre Dame, Ind.: University of Notre Dame Press, 1991), xv.

50. Ibid., 78–79.

51. Ibid., 257.
52. Ibid.
53. James Davison Hunter, *American Evangelicalism: Conservative Religion and the Quandary of Modernity* (New Brunswick, N.J.: Rutgers University Press, 1983), 9.

3

THE RHETORICAL AND THEOLOGICAL ANCESTRY OF OPERATION RESCUE

Evangelicalism and Fundamentalism in Francis A. Schaeffer's *A Christian Manifesto*

> *It is God's life-changing power that is able to touch every individual, who then has a responsibility to touch the world around him with the absolutes found in the Bible. In the end we must realize that the tide of humanism, with its loss of humanness, is not merely a cultural ill, but a spiritual ill that the truth given us in the Bible and Christ alone can cure.*
> —Francis A. Schaeffer and C. Everett Koop[1]

"Since the 1920s," observes church historian Timothy P. Weber, "fundamentalists have had an image problem. Many Americans equate fundamentalism with dogmatism, closed-mindedness, right-wing politics, and the 'paranoid style.'" Such equations, furthermore, have also been common among academics. "Until fairly recently," he continues, "most historians have seen fundamentalism as a movement of the socially backward, intellectually stunted, theologically naïve, and psychologically disturbed."[2] Clarence Darrow, the attorney who defended John Scopes in the 1925 "Monkey Trial," dismissed fundamentalists simply as "bigots and ignoramuses."[3]

Such characterizations are widely shared among scholars who have studied the pro-life movement and Operation Rescue in particular. In his study of the pro-life movement, sociologist Dallas Blanchard condemns fundamentalism, conceptualized as a cultural and religious ideology, as inherently misogynist, regressive, and violent. Writing that fundamentalists "worship a violent God" and "are more frequently wife abusers, committers of incest, and child abusers," he goes on to explain the "fundamentalist syndrome" as "authoritarianism, self-righteousness, prejudice against minorities, moral absolutism . . . and anti-analytical, anti-critical thinking."[4] Anthropologist Faye Ginsburg has suggested that fundamentalists and evangelicals more generally cannot be trusted to do their part to maintain a healthy pluralism in civic life.

Such characterizations are also echoed in studies of the abortion controversy done by rhetoric and communication scholars. Celeste Michelle Condit did make efforts to avoid unwarranted partisanship in her book-length treatment of the rhetorical dimensions of the abortion controversy. However, she was quick to denounce pro-life social protest, including picketing and "civil disobedience," as coercion and intimidation.[5] This denunciation, moreover, was not restricted just to protesters, but also extended to the pro-life movement as a whole. While discussing the foursome involved in the 1984 Gideon Project bombings in Pensacola, Florida, Condit declares that the ideology "from which the foursome acted" was essentially "the underlying ideology of the Right-to-Life movement as a whole. Such a hierarchical, authoritarian, coercion-focused, and militarist discourse is a partial pre-condition to violence." This "coercive ideology" was cast by Condit as waiting to be activated by other discursive conditions to engender a violent response.[6] The connection made here between pro-life beliefs—and, implicitly, the religious pattern of motivation that reinforces them—and violence is not much different from that made by *New York Times* columnist Anthony Lewis. He declared bluntly and simplistically that "[t]he hysterical rhetoric of the anti-abortion movement in this country is an invitation to violence."[7]

Other rhetorical studies have nourished the stereotype by making an explicit connection between pro-life discourse and the oppression of women. Analyzing the pro-life films *The Silent Scream* and *Eclipse of Reason*, rhetoric scholar Robert James Branham declares that "the films themselves eclipse reason" by "portraying women as ignorant, irrational, and gullible in order to deny them the ability to choose." The films, in his judgment, "subvert public discussion of the issue and reinforce demeaning and pernicious stereotypes of women."[8]

Such studies, then, generally draw from a conventional/scholarly wisdom about the pro-life movement, about pro-life motivation, and about the nature of the evangelicalism and fundamentalism that arguably give rise to such motivation. Those drawing upon such a wisdom seemingly cannot help but to maintain simplistic and unfair stereotypes that cathartically reaffirm their own ideological, "progressive" sensibilities.

It would be a mistake, however, to dismiss such studies completely. While overdetermined and to a significant degree unfair, these studies do make clear that there are indeed features of the conservative evangelical and fundamentalist Christian traditions in America that ill-equip such Christians to engage meaningfully and productively in public dialogue and political activism. According to Thomas and Dobson, these problems stem not from the particular beliefs these Christians hold, but rather from how these Christians have been encouraged to interpret and apply these beliefs to their lives and to the world in which they live. In particular, they have cautioned against the danger of thinking that successfully living out one's Christian faith is done primarily or even exclusively "by shortcuts through the dark and deep political jungle."[9]

This perspective on the problems of these faith traditions is shared by evangelical writer Os Guinness. In Guinness's view, American conservative evangelical and fundamentalist Christians have blundered badly in acknowledging and engaging the "pluralistic reality" of both the past and the present.[10] In particular, Christians within these faith traditions have (1) confused pluralism and relativism,[11] (2) confused or ignored the relationship between means and ends,[12] and (3) succumbed to the political stances of victimhood and resentment.[13] "Without a clear commitment to the common vision for the common good," he concludes, "evangelical and fundamentalist engagement in the public square serves neither America's interests nor their own."[14]

In my view, these insights point not to an *inherent* problem with these faith traditions, but rather a *rhetorical* problem: a problem of perspective with respect to what Christian faith means and how to live within Christian faith authentically. These rhetorical problems make it all too easy for conservative evangelical and fundamentalist Christians to adhere to an overall perspective of their faith that functions as a "trained incapacity"—in their engagement with others and with the larger culture of which they are a part. A major purpose of this chapter is to show what these features are, as well as how these features are reflected in Operation Rescue.

I begin the chapter by explaining briefly how I am conceptualizing *evangelicalism* and *fundamentalism* in this book. I then examine what I consider to be two problematic features that have marred the evangelical and fundamentalist Christian faith traditions in the United States: *anti-*

intellectualism and *the impulse to hegemony*. While these problematic features are not inherent to these faith traditions, they have been recurrent and persistent throughout the past two centuries.

Following this I turn my attention to an examination of Francis A. Schaeffer's influential book, *A Christian Manifesto*.[15] I have chosen Schaeffer as a case study for two reasons. First, Schaeffer is generally considered the most influential and best-known philosopher of the Christian Right. According to historian Grant Wacker, Schaeffer "probably qualifies as the official intellectual" of what Wacker describes as the "Evangelical Right."[16] Schaeffer's official connection with Moral Majority founder Jerry Falwell, during the rise of the Christian Right, was substantial.[17] And it is Schaeffer who is generally credited with introducing to the larger evangelical community the key term "secular humanism," the opposition to which has been a rallying cry and a defining feature of the Christian Right.[18] "As fundamentalists and evangelicals saw Schaeffer's films and read his numerous books," observes sociologist William Martin, "secular humanism came to be regarded not simply as an increasingly widespread way of looking at the world, but as a coherent movement diabolically bent on luring their children into every sort of immorality and unbelief in the course of undermining America's moral and spiritual foundations."[19] This influence has been particularly strong with *A Christian Manifesto*, which, according to political scientist Michael Lienesch, "remains the single most significant statement of Christian conservative political thinking."[20]

Schaeffer is important to investigate not just because of his pivotal influence on the Christian Right and on evangelicalism more generally, but also because of the influence his work has had on Randall Terry, founder of Operation Rescue. Martin has credited Schaeffer's work—specifically *A Christian Manifesto*—as key in Terry's turn from the duty to "evangelize others" to the duty to "get involved in controversial social issues" such as abortion.[21] This influence is also acknowledged by others who have written about Randall Terry and Operation Rescue.[22] Freelance writer Marian Faux characterized this influence, which she considers insidious, even more explicitly. "In Francis Schaeffer," she states, "eager young religionists like Randall Terry, who sensed that a new day was coming, had found their philosopher-king."[23]

In my analysis of *A Christian Manifesto*, I find the same two problematic elements of anti-intellectualism and the impulse to hegemony. More specifically, I argue that the text functions to invite the reader to identify with a conception of the evangelical Christian faith in which these two problematic elements figure prominently. In this way, I hope to establish the historical and theological foundations for the rhetoric of Operation Rescue, contextualizing the rhetorical problems of Operation Rescue with the more enduring problems within the evangelical and fundamentalist faith traditions.

Evangelicalism

In conceptualizing American evangelicalism, care must be taken not to elide the tradition's considerable diversity. Still, though, there are common features that make a broad sketch of the tradition possible.

Political scientist J. Christopher Soper observes, "Evangelicals are Protestant Christians who emphasize salvation by faith in the atoning death of Jesus Christ through personal conversion and the authority of scripture in matters of faith and Christian practice."[24] Evangelicalism, states sociologist James Davison Hunter, "may best be understood as a religiocultural phenomenon" featuring a worldview that "is deeply rooted in the theological tradition of the Reformation, in northern European Puritanism, and later in American Puritanism and the First and Second Great Awakenings in North America."[25]

A primary distinctive of evangelicalism is its view of the Bible. Hunter writes that "[p]erhaps the most important element of Evangelical theology is its particular conception of the Bible as the literary vehicle for God's revelation, both of his own nature and of his intentions in human history. As the inspired testimony of a perfect and supreme deity, [the Bible is] the final authority in matters that pertain to spiritual and everyday reality" and "is to be trusted as the sole authoritative testimony to absolute truth."[26] "Evangelicals," declares Soper, "invariably focus on the Bible as the final test of whatever claims to be the voice of God."[27] Gordon D. Fee and Douglas Stuart, as evangelical theologians, affirm the overriding commitment to biblical authority on the part of evangelicals in this succinct way: "In the words of the child that moved Augustine to read a passage at his conversion experience, we say, '*Tolle, lege,* Take up and read.' The Bible is God's eternal Word. Read it. Understand it. Obey it."[28]

Second, evangelicalism is distinguished by particular views on the nature of Jesus Christ and the nature of salvation. "Evangelicals," affirms Soper, "are distinctive among Christian believers because of their emphasis upon a personal faith in Jesus as the only way to salvation. A person can only be 'saved' by understanding and believing that Christ died on the cross for his or her sins."[29] To evangelicals, Christ is God-incarnate, God in human form, fully divine and fully human. Christ's death and resurrection, therefore, has made possible salvation from our fallen condition, separation from God, and eternal judgment. Evangelicals also insist that this salvation is individual, not social, in nature.

Third, evangelicals are distinguished by what Soper describes as "an emphasis on integrating religious beliefs and personal conduct," a belief that "they have an obligation to pattern their lives according to the will of God."[30] One's Christian beliefs, in other words, are not to remain merely a matter of intellectual assent, but are instead to be the guiding principles for the living of life in its entirety. To evangelicals, this entails not only personal growth and maturation in one's relationship with God, but also evangelism, social action, or some combination of both.

While certain core beliefs specific to evangelicalism can be readily identified, the history of evangelicalism is somewhat less clear. Since the term *evangelical* did not emerge as a common term in public dialogue until the public success of Billy Graham in the 1950s, the length and nature of evangelical history depend largely upon how evangelicalism is specifically defined. "Narrow" views of evangelical history, which date evangelicalism only back to the middle of the twentieth century, correspond with a conception of evangelicalism as a contemporary sociopolitical phenomenon. Reflecting this view, theologian Mark Ellingsen has conceptualized evangelicalism specifically as a visible movement consisting of "organizations like the National Association of Evangelicals (and a number of its member denominations), the periodical *Christianity Today*, and even Billy Graham and his organization."[31] The evangelical "movement," from this perspective, is best seen as a moderating response to the militance of American fundamentalism, which had been in disrepute since the mid-1920s. While evangelicalism grew out of fundamentalism and still seeks to preserve the "fundamentals of faith" against liberal theology and secular culture, evangelicals assume a "more constructive and less defensive separatist stance ... engaging modern society in order to influence and transform it."[32]

My sympathies, by contrast, lie with "broad" views of evangelical history that tend to conceptualize evangelicalism primarily in terms of its theological outlook, as briefly sketched above. In this theological sense, evangelicalism in America dates back to the Puritans. Toward the end of the eighteenth century, evangelicalism consisted of theologically conservative Protestantism that was increasingly coming under the influence of revivalism, marked particularly by the First Great Awakening (in the 1730s and 1740s) and the influence of revivalist preacher George Whitefield.[33]

Conceived this way, evangelicalism also represents the conservative Protestantism that held sway in America throughout much of the nineteenth century. Especially in the wake of the Second Great Awakening, theological evangelicalism was the basis for broad social, cultural, and political consensus in America during this time. "During the decades from the post-Revolutionary revivals at least through the Civil War," states historian Mark Noll, "the country's ethos was predominantly evangelical. In a number of particulars, this was indeed the era of 'Christian America' as evangelical Protestants would use the term."[34]

Conceived this way, evangelicalism is not a response to fundamentalism—as Ellingsen has suggested—but instead the other way around. "[T]o understand fundamentalism," declares historian George Marsden, "we must ... see it as a distinct version of evangelical Christianity uniquely shaped by the circumstances of America in the early twentieth century." In his view, a full understanding of fundamentalism depends upon an understanding of "how individuals who were committed to typically American versions of evangelical Christianity responded to and were influenced by the social, intellectual, and religious crises of their time."[35]

Both views on the origins of evangelicalism are correct, depending primarily upon how the definitional boundaries for evangelicalism are drawn. Common to both views of the evangelical tradition or movement, moreover, is an essentially consistent, conservative, Protestant theological outlook. This outlook is shared in the related tradition of fundamentalism.

Fundamentalism

"A fundamentalist," quips Marsden, "is an evangelical who is angry about something." Elaborating, he declares that "an American fundamentalist is an evangelical who is militant in opposition to liberal theology in the churches or to changes in cultural values or mores. Fundamentalists are not just religious conservatives, they are conservatives who are willing to take a stand and to fight."[36]

Fundamentalism can be difficult to define precisely, since it can be seen both as a religious and political movement in the late nineteenth and early twentieth centuries, and as a reasonably coherent theological perspective on authentic Christian faith. While there is some overlap, they are not the same. There is universal consensus neither on how to conceptualize fundamentalism, nor on how to draw the relevant theoretical and historical boundaries. As with evangelicalism, nonetheless, there are some generally accepted defining features of the fundamentalist faith tradition and its history. In what follows, I discuss four such features: (1) premillenial dispensationalism, (2) reaction against the "liberal" turn in American Protestantism, (3) the Fundamentalist-Modernist controversy, and (4) separatism.

Premillenial Dispensationalism

The first of these features is the prominence of premillenial dispensationalism, both as a theological system and as a basis for a social and political outlook. In his classic study, historian Ernest R. Sandeen emphasizes the preeminence of theological considerations in understanding fundamentalism.[37] In Sandeen's view, fundamentalism was the result primarily of the importation of millenarianism from Britain.

Millenarianism is a theological perspective on Christianity that emphasizes the second coming of Christ and the nature of the end of history. Central to this perspective is the "millenium," described in Revelation 20, in which Christ is said to reign directly over the earth for a thousand years.[38] The historical relationship between the millenium and the second coming of Christ is the basis of a fundamental distinction between the "postmillenial" and "premillenial" views.

During much of the nineteenth century in the United States, the primary manifestation of millenarianism was "postmillennialism," which holds that the second coming of Christ takes place *after* the millenium. In the postmillenial view, the millenium is not a literal one thousand years, but instead an indefinite and long period of time. In this view, further, the millenium began at the start of the church age (when Christianity was born) and continues into the present. This view of postmillennialism coincides with a progressive view of history in which Christians are able, incrementally, to perfect human society and usher in the Kingdom of God on earth. Postmillenialism fit well with the cultural and political dominance of Protestantism in the United States throughout much of the nineteenth century. "On the face of it," observes Noll, "it would be hard to imagine a nation more thoroughly biblical than the United States between the American Revolution and the Civil War."[39] Marsden declares, "In 1870 almost all American Protestants thought of America as a Christian nation.... Protestant evangelicals considered their faith to be the normative American creed."[40]

There emerged, nonetheless, the challenges of modernization and industrialization, along with the ascendance of Darwinism and liberal "higher criticism" of the Bible. These developments, seen by Protestant evangelicals as unmitigated attacks on the authority of the Bible, increasingly challenged evangelical Protestant optimism about American political and cultural development. Thus, these events and perceptions provided fertile ground for the opposing, premillenial view, which holds that the second coming of Christ, and the cosmic judgment that accompanies that event, occurs *before* the millenium described in Revelation. With such a view comes a pessimistic outlook on social and cultural development, in which society and culture progressively degenerate until Christ personally returns and renders judgment. Such a view, in Marsden's words, "offered a plausible explanation of the difficulties the church was facing"—difficulties that included "the secularization of the culture" and "the apostasy (liberalism) within the churches themselves."[41]

There was also the refinement and increasing acceptance of the "strikingly antimodernist" theological system of "historical" dispensationalism.[42] Theologically, historical dispensationalism has two distinguishing features: (1) a strict separation between historical Israel and the Christian church, so that God's promises to Israel in the Old Testament do *not* apply to Christians; and (2) a segmented view of history, with distinct eras—"dispensations"—in which, according to Sandeen, "the mode of God's operations, if not nature's, was unique."[43]

More interesting, though, is the particular approach to the reading and interpretation of the Bible that underlies historical dispensationalism. Following from the beliefs that the Bible is strictly inerrant (i.e., everything in the Bible is completely and literally true) and unitary (i.e., everything in the Bible is equally true and must be equally considered), historical dispensationalism approached the Bible with a hyper-Baconian, "inductive" hermeneutic that, in Marsden's view, combines the "supernatural" and the "scientific."[44] "Since the Bible could be 'proved' to be inspired through careful induction," relates Timothy Weber, "the theologian was free to use it as the scientist did the data in his laboratory. Because the Bible was inerrantly inspired in its entirety, each passage was the stuff out of which theology was made. Every proposition had to be sifted, analyzed, compared, and examined until larger connections emerged."[45]

Reaction against the "Liberal" Turn in American Protestantism

The fact that this particular biblical hermeneutic requires a strict and literal inerrancy helps to explain the severity of the reaction to the "liberal" turn in American Protestantism, a turn that resulted in what we now know as the "mainline" denominations. In addition to Darwinism, the latter half of the nineteenth century saw the development of "higher criticism" as a sustained line of biblical inquiry that functioned to cast significant doubt or even aspersion on the long-cherished "inerrancy" of the Bible. By 1890, claims religion scholar Grant Wacker, traditional views regarding "the source and the authority of Scripture" were facing serious challenge.[46]

The reaction against this "liberal" theological turn culminated in the namesake and most recognizable artifact of historical fundamentalism. I refer to *The Fundamentals*, an irenic yet bold twelve-volume set of articles published between 1910 and 1915, in which "orthodox" theologians sought to provide a coherent and compelling answer to theological liberalism.[47] The scope of influence envisioned by these writers was grand, and the number of these books distributed was in excess of three million.[48] To be sure, *The Fundamentals* utterly failed to realize the hopes of neutralizing the influences of modernism and theological liberalism. They did, however, have a long-term impact. In Marsden's judgment, they "became a symbolic point of reference for identifying a 'fundamentalist' movement,"[49] which then enabled the proponents of theological orthodoxy to provide a more unified response against modernism and theological liberalism. In fact, the term *fundamentalist* was first coined by Curtis Lee Lewis, editor of the Baptist periodical *The Watchman-Examiner*, in describing those who were ready "to do battle royal for the Fundamentals."[50]

The Fundamentalist-Modernist Controversy

This description implies the third distinguishing feature of fundamentalism: the fundamentalist-modernist controversy of the early 1920s. This struggle was waged for control of particular Protestant denominations, including the Northern Baptist Convention, the Presbyterian Church in the U.S.A., and the Disciples of Christ.[51] Included among the belligerents were notables such as Princeton theologian J. Gresham Machen and liberal Baptist preacher Harry Emerson Fosdick. In 1922, Fosdick lambasted the defenders of theological orthodoxy with a provocative and well-publicized sermon titled "Shall the Fundamentalists Win?"[52] The following year, Machen responded with his classic work *Christianity and Liberalism*, in which he argued that theological liberalism amounted to a different religion entirely, and that liberals should therefore be expelled from the churches.[53]

The fundamentalist-modernist controversy is widely considered to have culminated in the famous 1925 Scopes Trial in Dayton, Tennessee. A biology teacher, John T. Scopes, was put on trial for teaching evolutionary theory in violation of state law. This trial was a prominent public clash between fundamentalism and modernism, particularly since Democratic politician and former presidential candidate William Jennings Bryan—one of the most famous public advocates of fundamentalism—agreed to serve as chief prosecutor for the case. While Scopes was found guilty and fined, fundamentalists won a painfully hollow victory. Defense attorney Clarence Darrow humiliated Bryan to the point that the prominent apologist for fundamentalism was reviled in the press as "backwoods" and "ignorant."[54]

The trial represented a resounding and unrecoverable defeat not just for Bryan, but for fundamentalism as well. According to Ellingsen, "The Scopes Trial placed the Fundamentalist movement's prestige on the line, because the movement had invested so much support in the crusade against the theory of evolution."[55] In the wake of the trial and the acutely hostile press coverage, observes Marsden, "it became increasingly difficult to take fundamentalism seriously."[56]

Separatism

Following the public humiliation of the Scopes Trial, fundamentalism (including theologically conservative evangelicalism as described in this book) retreated into a lengthy period of political disengagement. Fundamentalists, according to historian Joel A. Carpenter, "began to take on an alienated 'faithful remnant' stance toward the culture."[57] This stance seemed to fit well with their exposure to what Richard John Neuhaus and Michael Cromartie describe as "the half century of ostracism and ridicule . . . in all 'respectable' circles of public discourse—the mainline Protestant churches, the academy, the prestige media, the scientific community, and both major political parties."[58] William Martin states, "Fundamentalist Christianity did indeed pass through a wilderness, but it did not enter the grave," instead undergoing a "transformation" that involved "shifting, realigning, and reorganizing its base. Since they had lost the fight for control of denominations and seminaries, fundamentalists set about creating a whole new set of institutions and structures in which the true, pure, and unadulterated Christian message could be preserved and preached."[59]

Though evangelicals would begin again to enter the public sphere and regain public respectability as early as the 1950s, with the emergence of Billy Graham, fundamentalists as a group did not decisively plunge again into overt political involvement until the 1980 Presidential election. Since that time, however, their influence has been significant, as those writing about the Christian Right acknowledge.

In what follows, I follow Marsden in conceptualizing evangelicalism broadly, with fundamentalism as a specific historical and contemporary manifestation of evangelicalism. Having sketched evangelicalism and fundamentalism, I now turn to a discussion of what I call "problematic features" of these faith traditions. These features—anti-intellectualism and the impulse to hegemony—are not inherent to these faith traditions; they are, however, recurring features of their historic expression.

Problematic Features of Evangelicalism and Fundamentalism

Anti-Intellectualism
C. S. Lewis protégé Harry Blamires declared:

> There is no longer a Christian mind. There is still, of course, a Christian ethic, a Christian practice, and a Christian spirituality. But as a *thinking* being the modern Christian has succumbed to secularization. Except over a very narrow field of thinking, chiefly touching questions of strictly personal conduct, we Christians in the modern world accept, for the purpose of mental activity, a frame of reference constructed by the secular mind and a set of criteria reflecting secular evaluations.[60]

In some respects Blamires's claims go beyond the specific problem I am seeking to articulate here. He has intended his comments to include more than just the traditions of evangelicalism and fundamentalism as described in this book. Further, much of his critique presumes a fairly strict Christian-secular opposition; while that is not necessarily a problem, this opposition is beyond the purview of anti-intellectualism as I am developing it.

Nonetheless, Blamires's critique is quite useful in that he articulates a recurring problem throughout the evangelical Christian tradition: the divorce of the faith from the intellect. It is this divorce that also characterizes the anti-intellectualism of the evangelical and fundamentalist traditions. This recurring problem is also articulated by historian Mark Noll, who declares that "[t]he scandal of the evangelical mind is that there is not much of an evangelical mind. American evangelicals are not exemplary for their thinking, and they have not been so for several generations."[61]

Noll's book *The Scandal of the Evangelical Mind* offers a systematic critique of this tendency within evangelicalism to divorce the faith from serious, sustained thinking. In particular, he has harshly judged historical fundamentalism as an "intellectual disaster" reinforcing unreflective and damaging "intellectual instincts that still . . . exert a pervasive influence over the thinking of evangelicals."[62] Fundamentalism, "was important for encouraging several kinds of simple anti-intellectualism, for reinforcing some of the questionable features of the nineteenth-century American evangelical synthesis, and for promoting right conclusions with the wrong kind of thought." "The result," he claims, "was a tendency toward a docetism in outlook and a gnosticism in method," both of which discourage sustained and fruitful intellectual activity.[63]

It is in response to perceived crisis that the intellectual habits of historical fundamentalism have exerted a particular influence upon contemporary evangelicalism. "When faced with a crisis situation," states Noll, "we evangelicals usually do one of two things. We either mount a public crusade, or we retreat into an inner pious sanctum. Not since the mid-nineteenth century have evangelicals characteristically tried to meet crises with a combination of voluntaristic activism, personal spirituality, and hard theological effort."[64]

The simplicity in thinking that gives rise to such approaches is not just the intellectual legacy of historical fundamentalism. Rather, it is more generally a product of an evangelical tradition that enjoyed virtually unchallenged legitimacy throughout American history up to the latter portion of the nineteenth century. In significant part because of this unchallenged legitimacy, evangelicals during this time "mostly just took for granted a fit between their faith" and the "ideals of the American situation." "Little need was felt to exercise the mind for Christ," Noll observes, "since evangelism and fervent moral activism seemed so successful at meeting the church's immediate needs." When the profound cultural and intellectual challenges came toward the end of the nineteenth century, evangelicals "turned to their intellectual resources" and "found that the cupboard was nearly bare."[65] In response to this crisis, unfortunately, evangelicals as a whole chose the easier road of cultural non-engagement, by way of either unreflective confrontation or unreflective avoidance. Thus began a pattern that has persisted to this day.

In *No Place for Truth*, theologian David F. Wells has offered a similar critique in more expressly theological terms, lamenting what he has called the "disappearance" of evangelical theology. Contemporary evangelicals, he claims, have "less biblical fidelity, less interest in truth, less seriousness, less capacity to speak the Word of God to our own generation in a way that offers an alternative to what it already thinks." In contrast to the "older orthodoxy," which was "driven by a passion for truth" and thus emphasized theology, "[t]he newer evangelicalism is not driven by the same passion for truth, and that is why it is often empty of theological interest."[66] In his critique, Wells points not only to intellectual habits of the type described by

Noll, but also to specifics of evangelical accommodation to modernism and to secular culture that have at least in part followed from this lack of concern for theological truth, as well as from the lack of concern for sustained and critical thinking more generally.

Theologian Millard Erickson has documented similar problems in support of his claim of a contemporary "resurgence of anti-intellectualism." To Erickson, this anti-intellectualism has taken two major and interrelated forms. The first form relates to the lowering of academic standards for education and pastoral ministry. While the evangelical tradition in the mid-twentieth century did take such concerns seriously, these goals are being increasingly abandoned. As evidence of this, he discussed the devaluation of seminary education by "megachurches" and the proliferation of "educational shortcuts" like the doctor of ministry (D.Min.) degree.[67] The second major form of this resurgent anti-intellectualism, according to Erickson, is the anti-intellectual philosophy of "pragmatism." This philosophy has encouraged evangelical churches and ministries to "not ask so much whether ministry is doctrinally sound and in keeping with the basic theological position of the church, but what results it is providing." This corresponds with the current "tendency not to wrestle with the really difficult issues of the faith."[68]

This anti-intellectualism that marks contemporary evangelicalism is confluent with a number of other trends that Erickson has identified as troubling. These include the increasing dominance of emotionalism in worship, the emphasis on counseling and pastoral care at the expense of exposition and instruction, the increasing popularity of the "seeker-sensitive" model of church worship and evangelism, a disproportionate focus on supernaturalism, and a lack of social concern—a concern that would have its vibrant source in "the social application of the gospel."[69] These confluences give rise to a more general concern articulated by Erickson, that "modern evangelicalism has retained some of the less desirable features of the old fundamentalism, and adopted some of the poorer qualities of the modernism which fundamentalism opposed."[70] Such features serve the evangelical faith tradition, and arguably the world, poorly.

The recurrent anti-intellectualism in the evangelical faith tradition can further be seen in part as a product of American culture. In *The Democratization of American Christianity*, historian Nathan O. Hatch has argued for the critical importance of "the transitional period between 1780 and 1830" in understanding the particular development of American Christianity, particularly evangelicalism."[71] Throughout his book Hatch emphasizes how the Revolutionary ethos fostered a significantly broad anti-authoritarian impulse in evangelicalism. Consistent with the cultural ethos of the young republic, there was profound emphasis placed upon the wisdom of the "common" and "unlearned" people, the corruption of the respected and the elite, the mistrust of authority, and the inviolability of the individual. This radically democratic religious climate explains at least in part the success in America of renegade, itinerant preachers such as Lorenzo Dow and William Smythe Babcock.[72]

It is not difficult to see how this religious climate could foster and reinforce attitudes of anti-intellectualism. Within such a climate, a concern with the life of the Christian mind—honoring God with the mind—is all too easily understood as elitist and anti-freedom. Hatch's discussion of the emergence of the Disciples of Christ is instructive in this regard. Seeking "a radical simplification of the gospel," the leaders of this movement "demanded, in light of the American and French revolutions, a new dispensation free from the trammels of history, a new kind of church based on democratic principles, and a new form of biblical authority calling for common people to interpret the New Testament for themselves."[73] Among other things, they called for the explicit rejection of "the traditions of learned theology altogether," and in their place they called for "a populist hermeneutic premised on the inalienable right of every person to understand the New Testament for him- or herself."[74]

The recurrent anti-intellectualism that marks the evangelical and fundamentalist faith traditions can thus be seen as a confluence of particular beliefs and habits of thought: (1) the belief that faith and thinking are separate and to a significant degree mutually exclusive; (2) the belief that thinking and theological effort are irrelevant, elitist, and therefore of little to no value; (3) the valuation of pragmatism, emotionalism, and individualism; and (4) the tendency to interpret and apply the Bible in a literal and simplistic way.

The Impulse to Hegemony

Distinct from, but related to, the recurrent spirit of anti-intellectualism, the impulse to hegemony in evangelicalism and fundamentalism is a distinctly rhetorical construction in that it reflects a particular view of the past, the present, and the future. It is a locus of motives that stems from a particular understanding of history, a particular understanding of the advancement of God's Kingdom, and a particular understanding of those who are seen as standing in the way of the advancement of that Kingdom.

Though writing as a non-conservative evangelical expressing concern that "the American evangelical movement" is "slowly being politicized and co-opted by the religious right,"[75] Tom Sine offers a keen illumination of the contemporary manifestation of this impulse to hegemony within the evangelical tradition. He does so by focusing on the rhetoric of the religious right.

One particularly significant feature of this rhetoric is its characterization of the religious right's adversaries. Their adversaries are characterized as, in short, a profound and somber threat both to the nation and to the future of Christianity. "'The humanists are coming, the humanists are coming!' has been the rallying cry of the religious right for two decades," Sine declares. "Leaders on the Christian right have convinced themselves that a liberal humanist elite is intent on destroying the family, undermining Christian faith, and collectivizing America to participate in a one-world gulag."[76] But while this enemy is powerful, it is also vulnerable. Many fundamentalists and conservative evangelicals, wrote Sine, "seem to believe that if somehow they can take back America politically, they can forestall the liberals and humanists from destroying our families, undermining our faith, and further socializing America. And then perhaps God can use America to head off the collectivization of the planet."[77]

As communication scholar Marsha Vanderford has pointed out, this "paradoxical" characterization of an enemy who is both powerful and vulnerable is an important function of vilification that encourages and sustains activism.[78] Sine observes, "It is difficult to exaggerate the importance of this vision for the remarkable growth of the religious right. It directly contributed to the ... politicization of millions of fundamentalists and evangelicals."[79] It has also ensured the large-scale success of groups like Jerry Falwell's Moral Majority and, later, Pat Robertson's Christian Coalition.

While this sort of vilification does encourage activism, it also rigidifies views of what the Christian faith means and for what Christians should strive. "There is a growing conviction among many [conservative evangelicals] that their primary mission as Christians is no longer to share God's love with the world but to try to save God's bacon and take back America."[80] In other words, the goal for which evangelical Christians should strive is represented primarily as "winning" in the political realm. A goal such as this only nurtures and reinforces yearnings of social and political hegemony.

This conflation of religion and politics stems from an idealized view of America's past. This view of the nation's past characterizes the nation as the "new Israel," as God's chosen nation. "I believe America has reached the pinnacle of greatness," declared Jerry Falwell, "unlike any nation in human history because our Founding Fathers established America's laws and precepts on the principles recorded in the laws of God, including the Ten Commandments. God has blessed this nation, because in its early days she sought to honor God and the Bible, the inerrant Word of the living God."[81] Pat Robertson subscribes to the same view. After taking stock of the United States's greatness, he likewise pointed out that "these things did not happen by accident, nor did they happen somehow because the citizens of America are smarter or more worthy than the citizens of any other country. It happened because those men and women who founded this land made a solemn covenant that they would be the people of God and that this would be a Christian nation."[82]

As seen in the above discussions of evangelicalism and fundamentalism, the temptation to view the United States and its past this way is by no means limited to the contemporary Christian Right. Marsden states that even in the Gilded Age, "[f]ew Protestants doubted that theirs was a 'Christian nation.' Though religion in America was voluntary, a Protestant version of the medieval ideal of 'Christendom' still prevailed. American civilization, said Protestant leaders, was essentially 'Christian.'"[83]

As seen above, this predominant view produced profound shock within evangelicalism in the face of the late-nineteenth century's profound social and theological challenges. These challenges, and the resulting collective shock, are in significant part what precipitated the rise of fundamentalism in the first place.

In several important respects, therefore, scholars are justified in linking the contemporary Christian Right with historical fundamentalism. In both, America is seen as a distinctly and uniquely Christian nation; in both, perceived challenges to this status are interpreted as fundamental threats; in both, maintaining or regaining a hegemony of Christian principles is seen not as coercive, but as reinforcing freedom and fulfilling a fundamental purpose of the Christian community. In both, finally, these beliefs create and sustain an impulse to hegemony.

These views, however, do not hold up under scrutiny. Noll, Hatch, and Marsden remarked, "We feel that a careful study of the facts of history shows that early America does not deserve to be considered uniquely, distinctly or even predominantly Christian, if we mean by the word 'Christian' a state of society reflecting the ideals presented in Scripture. There is no lost golden age to which American Christians may return."[84]

This does not mean that evangelicals and fundamentalists who have held this view are simply and completely mistaken about the existence of a Christian role in American history. It does mean, though, that they have misread the particulars to draw unwarranted conclusions about the religious heritage of the country. In this regard, Noll has made a useful distinction between "strong" and "weak" views of Christian America. In a "weak" sense the conception of Christian America may be justified. "In certain respects and at certain periods," he observes, America can be seen as "at least in reasonable conformity to Christian norms."[85] The "strong" view discussed thus far, however, is "misguided at best" and "pernicious at worst."[86]

Having described the recurrent problems of anti-intellectualism and the impulse to hegemony, I now show how these problematic features of the evangelical faith tradition are reflected in Schaeffer's *A Christian Manifesto* and, consequently, got passed on to Operation Rescue.

Problematic Features in Schaeffer

Prior to writing *A Christian Manifesto*, Francis Schaeffer had already gained ascendance as a contemporary Christian philosopher and catalyzed the return of fundamentalists and conservative evangelicals to political activism. *How Should We Then Live?* (1976) provides a sweeping analysis of Western culture that focuses on the Renaissance, as a source of anti-Christian humanism, and the Reformation. *Whatever Happened to the Human Race?* (1979), co-authored with C. Everett Koop, focuses on abortion as the most overt symptom of the cultural decline brought on by the hegemony of secular humanism.

In *A Christian Manifesto* (1981), Schaeffer shifted from an emphasis on cultural analysis to an emphasis on practical and political action, addressing (among others) the following questions: How should Christians respond to the increasing domination of secular humanism in American culture? What are their duties to resist? And what are the proper limits to that resistance?

The opening section of the book provides a reminder of the essential theme of much of his previous work. Secular humanism is becoming increasingly dominant in American culture, and this threat requires a Christian response. "The basic problem of the Christians in this country in the last eighty years or so," begins Schaeffer, "in regard to society and in regard to government, is that they have seen things in bits and pieces instead of totals." They have noticed social ills such as pornography and abortion, but they "have failed to see that all of this has come about due to a shift in world view. This shift has been *away from* a world view that was at least vaguely Christian in people's memory . . . *toward* something completely different—toward a world view based upon the idea that the final reality is impersonal matter or energy shaped into its present form by impersonal chance."[87]

Building upon this reminder, Schaeffer offered a rationale for Christians to fight and reverse this dominance of secular humanism by engaging in social and political activism. He did this by arguing that the political principles by which the United States was founded are firmly rooted in the Christian tradition. Christian beliefs, to Schaeffer, are considered central not just to the development of the "rule of law" more generally,[88] but also to the development of the particular political balance in the United States between freedom and authority. In short, the freedom that makes pluralism (as opposed to religious tyranny) possible comes from the "Christian consensus" behind the nation's founding.

These characterizations build this rationale in two important ways. First, they establish the legitimacy of working to advance Christian principles in America's political sphere because these principles are normative: they are true to the founding of the country, and they are responsible for the freedom our country has enjoyed. Second, these characterizations magnify the threat of secular humanism to this "consensus," which is clearly portrayed as placing in jeopardy the futures of both Christianity and the nation itself.

Finally, Schaeffer offered a particular vision and rationale for civil disobedience by Christians. Having taken note of the American political scene in 1981, Schaeffer expressed optimism that this important work of resistance and reversal could be done through established legal and political channels. "[T]he fact of the conservative swing in the United States in the 1980 election," Schaeffer suggests, constituted an "open window" for such resistance and reversal. "Now the window is open," he declares, "and we must take advantage of it in every way we can as citizens, as Christian citizens of the democracy in which we still have freedom. We must try to roll back the other total entity [secular humanism]."[89]

Apparently keeping in mind the possibility that the "window" will not remain open, though, Schaeffer writes that "[i]t is time to think to *the bottom line*" of civil disobedience as did the Founding Fathers. Particularly since "[w]e have reached a place today which is violently opposed to what the Founding Fathers . . . had in mind when they came together and formed the union," Christians must realize that "*[t]he bottom line* is that at a certain point there is not only the right, but the duty, to disobey the state."[90] This is so because "God has ordained the state as a *delegated* authority; it is not autonomous. The state is to be an agent of justice, to restrain evil by punishing the wrongdoer, and to protect the good in society. When it does the reverse, *it has no proper authority*."[91] He emphasized later that if Christians "do not practice *the bottom line* of civil disobedience on the appropriate level"—a level that sometimes will include "force in some form"—"when the state has abrogated its authority," then they are "not living under the Scripture."[92]

In making his case for political activism and civil disobedience by Christians, unfortunately, Schaeffer draws upon the same problematic features of evangelicalism and fundamentalism that I have discussed. In what follows, I show how *A Christian Manifesto* exhibits the same features of anti-intellectualism and the impulse to hegemony.

Anti-Intellectualism

Schaeffer's *A Christian Manifesto* replicates the recurrent strain of anti-intellectualism in evangelicalism and fundamentalism not by formally and explicitly scorning intellection. Rather, it does so by encouraging, within the form and appearance of intellection, the adoption of a simplistic, anti-intellectual framework for thinking about the Christian faith.

Conspicuous and foundational in this regard is the rhetorical use of the term *secular humanism*. Not just a mere identifier of a persistent cultural problem, in *A Christian Manifesto* it serves as the central term of what Kenneth Burke has called a "rejection frame"—a perspective or orientation that draws meaning and persuasive force from singular opposition to an idea or key term, or to symbols of authority.[93]

While rejection frames can carry with them a significant degree of rhetorical force, they also tend to be oversimplistic, inviting adherents of that frame to make connections of meaning that miss the complexities of the situation. "Frames stressing the ingredient of *rejection*," observes Burke, "tend to lack the well-rounded quality of a *complete* here-and-now philosophy. They make for fanaticism, the singling-out of one factor above others in the charting of human relationships."[94]

While I discuss more fully Burke's ideas regarding rhetorical "representation" in chapter 6, the essence of Burke's position can be seen here. Well-roundedness—scope—in a particular representation of reality is critical to avoid fundamental distortions or miscalculations of reality. Employing a rejection frame to represent authentic Christian faith, Burke might say, oversimplifies the meaning and essence of that faith. The oversimplification inherent in this rejection frame promotes anti-intellectualism in that it promotes simplistic responses to the challenges of the world, and in that it predisposes its adherents to avoid careful, sustained, and reflective connections between the essence of their faith and the "signs" of social and political culture.

This corresponding reduction of complexity to simplicity is reflected in Schaeffer's book in two noteworthy themes. The first theme I refer to as "total entities." It is inaugurated in Schaeffer's discussion of "parts and totals," which appears at the beginning of the *Manifesto*. As seen above, Schaeffer faults contemporary American Christians for seeing things "in bits and pieces" instead of "totals." While Christians have been observant of important social ills, he observes, "they have not seen this as a totality—each thing being a part, a symptom, of a much larger problem. They have failed to see that all of this has come about due to a shift in world view—that is, through a fundamental change in the overall way people think and view the world and life as a whole."[95] These "totals" are quickly revealed to be but two in number: the orthodox evangelical/fundamentalist "totality" and the secular humanist "totality."

The first "totality" is set up in terms of an absolute truth that covers not just matters of belief and faith, but all aspects of nature and reality. Responding to "pietist" Christianity that spiritualized the faith while implicitly judging itself irrelevant to other aspects of life and reality, Schaeffer writes:

> Many Christians do not mean what I mean when I say that Christianity is true, or Truth. When I say Christianity is true, I mean it is true to total reality—the total of what is, beginning with the central reality, the objective existence of the personal-infinite God. Christianity is not just a series of truths but *Truth*—Truth about all of reality. And the holding to that Truth intellectually—and in some poor way living upon that Truth, the Truth of what is—brings forth not only certain personal results, but also governmental and legal results."[96]

Fundamentally opposed to this first "totality" is humanism, which holds to "the material-energy, chance concept of reality." In this view of reality, "Man begin[s] from himself, with no knowledge except what he himself can discover and no standards outside of himself. In this view Man is the measure of all things as the Enlightenment expressed it."[97]

Schaeffer makes abundantly clear the diametrical opposition of these two "totalities." "These two world views," he states, "stand as totals in complete antithesis to each other in content and also in their natural results—including sociological and governmental results, and specifically including law.[98] There is no way to mix these two total world views," he declares. Liberal theology, according to Schaeffer, has repeatedly tried to synthesize the two. "But in each case when the chips are down," he writes, "these liberal theologians have always come down, as naturally as a ship coming into home port, on the side of the non-religious humanist."[99]

The totalized nature of this opposition leads logically to a division between absolute faithfulness to reality and absolute faithlessness to reality. While the Christian totality is completely true to what reality is, secular humanism is quite another matter. "Christians," exclaims Schaeffer, "should be inalterably opposed" to this "false and destructive humanism, which is false to the Bible and equally false to what Man is."[100] The humanists, he writes, "not only do not know the truth of the final reality, God, they do not know who Man is. Their concept of Man is what Man is not, just as their concept of the final reality is what final reality is not. Since their concept of Man is mistaken, their concept of society and of law is mistaken, and they have no sufficient base for either society or law."[101]

My purpose here is not necessarily to render judgment with respect to Schaeffer's various positions—on transcendent truth; on the concern with secularization and humanism; and on the need for Christians to have a voice in cultural, social, and political affairs. What concerns me, rather, is the sheer simplicity with which the dynamics of history and culture are rendered. Life in Schaeffer's view mimics the melodramatic form all too thoroughly. History reflects a simple dualism. Individuals and collectives, on the surface quite complex, really have simple and easily discerned motivations. Certainty is within our grasp after all, and possible to achieve without too much mental exertion. This, it seems to me, is the stuff of anti-intellectualism—an anti-intellectualism that results in a significant misreading or failure to discern the complexities of the evangelical faith.

This reduction of complexity to simplicity in Schaeffer can also be seen in the theme of "sounding the trumpet." This theme arises in Schaeffer's explanation of the shift from governance by the "Christian consensus" to "the takeover of our government and law by this other entity, the materialistic, humanistic, chance world view."[102]

This theme is drawn from the Old Testament notion of the "watchman," seen specifically in the book of Ezekiel. In Ezekiel 33, the prophet Ezekiel's responsibility to warn the nation of Israel of its waywardness is compared to the responsibility of a civic "watchman" to warn the people of an impending attack. If the watchman "blows the horn" to warn the people and the people do not take warning, then the responsibility for their deaths is theirs alone. If, however, "the watchman sees the sword coming and does not blow the trumpet to warn the people," then the watchman will be held accountable for their blood.[103]

In like manner, Schaeffer faulted members of the Christian community for failing to warn of the attack of secular humanism. "Now I have a question," he writes. "[W]here were the Christian lawyers during the crucial shift from forty years ago to just a few years ago? Within our lifetimes the great shifts in law have taken place. Now that this has happened, surely the Christian lawyers should have seen the change taking place and stood on the wall and blown the trumpets loud and clear."[104] Nor was this collective failure limited just to Christian lawyers. "The failed responsibility," he declares, "covers a wide swath. Christian educators, Christian theologians, Christian lawyers—none of them blew loud trumpets until we were a long, long way down the road toward a humanistically based culture."[105]

This theme of "sounding the trumpet" reinforces the oversimplistic views of culture, history, and the Christian faith that encourage anti-intellectual thinking. Presumed in this theme is the diametric opposition of "totalities," as discussed above. Also presumed in this theme, more significantly, is the ease of recognition with respect to these "totalities." The assault of secular humanism upon Christian-based culture is implied to be as easily discerned as an army just on the horizon, advancing toward a walled city.

These two themes exemplify a rhetorical invitation on Schaeffer's part to see culture, history, and the Christian faith in an oversimplified, reductionist manner. Making the invitation to this particular manifestation of anti-intellectual thinking more compelling, further, is the form in which it is presented. Schaeffer's general status as a philosopher within the evangelical and fundamentalist communities, combined with a writing style that roughly conforms to scholarly form, conveys to his readers the distinct impression of rigorous, sustained intellection. This perhaps functions to make Schaeffer's ideas more persuasive for those who have an initial predisposition to such views. Rhetoric scholar Randall Bytwerk observed a similar phenomenon at work in the public reception of Daniel Jonah Goldhagen's controversial book, *Willing Executioners: Ordinary Germans and the Holocaust*. Noting that it has been "a book that the public loves and scholars hate," Bytwerk explains that "[t]he experts almost uniformly reject Goldhagen's thesis because they know the sources.... To the ordinary reader, those 474 pages of text and 130 pages of endnotes look persuasive."[106]

More critically, though, this impression—this "form"—of intellection makes it easier for those persuaded by or sharing Schaeffer's thinking to rest assured that their thinking is intellectually sound, when that soundness is actually quite questionable.

The Impulse to Hegemony

The impulse to hegemony in Schaeffer arises in the constitution of particular motives for action—motives with respect to both the nation as a whole and one's Christian faith. These motives serve as the basis for a powerful goad to action.

Motives with respect to the nation are created by a particular rendering of the nation's history. The United States, according to Schaeffer, exhibits a particular "form-freedom balance." "There is form in acknowledging the obligations in society," he states, "and there is freedom in acknowledging the rights of the individual."[107] America, in his judgment, exhibits (or at least exhibited in the past) a most favorable balance between these two opposing elements, yielding liberty and human dignity in significant measure.

In the first part of his *Manifesto*, Schaeffer labors to establish that this favorable form-freedom balance set up by the founders is inextricably grounded in the Christian worldview. In his discussion of the influence of the "rule of law" on the Founders, for instance, Schaeffer argues that the concept of "certain inalienable rights" originated from the Judeo-Christian tradition. In answering the question, "Where do the rights come from?" Schaeffer declares that the Founders "understood that they were founding the country upon the concept that goes back into the Judeo-Christian thinking that there is Someone there who gave the inalienable rights. They publicly recognized that law could be king because there was a Law Giver, a Person to give the inalienable rights."[108] Because of this, reasons Schaeffer, "[t]o have suggested the state separated from religion and religious influence would have amazed the Founding Fathers."[109]

In this respect, Schaeffer also advances the argument that the British Common Law, the foundation for law in America, is grounded in the Christian worldview. To advance this argument, he mentions Sir William Blackstone, author of the influential work *Commentaries on the Law of England*. In Blackstone's view, Schaeffer relates, "there were only two foundations for law, nature and revelation, and that he stated clearly that he was speaking of the 'holy Scripture.'"[110]

The essential connection made by Schaeffer between the Christian worldview and the proper form-freedom balance is strengthened not just by articulating the influence of Christian principles in creating it, but also in making clear the inability of humanism to create or sustain it. Schaeffer bluntly states:

> The materialistic-energy, chance concept of final reality never would have produced the form and freedom in government we have in this country and in other Reformation countries. The humanists push for "freedom" but having no Christian consensus to contain it, that "freedom" leads to chaos or to slavery under the state (or under an elite). Humanism, with its lack of *any* final base or values or law, always leads to chaos. It then naturally leads to some form of authoritarianism to control the chaos. We have forgotten why we have a high view of life and why we have a positive balance between form and freedom in government, and the fact that we have such tremendous freedoms without these freedoms leading to chaos.[111]

He does not forget to remind the reader concerning where these views originated. Noting that "none of these is natural in the world," he further observes that "[t]hey are unique, based on the fact that the consensus was the biblical consensus."[112]

Interestingly, Schaeffer's use of the term *consensus* allows him to do more than ground the American ideal of freedom squarely within the Christian worldview. His use of this term also allows him to deflect charges that he is urging a formation of a Christian "theocracy" in America. This has been and continues to be a frequent charge made against fundamentalism and the Christian Right.

Schaeffer specifically addresses this issue in his later discussion of civil disobedience. In seeking to reverse the tide of secular humanism in America, he makes clear, "we must continually emphasize the fact that we are not talking about some kind, or any kind, of a theocracy. We must not confuse the Kingdom of God with our country," he declares, specifically adding that Christians "should not wrap Christianity in our national flag." "None of this, however," he then emphasizes, "changes the fact that the United States was founded upon a Christian consensus, nor that we today should bring Judeo-Christian principles into play in regard to government."[113] While the difference between *consensus* and *hegemony* in this context is somewhat difficult to discern, the former term allows Schaeffer to evade the objection while maintaining the other totalizing aspects of his representations.

The invitation given by Schaeffer, in all this, is for the reader to conclude that pluralism in any significant sense is impossible; it is either one total entity or another that dominates political and cultural life. More important, this invitation is also for the reader to conclude that such pluralism is undesirable. True pluralism—not the dominance of the humanist total entity in the guise of "pluralism"—is possible only within the context of the "Christian consensus." This is so because it is the Christian consensus that provides a positive maximum of freedom, the most favorable balance between "form" and "freedom."

Schaeffer grounded the commitment to "rolling back" secular humanism not just in terms of restoring the basis for freedom in America, but also in terms of Christian obedience. This is seen implicitly in his theme of "sounding the trumpet," as seen above. In a brief discussion of the Moral Majority, though, Schaeffer made this connection between such political activism and Christian obedience more explicit. "The Moral Majority has drawn a line between the one total view of reality and the other total view of reality and the results this brings forth in government and law," he states. "And if you personally do not like some of the details of what they have done, do it better. But you must understand," he emphasizes, "that all Christians have got to do the same kind of thing or you [sic] are simply not showing the Lordship of Christ in the totality of life."[114]

It is in these characterizations—regarding the United States and the evangelical Christian faith—that the impulse to hegemony is in significant measure cultivated. Those with the impulse do not see what they are doing as an exercise in greed, vanity, and/or self-righteousness. They see what they are doing as action to preserve the essence of the American nation and the freedom that has characterized it. Further, they see what they are doing as living out the implications of their Christian faith—living in obedience to God and affirming their identity as "authentic" Christians.

It is here that we are reminded of the truth of Kenneth Burke's observation that "motives are shorthand terms for situations."[115] My contention, therefore, is not with the motives of those who adhere to this line of thinking. Rather, it is with the flawed characterizations of the situations that give rise to those motives.

Conclusion

Throughout this chapter I have explored what I call the rhetorical and theological ancestry of Operation Rescue. Operation Rescue, as well as its rhetoric, cannot be fruitfully examined apart from the context of the evangelical and fundamentalist Christian faith traditions. I have also examined two recurring and problematic features of these closely related faith traditions. In discussing anti-intellectualism and the impulse to hegemony, I have hopefully made clear that these problematic features are not inherent to these faith traditions. The evangelical Christian faith, as with reality or any other perspective, can be represented more or less well. These problematic features, I contend, arise and are reinforced when that faith is represented less well.

Such is the case with Francis Schaeffer. And as will be seen in subsequent chapters—which address how the rhetoric of Operation Rescue represents the evangelical Christian faith and what the implications are regarding the group's participation in public dialogue—such is also the case with Operation Rescue.

Marian Faux has claimed that Randall Terry used *A Christian Manifesto* as "his model for the organization of Operation Rescue."[116] In their perspective on the evangelical Christian faith and in their rhetorical practice, unfortunately, Terry and Operation Rescue borrowed considerably more from Schaeffer than the model for civil disobedience.

Notes

1. Francis A. Schaeffer and C. Everett Koop, *Whatever Happened to the Human Race?*, 1979; reprint, in *The Complete Works of Francis A. Schaeffer: A Christian Worldview, Volume Five, A Christian View of the West* (Westchester, Ill.: Crossway Books, 1982), 410.

2. Timothy P. Weber, "The Two-Edged Sword: The Fundamentalist Use of the Bible," in *The Bible in America: Essays in Cultural History*, ed. Nathan O. Hatch and Mark A. Noll (New York: Oxford University Press, 1982), 101.

3. Clarence Darrow, quoted in George M. Marsden, *Fundamentalism and American Culture: The Shaping of Twentieth-Century Evangelicalism, 1870–1925* (New York: Oxford University Press, 1980), 187.

4. Dallas A. Blanchard, *The Anti-Abortion Movement and the Rise of the Religious Right: From Polite to Fiery Protest* (New York: Twayne Publishers, 1994), 45–46.

5. Celeste Michelle Condit, *Decoding Abortion Rhetoric: Communicating Social Change* (Urbana: University of Illinois Press, 1990), 151–53.

6. Ibid., 158.

7. Anthony Lewis, "What Is It about America that Nourishes Extremism over Abortion Issue?" *Houston Chronicle*, August 2, 1994, 21A.

8. Robert James Branham, "The Role of the Convert in *Eclipse of Reason* and *The Silent Scream*," *Quarterly Journal of Speech* 77 (1991): 423, 409.

9. Cal Thomas and Ed Dobson, *Blinded by Might: Can the Religious Right Save America?* (Grand Rapids, Mich.: Zondervan, 1999), 8.

10. Os Guinness, *The American Hour: A Time of Reckoning and the Once and Future Role of Faith* (New York: Free Press, 1993), 186.
11. Ibid., 186–89.
12. Ibid., 189–93.
13. Ibid., 193–97.
14. Ibid., 197.
15. Francis A. Schaeffer, *A Christian Manifesto*, 1981; reprint, in *The Complete Works of Francis A. Schaeffer*, 415–501.
16. Grant Wacker, "Searching for Norman Rockwell: Popular Evangelicalism in Contemporary America," in *The Evangelical Tradition in America*, ed. Leonard I. Sweet (Macon, Ga.: Mercer University Press, 1984), 303.
17. William Martin, *With God on Our Side: The Rise of the Religious Right in America* (New York: Broadway Books, 1986), 196–97.
18. See, for instance, Tom Sine, *Cease Fire: Searching for Sanity in America's Culture Wars* (Grand Rapids, Mich.: Eerdmans, 1995), 75; Gabriel Fackre, "Theology: Ephemeral, Conjunctural and Perennial," in *Altered Landscapes: Christianity in America, 1935–1985*, ed. David W. Lotz, Donald W. Shriver, Jr., and John F. Wilson (Grand Rapids, Mich.: Eerdmans, 1989), 262.
19. Martin, *With God on Our Side*, 196.
20. Michael Lienesch, *Redeeming America: Piety and Politics in the New Christian Right* (Chapel Hill: University of North Carolina Press, 1993), 177.
21. Martin, *With God on Our Side*, 321.
22. See, for instance, Faye Ginsburg, "Rescuing the Nation: Operation Rescue and the Rise of Anti-Abortion Militance," in *Abortion Wars: A Half Century of Struggle, 1950–2000*, ed. Rickie Solinger (Berkeley: University of California Press, 1998), 229; Blanchard, *The Anti-Abortion Movement and the Rise of the Religious Right*, 67; James Risen and Judy L. Thomas, *Wrath of Angels: The American Abortion War* (New York: Basic Books, 1998), 232.
23. Marian Faux, *Crusaders: Voices from the Abortion Front* (New York: Carol Publishing Group, 1990), 134.
24. J. Christopher Soper, *Evangelical Christianity in the United States and Great Britain: Religious Beliefs, Political Choices* (New York: New York University Press, 1994), 38.
25. James Davison Hunter, *American Evangelicalism: Conservative Religion and the Quandary of Modernity* (New Brunswick, N.J.: Rutgers University Press, 1983), 7.
26. Ibid., 61.
27. Soper, *Evangelical Christianity*, 42.
28. Gordon D. Fee and Douglas Stuart, *How to Understand the Bible for All Its Worth: A Guide to Understanding the Bible* (Grand Rapids, Mich.: Zondervan, 1982), 14.
29. Soper, *Evangelical Christianity*, 40.
30. Ibid., 43, 44.
31. Mark Ellingsen, *The Evangelical Movement: Growth, Impact, Controversy, Dialog* (Minneapolis: Augsburg Publishing House, 1988), 48.
32. Ibid., 97.
33. See, for instance, Mark A. Noll, *A History of Christianity in the United States and Canada* (Grand Rapids, Mich.: Eerdmans, 1992), 91–113; Harry S. Stout, *The Divine Dramatist: George Whitefield and the Rise of Modern Evangelicalism* (Grand Rapids, Mich.: Eerdmans, 1991).

34. Noll, *A History of Christianity in the United States and Canada*, 222.
35. Marsden, *Fundamentalism and American Culture*, 3.
36. George M. Marsden, *Understanding Fundamentalism and Evangelicalism* (Grand Rapids, Mich.: Eerdmans, 1991), 1.
37. Ernest R. Sandeen, *The Roots of Fundamentalism: British and American Millenarianism, 1800–1930* (Chicago: University of Chicago Press, 1970).
38. This assumes, of course, a quite literal reading of Revelation 20. In the "postmillenial" and "amillenial" views, this period of a thousand years is read symbolically to mean an indefinite but long period of time.
39. Mark A. Noll, "The Image of the United States as a Biblical Nation, 1776–1865," in *The Bible in America: Essays in Cultural History*, ed. Nathan O. Hatch and Mark A. Noll (New York: Oxford University Press, 1982), 39.
40. Marsden, *Fundamentalism and American Culture*, 11.
41. Marsden, *Understanding Fundamentalism and Evangelicalism*, 39–40.
42. Ibid., 41. It must be noted, though, that dispensationalism, as a theological system, still enjoys widespread acceptance within evangelicalism. Further, it has been considerably revised and nuanced since its appearance within historical fundamentalism. This is why I use the term *historical dispensationalism* to refer to this earlier form. See, for instance, Charles C. Ryrie, *Dispensationalism Today* (Chicago: Moody Press, 1965); Craig A. Blaising and Darrell L. Bock, ed., *Dispensationalism, Israel and the Church* (Grand Rapids, Mich.: Zondervan, 1992).
43. Sandeen, *The Roots of Fundamentalism*, 68.
44. Marsden, *Fundamentalism and American Culture*, 55.
45. Weber, "The Two-Edged Sword," 106.
46. Grant Wacker, "The Demise of Biblical Civilization," in *The Bible in America: Essays in Cultural History*, ed. Nathan O. Hatch and Mark A. Noll (New York: Oxford University Press, 1982), 123.
47. For a comprehensive listing of authors and articles in *The Fundamentals*, see David O. Beale, *In Pursuit of Purity: American Fundamentalism since 1850* (Greenville, S.C.: Unusual Publications, 1986), 41–45.
48. Ellingsen, *The Evangelical Movement*, 50.
49. Marsden, *Fundamentalism and American Culture*, 119.
50. Marsden, *Understanding Fundamentalism and Evangelicalism*, 57.
51. For more detailed discussions of the fundamentalist-modernist controversy, see Ellingsen, *The Evangelical Movement*, 85–92; Marsden, *Understanding Fundamentalism and Evangelicalism*, 164–84; Beale, *In Pursuit of Purity*, 153–61, 185–235.
52. Marsden, *Fundamentalism and American Culture*, 171; Beale, *In Pursuit of Purity*, 153.
53. For a more extended and particularly insightful discussion of J. Gresham Machen, see Marsden, *Understanding Fundamentalism and Evangelicalism*, 182–201.
54. Beale, *In Pursuit of Purity*, 221. For a more detailed and rhetorical analysis of Darrow's cross-examination of Bryan, see Kathleen Hall Jamieson, *Eloquence in an Electronic Age: The Transformation of Political Speechmaking* (New York: Oxford University Press, 1988), 31–42. See also the case study in Richard M. Weaver, *The Ethics of Rhetoric* (1953; reprint, Davis, Calif.: Hermagoras Press, 1985), 27–54.
55. Ellingsen, *The Evangelical Movement*, 90.
56. Marsden, *Fundamentalism and American Culture*, 191.

57. Joel A. Carpenter, "From Fundamentalism to the New Evangelical Coalition," in *Evangelicalism and Modern America*, ed. George Marsden (Grand Rapids, Mich.: Eerdmans, 1984), 5.
58. Richard John Neuhaus and Michael Cromartie, preface to *Piety and Politics: Evangelicals and Fundamentalists Confront the World*, ed. Richard John Neuhaus and Michael Cromartie (Washington, D.C.: Ethics and Public Policy Center, 1987), vii.
59. Martin, *With God on Our Side*, 17.
60. Harry Blamires, *The Christian Mind: How Should a Christian Think?* (1963; reprint, Ann Arbor, Mich.: Servant Books, 1978), 3–4.
61. Mark A. Noll, *The Scandal of the Evangelical Mind* (Grand Rapids, Mich.: Eerdmans, 1994), 3.
62. Ibid., 122.
63. Ibid., 122–23.
64. Ibid., 141.
65. Ibid., 106.
66. David F. Wells, *No Place for Truth: Or, Whatever Happened to Evangelical Theology?* (Grand Rapids, Mich.: Eerdmans, 1993), 12.
67. Millard J. Erickson, *The Evangelical Mind and Heart: Perspectives on Theological and Practical Issues* (Grand Rapids, Mich.: Baker, 1993), 195–97.
68. Ibid., 197.
69. Ibid., 197–200.
70. Ibid., 206.
71. Nathan O. Hatch, *The Democratization of American Christianity* (New Haven, Conn.: Yale University Press, 1989), 6.
72. Ibid., 34–46.
73. Ibid., 68–69.
74. Ibid., 71–73.
75. Sine, *Cease Fire*, 5.
76. Ibid., 75.
77. Ibid., 110.
78. Marsha L. Vanderford, "Vilification and Social Movements: A Case Study of Pro-Life and Pro-Choice Rhetoric," *Quarterly Journal of Speech* 75 (1989): 175–76.
79. Sine, *Cease Fire*, 111.
80. Ibid.
81. Jerry Falwell, quoted in Sine, *Cease Fire*, 118.
82. Pat Robertson, quoted in Sine, *Cease Fire*, 119.
83. Marsden, *Understanding Fundamentalism and Evangelicalism*, 10.
84. Mark A. Noll, Nathan O. Hatch, and George M. Marsden, *The Search for Christian America* (Westchester, Ill.: Crossway Books, 1983), 17.
85. Mark A. Noll, *One Nation under God? Christian Faith and Political Action in America* (New York: Harper and Row, 1988), 10.
86. Ibid., 8.
87. Schaeffer, *A Christian Manifesto*, 423.
88. See, in particular, Schaeffer's discussions of Samuel Rutherford's *Lex Rex* and the American adoption of British Common Law (431–36).
89. Schaeffer, *A Christian Manifesto*, 457.
90. Ibid., 467, 469.

91. Ibid., 468.
92. Ibid., 477, 495.
93. See Kenneth Burke, *Attitudes toward History*, 3rd ed. (Berkeley: University of California Press, 1984), 21–25.
94. Ibid., 28–29.
95. Schaeffer, *A Christian Manifesto*, 423.
96. Ibid., 424–25.
97. Ibid., 428, 427.
98. Ibid., 424.
99. Ibid., 425.
100. Ibid., 427.
101. Ibid., 428.
102. Ibid., 436.
103. Ezekiel 33:1–9. This and all subsequent citations to the Bible will be to the New International (NIV) translation.
104. Schaeffer, *A Christian Manifesto*, 440–41.
105. Ibid., 442–43.
106. Randall L. Bytwerk, "Is It Really that Simple? A Response to Goldhagen (and Newman)," *Rhetoric and Public Affairs* 1 (1998): 425, 432.
107. Schaeffer, *A Christian Manifesto*, 427.
108. Ibid., 432.
109. Ibid., 434.
110. Ibid., 435.
111. Ibid., 439, 430.
112. Ibid., 456.
113. Ibid., 485–86.
114. Ibid., 450.
115. Kenneth Burke, *Permanence and Change: An Anatomy of Purpose*, 3rd ed. (Berkeley: University of California Press, 1984), 29.
116. Faux, *Crusaders*, 135.

Part Three

Representations of the Evangelical Christian Faith

4

ABORTION AS AN ACUTE FAILURE OF THE CHRISTIAN COMMUNITY

Representations of History in the Rhetoric of Operation Rescue

We are in such an hour of crisis; an hour that is far darker and more grievous than the darkest hour endured by the original thirteen colonies under King George III; an hour with more cruelty, murder, injustice, and exploitation than the founders would have dreamed possible. This is why our people must act. Let the facts, therefore, be candidly submitted to the world.

—Randall Terry, founder of Operation Rescue[1]

Who controls the past controls the future; who controls the present controls the past.

—George Orwell[2]

"My name is Baby Jane Doe #741," wrote one Operation Rescue activist who had been imprisoned during the group's 1988 "Siege of Atlanta."[3] Admitting that she had never before been involved in the pro-life movement, she briefly related how she had gotten involved with Operation Rescue. "One Friday night," she recounted, "a friend called and asked if I was going to a meeting to be held at our church about the protests that was [sic] going on in Atlanta. I thought it was 'dumb,'" she continued, "that all these Christians were getting arrested—including a sweet lady from my church—over an 'old issue.' Sure, I agreed abortion was wrong from

ABORTION AS AN ACUTE FAILURE OF THE CHRISTIAN COMMUNITY

God's word, but it was a far away problem and a law I thought couldn't be reversed." Then came the dramatic realization. "I went to the Operation Rescue rally out of curiosity," she wrote, "to find out what the story was. It was so shocking to hear that 25 million babies have been aborted since the law was passed and reading from the Bible Proverbs 24:11 saying that even those who disapprove of an evil but don't *do* something to try to stop it are just as guilty as those who actually participate in the evil!"[4]

"Naw, it couldn't happen," pro-life activist Henry Irby was recorded as saying. "[T]hat," writer and pro-life activist Paul deParrie relates, "was Henry's first reaction to the infamous *Roe v. Wade* decision." After that, though, Henry Irby joined the pro-life movement to confront "the horror of abortion, which he calls aborticide." "Aborticide," Irby was quoted as saying, "is the basis for God's judgment on America . . . because the blood comes out from the ground."[5]

Prominent pro-life activist Joseph Scheidler states, "Over 26 million preborn babies have been slaughtered through legal abortion in the United States since the 1973 Roe v. Wade [*sic*] Supreme Court decision. Although this type of child-killing has become, effectively speaking, a part of the way of life in our society, still there are courageous individuals who have resisted the evil. They have sacrificed their private goals, and in some cases their personal freedoms, to counter the death trend."[6]

These instances of discourse are easily recognizable as consistent with the pro-life position with respect to the abortion controversy. The practice of abortion is characterized as child-killing, as evil, and as the basis for God's judgment upon the nation—all generally consistent with pro-life ontology.

Equally significant, but not equally obvious, is the consistent pro-life characterization of the 1973 *Roe v. Wade* United States Supreme Court decision. Rhetorician Celeste Michelle Condit observes, "Conventional wisdom has it that in 1973 the Supreme Court of the United States suddenly, unilaterally, and completely legalized abortion, bringing about a state of affairs unprecedented in the nation's history."[7] Sociologist Kristin Luker gave voice to the perception of many pro-life activists in writing that, to them, *Roe v. Wade* came "like a bolt out of the blue." "It seemed to them," she notes, "that the Court had suddenly and irrationally decided to undermine something basic in American life, and they were shocked and horrified."[8]

Luker and Condit both vigorously dismissed the historical accuracy of this "bolt from the blue" conception of *Roe v. Wade*. Luker declares, "Historically, the Supreme Court decision on abortion was in no way sudden or unprecedented. It was the result of over a decade of political activity, during which sixteen states, including California, had passed greatly liberalized abortion laws."[9] Condit, referring to the "conventional wisdom" described above, explains, "This is a far from accurate account. Until well after the Civil War, most abortions had been legal in this nation. Even between 1870 and 1950, as many as 30,000 abortions were done 'legally' each year in the nation's hospitals. Many more 'criminal' abortions were performed outside the hospitals. By 1971, well before the high court's decision in *Roe v. Wade*, the trickle of legal abortions had become a torrent—as many as 600,000 *legal* abortions were being done in the country each year."[10]

Despite the quibble over the historical accuracy of the "bolt from the blue" perception of *Roe v. Wade*, at least with respect to abortion practice in the United States, both authors have recognized the significance of the Supreme Court decision as a watershed event. "[T]he Supreme Court decision," Luker declares, "really did usher in a new era. Abortion was no longer a technical, medical matter controlled by professionals; it was now emphatically a public and *moral* issue of nationwide concern."[11] Condit judged the impact of the decision somewhat differently: "The revolutionary importance of the Court's decision rested in its character as a national symbolic act. The *Roe v. Wade* case officially legitimated a new set of shared meanings, which had been argued into place in the decade before the Court's decision."[12]

The *Roe v. Wade* decision, I contend, is vitally important in still other ways. For the pro-life movement in general, and for Operation Rescue in particular, the 1973 Supreme Court decision serves as a "flag symbol" by which the conceptions of the abortion "problem" and "solution" can be articulated both more easily and more emotionally.[13] More critically, though, *Roe v. Wade* functions as an organizing, "ultimate" term in a specifically pro-life historiography. How Operation Rescue—as a "confrontational" pro-life social protest group—makes use of *Roe v. Wade* as a symbol, and consequently how the rhetoric of Operation Rescue builds a particular representation of abortion history, are the concerns of this chapter.

The rhetoric of Operation Rescue encourages a particular view of abortion history, one that frames the abortion issue as an acute and severe exigence, a "crisis." Further, this "crisis" is imbued with certain features that function to strengthen commitment to the pro-life cause and to encourage a sacrificial level of participation in specifically Operation Rescue activism. This particular representation of history, of which the rhetoric of Operation Rescue tempts acceptance, involves specific characterizations of *Roe v. Wade*, of the abortion controversy, of the United States as a nation, and of the proper role of the Christian community.

This particular representation of history bears a striking resemblance to that of Francis Schaeffer, discussed in the previous chapter. The historical significance of abortion parallels the historical significance of Schaeffer's concept of "secular humanism." In fact, Schaeffer himself made the connection very clearly. To Schaeffer, abortion was a particularly prominent, public, and morally turpitudinous dimension of the ascendance of secular humanism in American culture. Both abortion and the rise of secular humanism represent an acute and profound failure of the Christian community. Both represent a grave threat to the future of our culture. And both must be countered by deliberate, even sacrificial Christian action. So is it also to Terry and Operation Rescue. The rhetorical analysis of this chapter, then, is intended to show a particular manifestation of certain problematic views of history in evangelicalism and fundamentalism, as well as the rhetorical utility of those views to gain and solidify commitment to Operation Rescue's means and ends.

I first reemphasize the conception of history as rhetoric, as well as the rhetorical uses of a given representation of history. Second, I survey the controversy of abortion history by expositing decidedly pro-life and pro-choice conceptions of abortion history. Finally, I detail Operation Rescue's representation of abortion history by conducting a rhetorical examination of Randall Terry's book, *Operation Rescue*.

History as Rhetoric

Historian Hayden White's observation that "there is no such thing as a politically innocent historiography," as well as rhetoric of inquiry scholars Allan Megill and Donald N. McCloskey's claim that "the writing of history is rhetorical," are virtually truisms in rhetorical studies.[14] Specifically with respect to the abortion controversy, Condit explained that established presentations of history serve a persuasive function in reaffirming the status quo. "[V]erbal reconstructions of the past," she states, "place the weight of a unified humanity against 'new' actions by identifying who 'we' are and thus, what it is that we should do."[15]

Condit's observation nicely points to an important aspect of history, as rhetoric, that should not be ignored. Put simply, a particular representation of history has a *constitutive* power to unite people into communities, a uniting that shapes and gives meaning to motivation and action. Maurice Charland's study, discussed in chapter 2, shows how a specific vision of history functions as a part of a "constitutive rhetoric" to create a new "collective subject," in this case, the *peuple québécois*.[16] The rapidly growing body of scholarship on "public memory" also makes clear that a shared history is a critical way by which individuals identify as part of larger communities.[17]

The affirmation of history as rhetorical is really but an extension of the generative conception of rhetoric assumed throughout this book. Rhetoric, as discussed in chapter 2, is fundamentally connected with the implicit or explicit proclamation of symbolically negotiated perspectives. Part of any such perspective, as Kenneth Burke made clear, is a particular conception of the past. An "orientation" is a "bundle of judgments"—not just of "how [things] are" and "how they may be," but also "how things were." In the same passage, Burke suggested the relationship between conceptions of the past and conceptions of the future, writing that "[a] sign, which is here now, may have got a significance out of the past that makes it a promise of the future."[18]

There is, then, an important connection between the particular way the past is understood (symbolically constructed and negotiated by means of rhetorical discourse) and the particular way(s) in which the "good life" can be realized. In what follows later, we shall see how Operation Rescue's particular version of abortion-related history—not just in its particular view of *Roe v. Wade* discontinuity; but also its historical view of the overall abortion controversy, of the United States, and of the Christian community—functions rhetorically to encourage identification with Operation Rescue's specific vision of what must be done. First, though, I lay the contextual groundwork by discussing the controversy of abortion history itself.

The Controversy of Abortion History

Since histories are rhetorical constructions, it should not be surprising to find that competing, incommensurable accounts of abortion history exist. I mention below two such competing accounts, both to provide some background on the abortion issue and to convey the substance of the historical controversy with respect to abortion. In this way, Operation Rescue's rhetorical appeals, functioning as history-making, are placed in a proper and heuristic context.

Abortion History as Moral: Glessner

"As the sixties matured," states Condit, "the vivid story of illegal abortion garnered support for change in abortion policies. . . . The dramatic reform narrative had begun to chip away at what seemed to be the American heritage—a largely inarticulate sense that abortion was 'wrong.' When such cultural presumptions are attacked, supporters of the status quo re-tell the 'story of our past' in order to re-invigorate the heritage, giving it enough force to combat the new tales."[19]

Referring to what she called the "pro-life heritage tale," Condit then remarks that "[t]his is precisely what the pro-Life rhetors hurried to do."[20] Using "a selective and coherent account portraying a specific strand of white, Western, Christian history as the authoritative and legitimate American heritage," the pro-life advocates "described how, throughout the Western tradition, abortion had been written and spoken against by important institutional and moral authorities. Although disagreements had occurred in the past, they indicated that there had been a clear path of 'moral improvement' through history—prohibitions against abortion had become more and more restrictive through time, as humankind became increasingly aware of the fact that abortion represented the killing of a human being."[21]

"Tales" such as this cast the history of abortion in primarily *moral* terms, with the determinative issue being the human life involved that exists between conception and birth. In these "tales," furthermore, the historical engagement on this determinative issue is given a clearly teleological emphasis, as Condit indicates. Condit spends considerable time discussing an exemplar of this abortion history, John T. Noonan's "An Almost Absolute Value in History,"[22] explaining the particular strategies by which the "cacophony" of historical voices could be more effectively represented as "a unified chorus."[23]

A more recent account of the same historical vision is given by pro-life attorney Thomas A. Glessner. In his book, *Achieving an Abortion-Free America by 2001*, he promotes the same moral view of history as does Noonan, a history in which a general connection is made between civilization and proscription of abortion. Although the author acknowledges that abortion was allowed in "some pre-Christian societies," he then describes laws proscribing abortion in a variety of non-Christian and pagan religious writings and legal codes. These include the Code of Hammurabi in Babylon, the Assyrian legal code under King Tiglath-Pileser, the legal codes of the Hittites, ancient Indian legal codes such as the Code of Manu, later Hindu tradition, Zoroastrian literature, and ancient Jewish tradition.[24]

To solidify the perception of a consistently pro-life historical witness, Glessner makes use of an opportune metaphor, that of a "wall." Throughout his chapter on pre-*Roe* abortion history, Glessner connects the historical data in terms of a "wall of protection" for the unborn, which encourages a vision of essential historical unity against abortion. The nineteenth-century appearance of anti-abortion statutes in the United States, as well as the physicians' "right-to-life" campaign in the latter half of that century, are similarly characterized as "support for the wall of protection." "Hence," declares Glessner, "up until the end of World War II, the wall of protection for the unborn was well established and the humanity of the unborn child was unquestioned."[25]

The historical unity emphasized in Glessner's account serves, among other things, to highlight the historical discontinuity of pro-choice ideology. Attempts to revise abortion laws in the 1950s and 1960s are summarily characterized as "the assault on the wall."[26]

In Glessner's account, moreover, the historical development of the abortion issue is not only unified, but also unified on primarily moral terms. After a discussion of the anti-abortion disposition of English common law, which was the basis for American law, Glessner notes that "[b]eginning in the nineteenth century, statutes began appearing which criminally punished abortion." The existence of such laws, of course, is not in dispute. However, Glessner eagerly attributes motives for the passage of those laws. "It is likely," he declares, "that the law was responding to the scientific discovery of the ovum in 1827. It was at this time that we learned how conception occurs. A greater appreciation developed for the unborn child who was understood to be a separate, distinct, and living being from the moment of conception."[27]

This connection—between greater medical knowledge and greater restriction of abortion—is important because it suggests a transcendent moral concern for the value of human life in the face of different levels of abortion restriction. Thus Glessner can ascribe a pro-life sentiment to the common law despite the fact that the common law, which proscribed abortion only after "quickening,"[28] rendered most abortions legal. He states that "[p]rior to [the above mentioned discoveries], the common law had made a distinction between prenatal life before and after quickening. The common law protected prenatal life after quickening because it is at this stage that there is actual evidence of life within the womb."[29] The implication, then, is that if the drafters of the common law had greater knowledge with respect to prenatal life, they would have been much more intolerant of abortion.

The primarily moral concern for life inside the womb, in Glessner's account, was also what motivated the American Medical Association's anti-abortion position throughout the second half of the nineteenth century. After relating statements by physicians of the period, he exclaims that "[s]uch statements put to rest the claim from modern-day abortion proponents that the anti-abortion laws of the nineteenth century were designed only to protect the woman from exposure to unsanitary surgery. While it is true (and ironic) that the pioneers of the feminist movement during this time period opposed abortion as an act which exploits women, the motivating factor behind the AMA's push for tighter abortion laws was its concern for the life of the unborn child."[30]

The "sudden" push for the easing of abortion restrictions is likewise characterized in moral terms. The basis for "the assault on the wall," Glessner suggests, was moral waywardness. "The impetus for this change," he proposes, "came from an increasing acceptance of American society of a humanist world view which considers mankind self-sufficient and not in need of a God who intervenes in human affairs. With man seen as self-sufficient, the medical and intellectual communities began to discuss the need to control the uncontrollable, including the ability to control one's reproductive capacities, once a hushed topic."[31]

Abortion History as Political: Luker

Glessner's brief history of the abortion controversy, then, gives historical witness an essentially unified, moral, pro-life voice. Luker's account, however, is profoundly and fundamentally different. To Luker, the historical witness on abortion—even within the Christian tradition—is essentially *fragmented*, not unified. Further, the motivation behind the conception and passage of America's anti-abortion laws was not at all moral, but instead *political*.

Luker vigorously contested this view of an essentially unified, pro-life historical witness, arguing instead that there was no cross-cultural consensus on the moral status of abortion even before the time of Christ. "Surprising as it may seem," she states, "the view that abortion is murder is a relatively recent belief in American history. To be sure, there has always been a school of thought, extending back at least to the Pythagoreans of ancient Greece, that holds that abortion is wrong because the [fetus][32] is the moral equivalent of the child it will become. Equally ancient however is the belief articulated by the Stoics: that although [fetuses] have some of the rights of already-born children (and these rights may increase over the course of the pregnancy), [fetuses] are of a different moral order, and thus to end their existence by an abortion is not tantamount to murder."[33] She also describes the practice of abortion in the Roman Empire as "so frequent and widespread" that it was commented upon by a number of writers, including Ovid, Juvenal, Seneca, and Pliny. Despite this widespread practice of abortion, though, the Roman legal system did virtually nothing to regulate it.[34]

Nor did the limit of this lack of consensus, according to Luker, apply only to pagan societies; there was division even within Christian church tradition itself. Although Luker acknowledges that abortion "was denounced in early Christian writings such as the Didache and by early Christian authors such as Clement of Alexandria, Tertullian, and St. Basil," she describes the inconsistency of punishment for abortion, noting that "church councils, such as those of Elvira and Ancyra, which were called to specify the legal groundwork for Christian communities, outlined penalties only for those women who committed abortion after a sexual crime such as adultery or prostitution.[35] More critically, though, she argued that "from the third century A.D. onward, Christian thought was divided as to whether early abortion—the abortion of an 'unformed' [fetus]—was in fact murder.[36] Different sources of church teachings and laws simply did not agree on the penalties for abortion or on whether early abortion was wrong."[37] Because of all this, "[n]ineteenth-century America," in Luker's judgment, "did not inherit an unqualified opposition to abortion."[38]

Luker's account of abortion history opposes Glessner's not just in her fragmentary view of historical witness on abortion, but also in her views of the nineteenth-century right-to-life movement spearheaded by physicians. In Luker's view, the physicians' motives were not moral, as Glessner has alleged, but primarily political. She notes that this movement, which took place between the 1850s and the 1890s, indeed advanced the claim that abortion in all stages of pregnancy is murder.[39] Her claim, though, is that the physicians were not acting primarily out of concern for unborn human life, but rather to legitimate their profession, which at that time was nothing like the well-established, restricted, licensed profession of today. She described a variety of factors that contributed to the profession's low status in the nineteenth century, such as a lack of entry restrictions and a lack of agreement with regard to both doctrine and practice.[40] "Members of the regular medical profession," she then observes, "were therefore caught in a dilemma. In order to upgrade the profession's status, they had to upgrade not only the standards of practice but also the education and qualifications of those who wished to practice. However, the prerequisite to such an upgrading—the restriction of the title of 'doctor' to only the best and the best-trained physicians—was difficult to meet because of the lack of licensing laws. Physicians faced the paradox that they could not obtain licensing laws until they were 'better' than their competition, but becoming 'better' depended on having licensing laws."[41]

Consequently, when abortion began to emerge publicly as a social issue in the second half of the nineteenth century, many physicians came to view abortion as the tool by which to resolve this professional paradox and establish legitimacy for their profession. According to Luker, the physicians used the abortion issue as a means to make an indirect, symbolic claim regarding their professional status. "By becoming visible activists on an issue such as abortion," she states, the physicians "could claim both *moral stature* (as a high-minded, self-regulating group of professionals) and *technical expertise* (derived from their superior training)." The emerging abortion issue was ideal for this task because "[u]nlike the other medico-moral issues of the time—alcoholism, slavery, venereal disease, and prostitution—only abortion gave physicians the opportunity to claim to be saving lives."[42]

The best evidence of the physicians' political motives, Luker claims, lies in the way they handled the issue after they had "alerted Americans to the 'fact' that abortion was murder." If they had held that abortion is "never morally right," then they would have had "no grounds for claiming it as a medical issue that required their *professional* regulation." Consequently, the anti-abortion physicians ended up "simultaneously claim[ing] both an *absolute* right to life for the [fetus] (by claiming that abortion is always murder) and a *conditional* one (by claiming that doctors have a right to declare some abortions 'necessary')."[43] The physicians' opposition to legislative attempts to define precisely what constitutes a medically necessary abortion further suggests, in Luker's view, that they "wanted to create a category of 'justifiable' abortion and make themselves the custodians of it."[44]

The opposition of Glessner's and Luker's views of abortion history, then, convincingly suggests the partisan, rhetorical nature of a particular representation of history, particularly abortion history. Operation Rescue, as we shall see, is no different. In what follows, I elaborate on three essential features of Operation Rescue's representation of abortion history. First, the *Roe v. Wade* decision is seen as a striking discontinuity in the political and social history of the United States, consistent with the overall pro-life perspective. Second, this discontinuity extends to the moral condition of the United States, both as a nation and as a culture. The United States is characterized as having a moral, near-ideal past. This past, however, has given way to the pernicious moral climate of the present. Third, the Christian community is claimed to have special, overriding responsibilities in "crises" like the present one. In this way, the link is established for would-be Operation Rescue activists between what has happened in the past and what should be done in the present.

Operation Rescue and Abortion History

Discontinuity of the Roe v. Wade *Decision*

As seen above, the discontinuous conception of *Roe v. Wade* is pervasive in the general pro-life movement, and Operation Rescue is no exception to this trend. This conception of *Roe* is seen, for instance, in two related hypothetical examples Terry uses in making a larger point about whether or not human governments can "legislate God." Seeking to validate the "Higher Laws" principle that justifies civil disobedience by Christians, Terry begins by writing, "Let's use our imaginations to make the point. Picture with me, if you will, a group of believers who are gathered in a church in 1963 before abortion was legalized." In Terry's hypothetical narrative, an angel appears to these Christians and leads them to trespass on the property of an "abortion mill" and stop an abortion that is about to take place. They arrive in time, stop the abortion from taking place, and call the police. "The police arrest the killer," Terry continued, "and congratulate the rescuers for a job well done. The mothers find help in their crisis, the babies are saved from certain death, the press writes a front-page story, and the believers become heroes in the community."[45]

"Now picture the same angel," Terry continues, shifting to his second narrative, "coming to the same group of people on January 23, 1973, the day after *Roe v. Wade* legalized abortion." After the angel relays the same mission, "[o]ne Christian sheepishly raises his hand and says, 'Uhum, mister angel, perhaps you haven't heard. Yesterday the Supreme Court legalized abortion in America.'"[46] After a brief dialogue between the angel and the "front desk" of Heaven, the angel is finally told, "God says you had better put Psalm 82:3, 4 and James 1:27 on hold right now. The same goes for Proverbs 24:11, Leviticus 20:1–5, and any other place you find the command to rescue the innocent. He says they're not valid or binding commands anymore. You know, 'Render unto Caesar what is Caesar's' and all that." After the angel flies away in resignation, one of the Christians in the crowd pipes up that "[w]hen the law is changed, then we'll be glad to rescue innocent babies from the hands of the abortionists. In the meantime, we'd better get on with our meeting. Now, what color should we choose for the new pew covers?"[47]

Terry's satirical—sarcastic—narration is designed to impress upon the reader that God's law is not invalidated by human law, and therefore to point out the inconsistency of pro-lifers who do not support civil disobedience. "[I]f God's Word still applies in America today," Terry asks, "and if His commands are still in effect, why then are so many Christians thinking and acting as if God has made a new decree—and murdering children is now fine with Him?"[48] Assumed throughout the narrative, however, is a stark contrast in abortion law before and after the *Roe v. Wade* decision. Before January 22, 1973, it assumes that abortion law was essentially monolithic in its *proscription*. After January 22, 1973, it assumes that abortion law became essentially monolithic in its *license*.

The discontinuous conception of *Roe v. Wade* is seen even more clearly in an appendix to Terry's book, entitled, "A Declaration: July Fourth in The Year of Our Lord Nineteen Hundred Eighty-Eight."[49] Intentionally modeled on Thomas Jefferson's historic "Declaration of Independence," Terry's "Declaration" explicitly characterizes contemporary abortion circumstances as acute, discontinuous, and grave.[50] "When in the course of a nation's history," Terry begins, "it becomes necessary for the God-fearing citizens of that nation to take actions which in times of peace would be considered drastic or extreme, a decent respect to the opinions of their countrymen requires that they should declare the causes that compel them to act." As in Jefferson's Declaration, Terry's "Declaration" puts forward self-evident truths that, when forsaken by governments and rulers, justify extraordinary measures. "[A]ll men and women, in-utero and out, are endowed by their Creator with certain inalienable rights, the first and foremost being the right to life." When governments "stray from their Divinely appointed purpose," Terry continues, "and tolerate or participate in the oppression and slaughter of its innocent people . . . courageous efforts from within or without must be made to break the bonds of tyranny. In such hours of crisis, it is the right and the duty of a nation's citizens to act."[51]

In declaring that "[w]e are in such an hour of crisis," Terry points clearly to the *Roe v. Wade* decision as the essential starting point. "In 1973," he states, "a bloodbath was unleashed in all fifty states by the barbaric *Roe v. Wade* decision. Seven despots, whose tender mercies are cruel, forsook their Constitutional responsibilities, and against all decency, common sense, scientific evidence, and natural and Divine Law, stripped our in-utero countrymen of their rights. They declared these children non-persons who could be slaughtered through the sixth month of gestation, for any reason, and until birth for the so-called 'health' of the mothers." In the Jeffersonian form of specific "grievances," Terry goes on to enumerate specific abortion practices and consequences. Before doing that, though, he makes it clear that these practices stemmed from the 1973 Supreme Court decision. "In the wake of this barbarism," he states, "doctors turned executioners have developed numerous insidious means of destroying the defenseless. Let them be plainly told."[52]

Operation Rescue, then, subscribes to a vision of history in which the *Roe v. Wade* decision is an extraordinary act of moral turpitude that completely changed the trajectory of abortion in America. With it, according to Operation Rescue's account, began a horrific state of affairs unlike any other in American history. Joseph Scheidler expressed this sentiment well when he declared, during Operation Rescue's 1992 "Summer of Love" campaign, that *Roe* "has given us an outrageous attack on a whole class of people."[53] This sudden shift with respect to abortion, furthermore, is also applied to the moral condition of the nation.

Moral Condition of the United States

The conception of *Roe v. Wade* as an essentially discontinuous historical event, as seen above, is relatively common to the pro-life movement generally. More specific to Operation Rescue, though, is the conception of a discontinuity in the moral status of the United States. In Operation Rescue's historical vision, the state of abortion law was not the only thing that changed radically in 1973. Indeed, Terry devotes considerable space in his book to condemning the United States as a morally depraved nation that is under the threat of God's imminent judgment.

As one might have guessed, the abortion "bloodbath" is the primary cause of this current depravity. Scheidler nicely echoes this theme that "God is not mocked. God did not accept *Roe v. Wade* ... He came first, and He has His laws. And when you disobey God's laws, you are in big trouble. This nation is in big trouble."[54] To make clear this connection between abortion and national depravity, Terry first argues that the United States, like any other nation, is ultimately accountable to God and is required to obey him. In a short section entitled "Does It Apply to America?" Terry very briefly rehearses the argument "that Israel's historical lessons are not applicable in America because Israel was a theocracy in covenant with God." "Why then," he counters, "do we have the books of Jonah, Nahum, and Obadiah? All three prophecies were to heathen nations. Because God is 'the God of all flesh,' [w]e err if we think that God does not demand even heathen nations to obey Him. He does." It is precisely because of this truth that the Christian community is urged to "follow the prophet's example" and "take the Word and precepts of our God into America's political spectrum."[55]

ABORTION AS AN ACUTE FAILURE OF THE CHRISTIAN COMMUNITY

On the basis of this conclusion, Terry then makes connections between America's abortion practices and the cultivation of God's wrath. "One and one-half million children a year are murdered on the altar of convenience, pleasure, and 'freedom of choice' while most Christians sit idly by and look the other way." God, however, does not look the other way. "God watches them agonize, struggle, and fight; He hears their silent screams; He watches as they slowly go into shock and die at the hands of hired killers. God sees it all and to Him abortion is no different from sacrificing a child on an altar.... Both are an abomination to Him that kindles his wrath."[56] And a Satanic abomination it is. Although most "never hear" the "silent screams" and "rarely see" the "brutalized remains," Terry bluntly states, "[y]ou can be sure that the powers of darkness hear and see with pleasure. Satan receives the blood of these little ones as human sacrifice, and he is not going to give up this stronghold and demonic altar without a fight. The cry of [unborn babies'] blood must ascend as a deafening chorus in the courts of heaven. An atrocity of this magnitude does not go unnoticed by the Almighty."[57]

In Terry's book, the nature of this atrocity is emphasized by comparisons to the Nazi Holocaust. The abortion "holocaust," Terry states, is "of such major proportions that it's now five times greater than the Nazi slaughter of the Jews."[58] To be sure, comparisons between abortion and the Nazi Holocaust are not particular just to Operation Rescue; as Condit points out, they have been common in pro-life rhetoric since 1960.[59] What is particularly important about this comparison, though, is the way in which it reinforces the discontinuity between abortion in the past and abortion in the present. Like the Nazi Holocaust, the current abortion "holocaust" is a historical anomaly, a unique and horrific exigence that demands a particular and compelling set of responses.

The comparison also reinforces Terry's characterization of contemporary America as morally depraved. Terry declares,

> America is racing toward God's judgment. The sex-related sins of pornography, the sexual exploitation of children, homosexuality, immorality, and adultery probably make us look like Sodom and Gomorrah before God. Our public school systems have banned prayer, treated the Scriptures with contempt, and ridiculed strict moral teaching as old-fashioned and obsolete. Instead, children are gradually brainwashed with situational ethics and liberal, atheistic morals. Parental authority is undermined or ignored.... America lies in a very serious, even critical state morally ... sink[ing] in a swamp of immorality and cruelty.... [Though the United States] has access

to more preaching than any other nation [it has nonetheless] become the moral cesspool of the world.[60]

Yet the nation was not always this way. A bit more implicit in Terry's book is a vision of America as a previously virtuous nation, a vision essentially consistent with what many others have called the "New Israel" myth. This conception of pre-*Roe* American history works to provide a greater contrast to the contemporary state of affairs.

Terry's most overt affirmation of this idealistic vision appears in his "Declaration" described earlier. "Our once great nation," he declares, "though always with faults, was born of and founded on the concept of Higher Law; the belief that God, not man, was the Judge of the world, and that governments were accountable to Him."[61]

Though the nation is now currently on a course of reprobation, Terry wrote frequently of returning the nation to its now-lost moral stature. In one appeal, Terry wrote of the possibility of "turn[ing] America back to God." "[I]f we stand together," he exhorts, "time still exists to restore justice and to lead America out of moral chaos, turning her back to godliness and common decency."[62] Time still exists for "the church" to "provide God an avenue through which to bring restoration, blessing, and the reconstruction of our society."[63] Time still exists to "defeat the abortion holocaust, restore religious and civil liberties to individuals, bring justice to our judicial system, see common decency return, and the godless, hedonistic, sexually perverted mindset of today pushed back into the closet—and hopefully back to hell where it came from."[64] Time still exists for "the heart of this nation" to "again turn toward righteousness and compassion."[65] "What we *can* work for, believe for, and struggle for," he declares, "is a nation where once again the Judeo-Christian ethic is the foundation for our politics, our judicial system, and our public morality; a nation not floating in the uncertain sea of humanism, but a country whose unmoving bedrock is Higher Laws."[66]

The historical discontinuity of the present, along with the hope for restoration of the idealized past, gives rise to powerful motivations to act. But in the case of Operation Rescue, the historical discontinuity being discussed does more than hold out promise. It also holds out Christian responsibility.

Proper Role of the Christian Community

"It is a principle of drama," Kenneth Burke observes, "that the nature of acts and agents should be consistent with the nature of the scene."[67] A given

ABORTION AS AN ACUTE FAILURE OF THE CHRISTIAN COMMUNITY

response, in other words, must fit the situation. Herein lies an important connection between Operation Rescue's vision of abortion history and the group's motivational appeal. Having established contemporary abortion practices as a historically anomalous, uniquely pernicious exigence, Terry then offers a portrait of how the Christian community *should* behave in such situations. Put another way, how is Christian obedience conceptualized in extraordinary situations or "crises"? Terry provides a strategic answer: "God always calls His people to *action* in times of moral crisis."[68] The "action" Terry has in mind, of course, is participation in "rescues."

To bolster this connection between extraordinary circumstances ("moral crises") and extraordinary responses that constitute obedience in those circumstances ("action"), Terry offers short histories of Christians who responded well (as well as those who did not respond well) to other acknowledged historical crises. Amy Carmichael, for instance, is praised for her work in ending child prostitution in India.[69] Calvin Fairbank is praised for his work in helping operate the "Underground Railroad."[70] Corrie Ten Boom and the Ten Boom family are praised for their work in hiding Jews from the Nazis during World War II.[71]

While Terry's "heroes of faith" met the challenges to which they were called, most Christians did not. Missionaries thought Amy Carmichael was "off-base."[72] Abolitionists like Calvin Fairbank were hated by Southerners and Northerners alike. During the reign of the Nazis, Terry relates, "extolling Hitler, compromising with him, and ignoring the plight of the Jews was the *acceptable norm* for most Christians and church leaders."[73] In a short section titled "Whose Opinion Counts?" Terry takes these Christians and their churches to task. "Perhaps some of those churches had wonderful covered dish dinners or stirring seminars on eschatology," he muses. "But now, from a distance, the light of history casts a hue of contempt over their lives and ministries. Why? Because in a season of crisis, they failed to stand for the whole counsel of God, and they fled when faced with adversity."[74]

The abortion situation in America, as seen in Operation Rescue's historical vision, is just such a "season of crisis." "The number one social priority facing the church," Terry insists, "must be to end this slaughter of children. No other sin mentioned can match the level of shedding innocent blood. Halting this atrocity demands the immediate, concerted, and sacrificial effort of the church. The fate of America, and the future existence of the church, is bound up in the fate of the children."[75]

As a way of reinforcing the sheer urgency of this exigence—and therefore the need for extraordinary response—Terry introduced an extended analogy between the pro-life cause and warfare. He began this analogy by writing that "we need to 'declare war' on the child killing industry." "In a time of war," he continues, "a nation pulls together to defeat the enemy." Therefore, "everyone" in the Christian community "is called to do *something*," as "[t]he war is everyone's business."[76]

In developing the analogy, Terry emphasizes that while Christians will have different roles to play and different levels of commitment, *all* must be involved. "During war," he states, "the whole nation has certain responsibilities. Some are front-line soldiers, some are medics, others do recruiting, and some make ammunition." "Everyone who works," he elaborates, "pays taxes to support the troops. There are diplomats and family members. Everyone prays." He then makes the connection even more explicit by elaborating on the specific parallels between pro-life roles and warfare roles. Those who "rescue" at abortion clinics, for instance, are characterized as "front-line soldiers."[77] "[T]hose who educate churches, schools, and civic groups on the horrible truth about abortion" are characterized as "recruiters." Pro-life pamphlets, cassettes, films, and videos are characterized as "ammunition." Those helping at crisis pregnancy centers are characterized as "medics."[78] And the list of comparisons goes on.

Therefore, the perception of contemporary abortion practices as a "moral crisis" and the historical vision that reinforces that perception are made to support appeals to action and sacrifice, notably Operation Rescue activism. This perception is also used as a means to deflect any objections about the legitimacy of Operation Rescue's vision.

The actions of the "heroes of faith," for instance, are mentioned repeatedly throughout Terry's book to break down objections to engaging in Operation Rescue's brand of civil disobedience. For instance, while acknowledging that physical intervention "on behalf of children about to be sacrificed" would look like aggression, Terry counters: "Isn't this similar to what the Ten Boom family faced? They were not being asked to participate in killing Jews. They were being asked to shut up and sit idly by while the Nazis killed Jews. They were told to mind their own business, and to not interfere with the German government's right to murder innocent people." Explicitly stating that "Christians in America are facing this exact issue in regard to the abortion holocaust," Terry then asks, "Why don't we sense the same urgency that the Ten Booms felt in rescuing the innocent from slaughter?"[79]

Terry made use of these examples again in a more explicit appeal to become involved in "rescuing." "Christians have a tendency," Terry relates, "to fantasize about helping Corrie Ten Boom or the Underground Railroad. What makes us think we would have aided them, when it might have cost us years in prison or even death? Today you can save a life, and all it costs is maybe your reputation, a small fine, or a few hours or days in jail."[80] In other words, Christians like to think that in extraordinary situations such as the Nazi Holocaust, they would have been obedient to God and acted extraordinarily (risked one's life and security in the pursuit of "higher laws"). The clear implication, then, is that "ordinary" responses (or the avoidance of "extraordinary" responses) in the face of an "extraordinary" situation are not obedience, but rather *disobedience*—a betrayal of the faith.

Terry emphasized this implication in his appropriation of the "good Samaritan" parable.[81] Terry retold the parable to reflect contemporary circumstances. "A certain man," Terry begins, "was going down from Queens to the Bronx, and he fell among robbers. They stripped him and beat him and left him half dead. By chance a certain clergyman was traveling on that road, and when he saw the injured man, he was too busy with the work of the Lord to help him, so he passed by on the other side." The clergyman went home and "pondered what had become of society that such an unjust and barbaric crime could be committed." That clergyman, in Terry's narrative, ended up writing a bestseller on the problem of ditch beatings. "He was a hero!" Terry exclaims. "Well," he wryly adds, "a hero to everyone but the man in the ditch."[82]

Terry then returns to the storyline of the original parable. "Shortly after the clergyman passed by," he relates, "a gospel singer came upon the beaten man. Since he did not feel that God had called him to 'social issues,' he said a prayer for the man, passed by on the other side . . . and continued on his way." Because the incident ate on his conscience, though, he recorded a song about what had happened. "He won a Dove and a Grammy award for the best religious song. He became a hero. Unfortunately, the man in the ditch died."[83]

The two individuals Terry described in his version of the parable were engaging in important and praiseworthy activities, in the face of an *ordinary* set of circumstances. However, in the face of an *extraordinary* set of circumstances (such as facing someone who will die without immediate intervention), those same activities are rendered useless and unimportant. Instead, what is called for is an *extraordinary* response (putting everything else on hold and acting to save that person's life). In this extraordinary situation, not responding properly is dishonorable and, more significantly, disobedient to the precepts of the evangelical Christian faith. Though engaging in normally honorable activities, the clergyman and the gospel singer are harshly judged in Terry's "parable" because they did not do what needed to be done in that situation. "We must understand," Terry states a bit later, "that men and women have different ministries and callings. But in a time of crisis, all are called to sacrifice."[84]

So it is also with abortion, according to the rhetoric of Operation Rescue. In this way, then, failure to act or intervene with respect to abortion constitutes similar disobedience with respect to the evangelical faith. Therein lies a powerful motivational appeal.

Conclusion

Terry's historical visions of the United States, of the abortion issue, and of the Christian community in "crisis," all work together to forge a vision of what constitutes "obedience" for the Christian community. It is in the forging of this vision that Operation Rescue makes claims on those identifying with the Christian faith. This "crisis," as depicted in the rhetoric of Operation Rescue, demands immediate attention and sacrificial, interventionist action. In this way, the rhetorical function of a particular representation of history is clearly on display. A given rendering of history is not just political (expressing a partisan point of view) but is also explicitly rhetorical (making claims on the attitudes and behavior of its adherents).

The historical vision of Operation Rescue as rhetoric, then, encouraged its recipients to make essential and exclusive connections between Operation Rescue activism and the authentic expression of evangelical Christian faith. These rhetorical invitations exhibit more clearly the essential connection between Operation Rescue and the evangelical and fundamentalist faith traditions. The rhetorical function of Operation Rescue's representation of history, further, suggests how representations of the Christian faith function as "equipment for living" in the lives of Operation Rescue activists. The next two chapters elaborate more fully on this point.

Notes

1. Randall A. Terry, *Operation Rescue* (Springdale, Pa.: Whitaker House, 1988), 279–80.
2. George Orwell, quoted in Howard Kahane and Nancy Cavender, *Logic and Contemporary Rhetoric*, 8th ed. (Belmont, Calif.: Wadsworth Publishing Company, 1998), 315.

3. During the Atlanta protests of July and August 1991, Operation Rescue activists generally refused to give their names to police when arrested. Rather, they used the pseudonym "Baby Jane Doe" or "Baby John Doe." See James Risen and Judy L. Thomas, *Wrath of Angels: The American Abortion War* (New York: Basic Books, 1998), 273. For a defense of this tactic, see Mark Belz, *Suffer the Little Children: Christians, Abortion, and Civil Disobedience* (Westchester, Ill.: Crossway Books, 1989), 118.

4. "Testimonies from Jailed Rescuers," unpublished collection, Josephine County [Oregon] Right to Life, [1988], 1.

5. Paul deParrie, *The Rescuers* (Brentwood, Tenn.: Wolgemuth and Hyatt Publishers, 1989), 42.

6. Joseph Scheidler, foreword to *Pro-Life Christians: Heroes for the Pre-Born*, by Joe Gulotta (Rockford, Ill.: Tan Books and Publishers, 1992), x.

7. Celeste Michelle Condit, *Decoding Abortion Rhetoric: Communicating Social Change* (Urbana: University of Illinois Press, 1990), 22.

8. Kristin Luker, *Abortion and the Politics of Motherhood* (Berkeley: University of California Press, 1984), 126.

9. Ibid., 127. For a more exhaustive account of abortion law "reform" efforts prior to the handing down of *Roe v. Wade*, see Suzanne Staggenborg, *The Pro-Choice Movement: Organization and Activism in the Abortion Conflict* (New York: Oxford University Press, 1991), 13–54.

10. Condit, *Decoding Abortion Rhetoric*, 22.

11. Luker, *Abortion and the Politics of Motherhood*, 127.

12. Condit, *Decoding Abortion Rhetoric*, 22.

13. The idea of a "flag symbol" here is based upon the ideas of "flag issues" and "flag individuals." See John W. Bowers, Donovan J. Ochs, and Richard J. Jensen, *The Rhetoric of Agitation and Control*, 2nd ed. (Prospect Heights, Ill.: Waveland Press, 1993), 34–35.

14. Hayden White, "Rhetoric and History," in *Theories of History: Papers Read at a Clark Library Seminar, March 6, 1976*, ed. Hayden White and Frank E. Manuel (Los Angeles: William Andrews Clark Memorial Library, 1978), 24; Allan Megill and Donald N. McCloskey, "The Rhetoric of History," in *The Rhetoric of the Human Sciences: Language and Argument in Scholarship and Public Affairs*, ed. John S. Nelson, Allan Megill, and Donald N. McCloskey (Madison: University of Wisconsin Press, 1987), 222.

15. Condit, *Decoding Abortion Rhetoric*, 44.

16. Maurice Charland, "Constitutive Rhetoric: The Case of the *Peuple Québécois*," *Quarterly Journal of Speech* 73 (1987): 133–50.

17. For discussion of the growing body of "public memory" scholarship, see Barbie Zelizer, "Reading the Past against the Grain: The Shape of Memory Studies," *Critical Studies in Mass Communication* 12 (1995): 214–39; Stephen H. Browne, "Reading, Rhetoric, and the Texture of Public Memory," *Quarterly Journal of Speech* 81 (1995): 237–50. For examples of such scholarship, see, for instance, John Bodnar, *Remaking America: Public Memory, Commemoration, and Patriotism in the Twentieth Century* (Princeton: Princeton University Press, 1992); Michael Kammen, *Mystic Chords of Memory: The Transformation of Tradition in American Culture* (New York: Alfred A. Knopf, 1991).

18. Kenneth Burke, *Permanence and Change: An Anatomy of Purpose*, 3rd ed. (Berkeley: University of California Press, 1984), 14.

19. Condit, *Decoding Abortion Rhetoric*, 43.
20. Ibid.
21. Ibid., 44.
22. John T. Noonan, Jr., "An Almost Absolute Value in History," in *The Problem of Abortion*, ed. Joel Feinberg (Belmont, Calif.: Wadsworth Publishing Company, 1984), 9–14.
23. Condit, *Decoding Abortion Rhetoric*, 44. For discussion of Noonan's historical account, see Condit, *Decoding Abortion Rhetoric*, 44–55.
24. Thomas A. Glessner, *Achieving an Abortion-Free America by 2001* (Portland, Ore.: Multnomah Press, 1990), 24–26.
25. Ibid., 25.
26. Ibid., 29.
27. Ibid., 27.
28. This claim is arguable, but the key distinction in common law with respect to abortion—quickening—is still acknowledged. See, for instance, Condit, *Decoding Abortion Rhetoric*, 36n; Luker, *Abortion and the Politics of Motherhood*, 14–15; James C. Mohr, *Abortion in America: The Origins and Evolution of National Policy, 1800–1900* (New York: Oxford University Press, 1978).
29. Glessner, *Achieving an Abortion-Free America by 2001*, 27–28.
30. Ibid., 29.
31. Ibid.
32. Recognizing that "a choice of terms is a choice of sides" (2n), Luker used the term *embryo* in place of *fetus* (a pro-choice term) or *baby* (a pro-life term), as an attempt to gain a higher sense of objectivity. In this discussion I am restoring the term *fetus* in place of her term *embryo*, since I believe the term *embryo* in this context to be not only unnecessarily confusing, but also more dehumanizing than the term *fetus*.
33. Luker, *Abortion and the Politics of Motherhood*, 11.
34. Ibid., 12.
35. Ibid.
36. Luker elaborated on the notion of the "unformed" (fetus) in a footnote: "The distinction between the formed and the unformed [fetus], which drew on Aristotelian beliefs about pregnancy, was first introduced in the Septuagint, the Greek translation of the Bible. Though rejected by some (e.g., St. Basil), it was formally entered into legal and theological arguments by Tertullian in *De Anima*, where abortion was held to be murder only if the [fetus] was formed; later this holding was ratified by Jerome, Ivo of Charles, and Gratian" (*Abortion and the Politics of Motherhood*, 13).
37. Ibid. For an example of an opposing argument, see Michael J. Gorman, "Ahead to Our Past: Abortion and Christian Texts," in *The Church and Abortion: In Search of a New Ground for Response*, ed. Paul T. Stallsworth (Nashville: Abingdon Press, 1993), 25–43.
38. Luker, *Abortion and the Politics of Motherhood*, 13.
39. Ibid., 14.
40. Ibid., 17–18.
41. Ibid., 18.
42. Ibid., 31.
43. Ibid., 32.
44. Ibid., 33.
45. Terry, *Operation Rescue*, 128–29.

46. Ibid., 129.
47. Ibid., 131.
48. Ibid.
49. Ibid., 279–83.
50. For a discussion of the rhetorical effectiveness of the Declaration of Independence, see Stephen E. Lucas, "Justifying America: The Declaration of Independence as a Rhetorical Document," in *American Rhetoric: Context and Criticism*, ed. Thomas W. Benson (Carbondale: Southern Illinois University Press, 1989), 67–130.
51. Terry, *Operation Rescue*, 279.
52. Ibid., 280.
53. Joseph Scheidler, address at July 11, 1992 Wichita "Summer of Love" (Operation Rescue) tent rally, *Wichita Summer of Love, Part III*, Christian American Family Life Association, 1992, videocassette.
54. Ibid.
55. Terry, *Operation Rescue*, 53–54.
56. Ibid., 122–23.
57. Ibid., 141–42.
58. Ibid., 22.
59. Condit, *Decoding Abortion Rhetoric*, 51. For an extended example of this comparison, see William Brennan, *The Abortion Holocaust: Today's Final Solution* (St. Louis: Landmark Press, 1983).
60. Terry, *Operation Rescue*, 181, 35, 146.
61. Ibid., 283.
62. Ibid., 42.
63. Ibid., 163.
64. Ibid., 178.
65. Ibid., 215.
66. Ibid., 178.
67. Kenneth Burke, *A Grammar of Motives* (1945; reprint, Berkeley: University of California Press, 1969), 3.
68. Terry, *Operation Rescue*, 36.
69. Ibid., 66–70.
70. Ibid., 105–6.
71. Ibid., 106–10.
72. Ibid., 70.
73. Ibid., 32.
74. Ibid., 34.
75. Ibid., 182.
76. Ibid., 183.
77. Ibid., 184.
78. Ibid., 185.
79. Ibid., 122.
80. Ibid., 128.
81. For the original parable of the "Good Samaritan," see Luke 10:25–37.
82. Terry, *Operation Rescue*, 38–39.
83. Ibid., 40.
84. Ibid., 41.

5

"A CLEAR TRUMPET HAS BEEN SOUNDED"

The Rhetoric of Operation Rescue as Theological

Rescue those being led away to death; hold back those staggering toward slaughter.

—Proverbs 24:11 (NIV)

"Since the *Roe v. Wade* decision legalized child killing in 1973," the narrator intones, "over twenty-five million children have been brutally murdered." "Christians," he continues, "are finally facing the reality that they share in the guilt of this holocaust, and that God is calling them to repent of their apathy and rescue the children." Later in the videotape, Operation Rescue founder Randall Terry appears on camera to offer a defining characterization of what his pro-life social protest organization is all about. "Operation Rescue," he declares, "is people who have responded to a move of God who are saying, 'I'm responsible to love my neighbor. I'm responsible to rescue the innocent.' And it is producing revival in people's hearts. People who get involved in the rescue movement become transformed, because it takes their eyes off themselves and puts their eyes on Christ and on other people's needs."[1]

Such declarations provide an important reminder about the sources of motivation for Operation Rescue activists. The pro-life movement historically has sought to cast its motivation and goals in broad, inclusive terms. Yet a distinctly religious, Christian motivation is apparent in the pro-life movement generally, and particularly so as the movement engages in more contentious forms of social protest. With Operation Rescue, such motivation is central.

Both political scientist J. Christopher Soper and sociologist Dallas Blanchard have explored the distinctly religious motivation behind certain social protest movements. Writing that "ideology and culture belong at the centre of the study of social movements," Soper claims that "evangelical political mobilization and activism cannot be understood unless the content and meaning of their ideology is plumbed."[2] More specifically, Soper affirms the centrality of religious motivation in the pro-life movement.

Blanchard has also made a very explicit connection between religious motivation and the pro-life movement, although he has taken a decidedly more antagonistic view. At the core of the pro-life movement, according to Blanchard, is an overarching ideology of "fundamentalism" that is regressive, prejudiced, and violent. He also suggests that adherents of this ideology are psychologically deficient. More specifically, he characterizes the "fundamentalist syndrome" as extending to individual "personality characteristics" such as "authoritarianism, self-righteousness, prejudice against minorities, moral absolutism (a refusal to compromise on perceived moral issues), and anti-analytical, anti-critical thinking."[3]

Throughout this book, I seek to present a more nuanced account of the relationship between Operation Rescue and the evangelical Christian faith tradition. An important part of that relationship is the way in which the rhetoric of Operation Rescue tempts its audience to buy into a particular representation of the evangelical Christian faith. In the previous chapter I began the larger discussion of how the evangelical Christian faith is represented in the rhetoric of Operation Rescue, focusing on representations of history. In this chapter, I continue this discussion by focusing on representations of theology.

Accordingly, in this chapter I am interested in exploring the theology of Operation Rescue as it is expressed rhetorically—in other words, how the rhetoric of the group functions theologically. I am interested in not only the particular theological claims that arise in the group's rhetoric, but also the manner in which these particular claims shape and constrain how an Operation Rescue activist—acting as an evangelical Christian—strives "to know and live Christianity in its authentic and divinely intended manner."[4] I am interested in how the "theology" of Operation Rescue, expressed in rhetorical discourse, shapes attitudes about the Bible, attitudes about the church, and attitudes about abortion—all as they provide connections of meaning between the professing evangelical Christian and the evangelical Christian faith.

To conduct this exploration, I focus my attention particularly upon one rhetorical artifact: a thirty-minute videotape produced by Operation Rescue, simply titled *Operation Rescue*. Produced in 1989 following the group's first significant national public attention, the video was intended to function as somewhat of a purpose statement, "present[ing] the vision, message, and growth of the Rescue movement" and "depicting those who have placed their bodies before abortion mills in order to rescue children and mothers from the American holocaust."[5] While more complete statements of the group's position exist, most notably Randall Terry's book *Operation Rescue*, the videotape is much better suited for a more widespread dissemination of the group's ideas and appeals. Videotape, for instance, is a much better format for dissemination at church forums, such as evening services or Sunday school classes, in which potential activists would most likely be recruited or otherwise exposed to Operation Rescue's vision. To examine the group's key claims and, consequently, how the rhetoric of Operation Rescue functions theologically, the videotape is a much more heuristic text for the purposes at hand.

The theology of Operation Rescue, as revealed in this text, is unique and significant in that it rhetorically constructs abortion as the single touchstone by which one identifies with the evangelical Christian faith. In other words, one's action (or lack of action) with respect to the abortion issue becomes the only significant means by which an evangelical Christian can determine whether or not he or she is truly living within the "will of God."

Accordingly, I examine the theology of Operation Rescue in terms of particular dispositions toward the faith that this rhetorical text encourages evangelical Christians to adopt. I focus on three elements that comprise the theology of Operation Rescue from a rhetorical point of view: the plainness of Scripture, the primacy of abortion, and the insularity of "conversion."

The Theology of Operation Rescue

The Plainness of Scripture

To explore how a pro-life social protest group like Operation Rescue appeals to evangelical Christians, who constitute a considerable majority of the group's membership, it is critical to reemphasize evangelical attitudes toward the Bible. As seen in chapter 3, evangelicals consistently hold a high view of Scripture. To evangelicals, the Bible represents divine revelation in full and complete form. As such, it is completely authoritative in matters of faith and practice.

Because of this high view of the Bible, it is not surprising that the rhetoric of Operation Rescue makes heavy use of the biblical text to ground its claims. Four biblical prooftexts appear in the videotape as a means of giving Operation Rescue the sanction of the evangelical Christian faith. The first, Deuteronomy 21:1–9, provides biblical support for *bloodguiltiness*, one of Operation Rescue's central doctrines. "The reason the child-killing industry is so strong in America," Terry explained during the 1991 "Summer of Mercy" campaign, "is because we've let it get that way, by our apathy, by our complacency, by our silence, by our inactivity. So we in the Christian community have blood on our hands." He emphasized, "If you want to understand Operation Rescue, you've gotta [sic] understand the whole concept of bloodguiltiness. Someone shares in the guilt of blood not only if they kill a person, but if they stand by and do nothing while a person is being killed."[6]

This idea of bloodguiltiness provides the important connection between abortion and the evangelical notion of repentance. Not surprisingly, it is given significant exposition in the videotape. Facing the videocamera, Terry declares that "God is saying to His people, the Church, those who call upon the name of the Lord Jesus Christ, He is saying one word: repent." As the visual shifts to an image of a dead fetus, the narrator poses the rhetorical question, "Some would say, 'repent of what?'" The answer, "bloodguiltiness," was reinforced orally and visually. The narrator then exposits the first prooftext: "Deuteronomy 21 teaches that for God's people to be absolved of bloodguiltiness, they had to be able to pray two things. 'O Lord, our hands have not shed this blood, nor did our eyes see it. Forgive Thy people, and set not the guilt of innocent blood in our midst.'" The narrator continues ominously, "The Church in America cannot pray this because our eyes have seen it. Amidst a flurry of religious activity, the Church for the most part has stood idly by while over 4,000 babies a day are being slaughtered."

The exposition of the videotape then leads into the second prooftext, Isaiah 1:12–15. "The prophet Isaiah," declares the narrator, "spoke of a people who excelled in religious duty but missed the heart of God and refused to protect the innocent." The narrator then shifts to an explicit statement of the prooftext: "'When you come to appear before me, who requires of you this trampling of my courts? . . . So when you spread out your hands in prayer, I will hide my eyes from you; Yes, even though you multiply prayers, I will not listen. Your hands are covered with blood.'"

The consequences of this bloodguiltiness, further, extend beyond the church to include the fate of the nation. "Besides the bloodguilt incurred by the church," the narrator states, "our entire nation is stained with the blood of these children, and is increasingly staggering under the weight of God's judgment. The Scriptures teach very clearly that if innocent blood is shed and unavenged, the entire nation may perish. For example, Judah was destroyed by invading armies because they were sacrificing their children." It is here that the third prooftext, 2 Kings 24:2–4, is employed: "The Bible says, 'So he sent them against Judah to destroy it . . . because of the sins of Manasseh, according to all that he had done, and also for the innocent blood, for which he shed, for he filled Jerusalem with innocent blood, and the Lord would not forgive.'" Included on the videotape is a segment in which Terry expounds this idea during a pro-life rally. "The twenty-five million children that are dead," he declares, "are enough to damn any nation to hell and to ultimate judgment, period. . . . [T]he blood that has been shed and now stains the garbage dumps, now stains the once Land of the Free and Home of the Brave, that blood is crying from the ground to the God of heaven and earth, saying 'How long, O Lord? How long?'"

Yet all is not lost. The fourth biblical prooftext, Isaiah 1:16–17, is used as a rationale for hope in the midst of this gloomy portrait, and hence for earnestness in activism. Following the judgment prooftext just described, the narrator asks, "Does this mean, then, that we are without hope, that nothing can be done to stay the wrath of God?" The narrator then quickly provides the hopeful answer: "If we repent and obey His commands, there is hope." He continues, making use of the fourth prooftext, "In the same passage quoted earlier Isaiah goes on to say, 'Wash yourselves, make yourselves clean; remove the evil of your deeds from my sight. Cease to do evil, learn to do good; seek justice, reprove the ruthless; defend the orphan, plead for the widow.'" Immediately following this statement of the prooftext, the visual shifts again to Terry, who explains the application of this idea. "And I ask you to stand," Terry exhorts, "in the name of Jesus, while there is still time to stand. And perhaps God will see from heaven, and He will look down upon us and say, 'These people have moved My heart. These people have given Me a reason to show mercy.' And I submit to you that the answer lies with you."

The exposition of these biblical texts on the videotape supports a coherent line of reasoning, leading one from (1) commitments to Christianity and the authority of the Bible in faith and life, to (2) commitments to be involved in Operation Rescue. The Christian church in America (read broadly to include all "genuine" Christians) has incurred "bloodguilt" and is consequently in a position of being harshly judged by God. Because of this "bloodguilt," the church needs to repent and beg God for mercy. Further, the

United States as a nation, also in a position of being harshly judged by God, is in great peril because of the many abortions that have been done since the *Roe v. Wade* decision. The only way this harsh judgment and destruction can be averted, consequently, is for Christians to repent of their apathy and "rescue the children," that is, participate in and/or otherwise support "rescue" activities.

Those Christians who find this line of reasoning convincing, then, have powerful motivations by which to act. They are acting not only to affirm the vitality and genuineness of their Christian faith, but also literally to save the nation from the destruction resulting from divine judgment. "A clear trumpet is being sounded," the narrator affirms near the end of the videotape. "Will the Church and other pro-life Americans repent, rise up, and make the sacrifices necessary to save the children, the mothers, and the very future of our nation?" It is this set of motivations that the above-mentioned biblical prooftexts are employed to create.

These uses of the Bible to support the imperatives of Operation Rescue rely on a particular attitude regarding how to glean authoritative truth from the pages of the Scriptures. In contrast to the claim set out in chapter 2 that *any* use of the Bible invariably involves interpretation, the rhetoric of Operation Rescue advances the implicit attitude that biblical meaning is *plain*—self-evident, not requiring any sort of explicit interpretation on the part of the reader.

This does not mean *literal*. Literalism is an arguably consistent hermeneutical stance that underlies both historical fundamentalism and the theological system of historical dispensationalism. As church historian Timothy Weber has pointed out, however, historical fundamentalists tended to conflate the "plain" and "literal" hermeneutical stances. On the one hand, historical fundamentalists believed not only that "lay people could read the Bible for themselves," but also that "lay people frequently understood what trained scholars could not," and that "the conclusions of the spiritually prepared but untutored Bible reader were preferable [*sic*] to the learned but spiritually deficient professor."[7] On the other hand, most historical fundamentalists insisted on the literal and "inductive" hermeneutical stance underlying historical dispensationalism. According to Weber, they "were convinced that dispensationalism provided a superior perspective from which to study the Bible and often claimed that non-dispensationalists were incapable of seeing the Scriptures in their fullness." Because the historical dispensational system is "anything but inductive"— anything but obvious—there lies the irony of fundamentalists who declare that "they can read the Bible by themselves," but who then "pore over Scofield's notes in order to discover what the text really means" and who "derive their greatest 'blessing' from hearing some notable Bible teacher tell them what the Bible really means."[8] The same problem pertains to the hermeneutical stance implied in the rhetoric of Operation Rescue.

The "plain" meaning of Scripture, as implied in the rhetoric of Operation Rescue, also helps to smooth over the at least apparent inconsistency between (1) the implied hermeneutic of historical dispensationalism, which suggests a premillenial perspective on cultural and political development, and (2) the postmillenial perspective implied by the jeremiad form in the rhetoric of Operation Rescue.[9] On the one hand, Operation Rescue offers a gloomy portrait of cultural and political degeneration. Our culture is cast as a "moral cesspool."[10] As previously described, our nation is cast as under the threat of destruction, as an act of divine judgment, for the atrocity of abortion. At the very beginning of the videotape, the narrator's opening lines—taken from Psalm 106—accompany images of dead fetuses. "They even sacrificed their sons and their daughters to the demons," he declares, "and shed innocent blood—the blood of their sons and daughters." As the visual shifts to a United States flag flying at full mast, he continues, "And the land was polluted with the blood." Put simply, our nation and our culture are not progressing; they are degenerating as part of a rush to divine judgment (consistent with a premillenial perspective).

On the other hand, though, Operation Rescue simultaneously offers a view of history in which society and culture progress (consistent with a postmillenial perspective) if only Christians would be faithful and obedient. Indeed, Terry articulates a causal link between "rescuing" and social change. In his book, *Operation Rescue*, Terry urges the reader to "[c]ommit . . . to make this vision"—a vision of "defeat[ing] the abortion holocaust," of "restor[ing] religious and civil liberties to individuals," of "bring[ing] justice to our judicial system," and of "see[ing] common decency return"—"a reality while we still have time." Terry also hints at Christian Reconstructionism in writing that "[w]hat we can work for, believe for, and struggle for is a nation where once again the Judeo-Christian ethic is the foundation for our politics, our judicial system, and our public morality; a nation not floating in the uncertain sea of humanism, but a country whose unmoving bedrock is Higher Laws."[11] It is Terry's commitment not just to social change along the lines of the pro-life position, but also to widespread transformation of society and culture, that led Blanchard to characterize him as a Christian Reconstructionist.[12]

Operation Rescue spokesman Joseph Foreman implies in the videotape that Operation Rescue's theology follows from a literal reading of the Bible, declaring that "[w]hen God says—I believe in the Bible literally—when God says rescue those being dragged away to slaughter, I don't think He's saying, if you have time, if you have a few minutes, by the way next Saturday maybe. But He's saying rescue them. Period. Categorically." A more accurate characterization of Operation Rescue's hermeneutic perspective, however, would be an *absence* of any explicit hermeneutic system for appropriating biblical truth. This absence, driven by a belief that biblical truth is self-evident, can be seen in the disregard of the context surrounding biblical texts.

In the biblical exposition on the videotape, this disregard of context can be seen in two particular ways. In the exposition of the Deuteronomy passage, for instance, the term "people of God" is employed rhetorically to eliminate, artificially, any conceptual distinction between the Israelites of the fifteenth century BCE (to whom the Mosaic Law was originally given) and evangelical Christians of this century. Since the historical Israelites and today's evangelical Christians are conflated under the term "people of God," what applied literally to the historical Israelites also applies, literally, without any contextual considerations, to evangelical Christians at all times and places.

In addition to the strategic use of the term "people of God," the disregard of biblical context can also be seen in selective quotation and application from the prooftext passages themselves. In the case of Isaiah 1:12–15, the narrator's quick move from "[W]ho has asked this of you, this trampling of my courts?" (v. 12) directly to "When you spread out your hands..." (v. 15), combined with the failure to mention anything else from the first chapter of Isaiah, reinforces the claim, "Your hands are full of blood," (v. 15) as the *sufficient* cause for God's impending judgment on Israel. This reinforcement of the linkage of blood with divine judgment, it must be pointed out, elides other contextual factors that might render the blood claim of the fifteenth verse (assuming it indeed refers to the shedding of innocent blood) a *contributing* cause rather than a sufficient cause.

A similar elision takes place with the 2 Kings 24:2–4 prooftext. This prooftext is employed in support of the claim that "Judah was destroyed by invading armies because they were sacrificing their children," which directly suggests that child sacrifice was a sufficient cause for the divine punishment. However, the phrase "because of the sins of Manasseh and all he had done, including the shedding of innocent blood" (vv. 3–4) suggests the distinct possibility that more was involved than the shedding of blood. A broader examination of the books of 1 Kings and 2 Kings, even a casual one, suggests that the primary offense of both Israel and Judah was a more fundamental rejection of God in the form of idolatry. Again, an even casual appreciation of the biblical text leads to the conclusion that the bloodshed described was a contributing cause for divine punishment, not a sufficient cause as the rhetoric of Operation Rescue suggests.

This disregard of context in expositing biblical passages reinforces the attitude that biblical meaning is *plain*—not requiring any explicit interpretation on the part of the audience to appropriate. This plainness of Scripture, moreover, is reinforced by non-textual cues (e.g., video and audio components) in the videotape message—cues that shape the expectations and attitudes of viewers. In this particular case, the attitude implied is a particular sacredness of the Bible that then implies a mystical, direct gleaning of biblical truth. A scene of a leather Bible being slowly opened is displayed as the narrator proclaims, "Deuteronomy 21 teaches that . . ." Further, whenever the actual text of the Bible is being read by the narrator, the text itself appears visually against the backdrop of an opened scroll. Together, these visual images work together to create this sacredness I have described, by resonating with those sharing a commitment to the Bible as God's authoritative inspiration. Among those sharing this commitment, the visual cues reinforce an attitude of "This is God's truth being communicated." This attitude encouraged by these formal elements downplays the act of interpretation, tacitly suggesting that in the case of God's truth, no interpretation is needed.

The audio cues accompanying the exposition of biblical text shape the perception of meaning in a similar way. When the "judgment" passages are exposited, there are ominous-sounding bass notes played on a minor scale, with a more intense, almost crashing sound as the last line of the passage is read. The attitude shaped and reinforced by this musical form, then, is that the unease of the judgment described in the passage also applies to the viewer. By contrast, when the "hopeful" exposition of Isaiah 1:16–17 takes place, the accompanying music is of a decidedly lighter, almost joyful disposition.

The Primacy of Abortion

The rhetoric of Operation Rescue, then, encourages a particular attitude toward the Bible and toward the task of how to read and obey it. As the above discussion of the biblical expositions may have foreshadowed, the rhetoric also encourages a particular attitude toward abortion, particularly as it relates to one's faith and one's identity as a Christian. Specifically, opposition to abortion and a determination to stop it are portrayed as at least *primary* or even exclusive means by which evangelical Christians affirm the identity and the authenticity of their faith.

The biblical expositions in the videotape, as seen above, support a line of reasoning that encourages potential activists to foreground the abortion issue in their perceptions of their evangelical Christian faith. The "plain," self-evident hermeneutic stance, discussed above, encourages evangelical Christians to see both themselves and the church as a whole in a position of divine judgment for "bloodguiltiness." If this particular reading of the Bible is persuasive, then specific action to stop abortion (particularly some form of participation in Operation Rescue activities) becomes an imperative by which evangelical Christians reaffirm their identity, their integrity, and their "right relationship" with God.

The primacy of abortion, encouraged by the biblical expositions, is supported and augmented at a number of other points on the videotape. Specifically, numerous other statements made on the videotape encourage this particular attitude toward abortion in three ways: statements about *identity* as a Christian, statements about Christian *obedience*, and statements about growing to *maturity* as an authentic Christian.

Dr. Beverly McMillan, a self-described former abortionist who also appeared on the pro-life film *Eclipse of Reason*, explicitly connects Operation Rescue activism with Christian identity. The "rescue movement," she declares on the videotape, "is the logical conclusion of what it means to call babies human, to call them our brothers and sisters, and to call ourselves a Christian [*sic*]." This claim of identity is also made by two church pastors featured on the videotape. Speaking of impending Operation Rescue protests, Rev. Van Guyton exclaims, "We are the people that have been born into the Kingdom of God for such a time as this, that we can as Christians come out of our shells, come out of our fears, come out of our religiosity, and step into the purposes of God." He then thunders, to loud cheering and applause, "We have been born for this day!" The Reverend Daniel J. Little, pastor of Terry's church in Binghamton, New York, declares in reference to Operation Rescue, "This is Middle America. This is the Church. We are forcing the gate open, and the gates of Hell cannot prevail against the Church."

This claim of identity is also articulated by connecting the work of Operation Rescue with the work of Jesus and of the Apostle Paul. Dr. Paul Lindstrom, in justifying civil disobedience for Christians, made the comparison between the work of Operation Rescue and the work of Christ Himself. "We see Jesus going into the temple," he declares, "and making a whip, turning over the money changers' tables. Now that wasn't exactly in accordance with the law, and I think we need to make some of those same whips, as it were, and get out onto the street, sit down, protest, and fight the good fight of faith for King Jesus, and . . . stop the murdering." Terry made the implicit comparison between the work of Operation Rescue and the work of the Apostle Paul. "We're at a place in this movement," he says, "where we need some people in jail for a day or two. The reason being again, as St. Paul said in Philippians, Chapter One, 'Do not be discouraged about my imprisonment, because it has caused the furtherance of the Gospel, because many of the brethren, seeing my bonds, have waxed bold in the cause of Christ.'" In this way, the imprisonment that Operation Rescue activists endure is endowed symbolically with the same essence and meaning as the imprisonment that the Apostle Paul endured. This linkage, as the one between Operation Rescue's acts and Christ's acts, provides an important, legitimizing affirmation of identity as an authentic Christian.

These claims of identity, moreover, carry a negative connotation. Not only is Operation Rescue activism connected with authentic Christian faith, but also lack of such activism is implicitly connected with a lack of authentic Christian faith. At a scene captured on the videotape just prior to a rescue, Terry prayed aloud with a group about to protest. "We are more guilty than the police when they drag us away," he prays, "because the police are not called to be the salt of the earth. We are." "Rescuing," in Terry's prayer, constitutes being "the salt of the earth"—an essential function of a Christian.[13] People who claim to be Christians but do not engage in "rescue" protests, it is implied, are not being "the salt of the earth," and therefore are not manifesting an essential characteristic of an authentic Christian.

Operation Rescue activism is also characterized in terms of obedience; consequently, refusal to engage in such activism is implicitly characterized as disobedience to God. On the videotape Joseph Foreman is shown declaring of Operation Rescue protests, "I would say this is normal Christian behavior. It's not radical. It's simple obedience." The videotape also shows a scene in which Rev. Keith Tucci prayed aloud with fellow activists during a rescue protest. "We thank you," he prays, "that we're here to please you, Father. We thank you for these babies that will be saved today. We thank you that they will have life nine months from now. But even then, Lord, that's not our ultimate reason for being here. We are here to do what's right, Father. That's our motivation, to serve you and please you."

The theme of loving one's neighbor as oneself, presented in Christ's parable of the Good Samaritan, is also used as a way of casting Operation Rescue activism as obedience to the God of the Bible. "When the Lord talked about loving your neighbor as ourselves [sic]," Terry declares on the videotape, "He set it up in the framework of rescuing someone from death. Remember, the priest and the Levite walked by while the man was dying in the ditch, but the good Samaritan saved his life." Making more explicit the parallel between the parable and the current situation, he continues, "So maybe the priest thought he was not called to a 'ditch ministry,' maybe he was saying 'Well, I'm called to preach the Gospel.' But the Lord said, 'He's not the one'—in so many words, said 'He's not the one who loved his neighbor as himself.' It was the good Samaritan who saved the man's life."

Finally, Operation Rescue activism is connected with growing to maturity as an authentic Christian. Father John McFadden is shown on the videotape testifying that "I really felt my Christian faith and my priesthood really alive in this incredible marketplace, in defending and trying to protect the lives of these unborn babies, and to save the mothers from their own victimization." Terry, in testimony previously described, declares that it is involvement with the "rescue movement" that is "producing revival in people's hearts" and transforming them, "because it takes their eyes off themselves and puts their eyes on Christ and on other people's needs." In this way, Operation Rescue activism is connected with the essential process of sanctification.

Testimony and the Insularity of "Conversion"

Finally, the *Operation Rescue* videotape makes extensive use of testimony from a wide range of people who have participated in Operation Rescue protests. This extensive use of testimony serves two important functions. First, it functions to portray Operation Rescue as a group enjoying a broad base of support, so as to defeat any conception of Operation Rescue as a fringe group. Second, and more important, it makes use of "conversion" itself as a rhetorical strategy.

As an implicit argument for Operation Rescue's broad base of support, the videotape features testimony from figures outside the evangelical tradition. Testimonies from Catholics and Jews, for instance, are prominently featured. In addition to the Catholics quoted above, the videotape features excerpts from Bishop Austin Vaughan and from Father Tony Mugavero. The latter figure reinforced the connection between Operation Rescue activism and Christian obedience by saying that "this is what He wants. This is what we have to do, and if we're not doing it, we're not being faithful to our brothers and sisters." Two Jewish rabbis are also included on the videotape. "It's absolutely a great merit to stand up against the most horrible injustice of all," Rabbi Yehuda Levin declares, "the injustice of the murder and elimination of poor innocent children." Rabbi Yosef Friedman appears on the videotape shortly afterward, stating that "[i]f a life will be saved by my arrest, it's a very small contribution for such a worthy cause." The implicit claim behind the inclusion of such testimony is that since Operation Rescue has support from a number of different religious traditions, then the group must enjoy moral and spiritual legitimacy.

For evangelical Christians, further, this implicit claim of legitimacy is augmented by the inclusion of testimony from prominent evangelical figures. "Every so often," Rev. Jerry Falwell declares on the videotape, "a pastor will call me and say, 'Surely you don't agree with that [Operation Rescue activism].' I said I sure do." Later in the videotape, Falwell is shown again to display his unqualified support of the group. "[A]fter fifteen years of efforts to judicially and legislatively correct the problem," he states, "Operation Rescue is a new and a fresh breath of air. Politicians don't respond to logic. Politicians never see the light until they feel the heat. . . . And that is exactly what Operation Rescue is doing." James Dobson, director of the prominent *Focus on the Family* radio program, testifies about Operation Rescue and the issue of civil disobedience by Christians. "You know, it's reminiscent for me, Nazi Germany, they forced the townspeople to come through those extermination camps and see the dead bodies, implying that there was some responsibility on the townspeople to oppose the law and to speak on behalf of those innocent people who were being killed." Dobson then linked that situation with today's abortion controversy, relating Operation Rescue's position that "children are being killed, and this is a law we should break, but break it peacefully." Dobson concludes, "It is interesting and a little bit discouraging to me that the Christian community is struggling over this issue, whether it's right or wrong," clearly implying that evangelical Christians should see the legitimacy of Operation Rescue's perspective and act accordingly. Finally, Melody Green, widow of the late Keith Green, gives her testimony of participation in, and therefore approval of, Operation Rescue.[14]

In addition to the use of testimony to suggest a broad base of support for Operation Rescue, the videotape makes use of testimony to advance the rhetorical strategy of "conversion." This particular strategy is similar to what rhetorician Robert James Branham describes as the "convert tale," in his analysis of the pro-life films *The Silent Scream* and *Eclipse of Reason*. The convert tale, according to Branham, functions not only to reaffirm the truth of the "new" perspective in its imitation of the spiritual conversion form, but also to imply the ignorance and/or malevolence of the "unconverted."[15] By making use of this insulating strategy, the rhetoric of Operation Rescue reinforces the legitimacy of the group while also providing a consistent explanation for the recalcitrance of the opposition.

One testimony on the videotape gives an account of conversion in the face of rationality and common sense. "Someone asked me a question once," declares Rev. Jesse Lee, "'If abortion is murder, why don't we act like it's murder?' And I couldn't answer the question very well with my own experience," he continued. "I couldn't give a good answer why I shouldn't act like it was murder. That question is what gripped me, and I couldn't see any difference in trying to save the life of a child in the womb from someone who was in the front of my church being murdered."

With the testimony of Larry Tomczak, the conversion account is presented in a somewhat more mystical way:

> Over the years, actually fifteen years now, I have done everything I know to do to express this conviction that an innocent human life has a right to live. I've participated in March for Lifes, petitions written to Congressmen. I've spoken publicly in seminars and conferences. I've written articles, supported crisis pregnancy centers. I've done everything I know how to do, even adopting a little abandoned child from another nation. But I sensed in my spirit that something of a next step was on the horizon for me. And as I heard of Operation Rescue, and the opportunity to prayerfully, peacefully, and physically place myself between an abortionist and a preborn victim, a child, I felt the time was now for me. And so I gave myself in this way.

The visual shifts to a scene of him being dragged away by police officers. He then gives evidence of the new perspective that conversion brings. "It was an honor. I was scared, I have to admit, but it was a very fulfilling experience, very rewarding, as I realized I was helping to stem the tide of the extinguishing of human life in this land." Tomczak thus communicates his own realization that a pro-life commitment—a product of a commitment to evangelical Christianity—leads logically and faithfully to Operation Rescue activism.

Conclusion

In discussing evangelical ideology and how that might shape mobilization in social protest movements, Soper explains that "[a]ctivism in the world assumes a religious significance for evangelicals, who believe that they have an obligation to pattern their lives according to the will of God."[16] It is this belief on the part of evangelical Christians that the rhetoric of Operation Rescue addresses. And it is this connection from which the most significant implications of this rhetoric are seen. These implications follow from the three essential features of the rhetoric of Operation Rescue explicated above.

First, the rhetoric of Operation Rescue encourages a view of biblical meaning as self-evident, as not requiring an interpretive frame nor interpretive work on the part of the audience. This attitude toward the Bible directly relates to other attitudes also encouraged by the rhetoric of Operation Rescue—attitudes toward the natures of truth and persuasion. As Operation Rescue activists are encouraged to see the understanding of the truths of Scripture as a self-evident process, so they are also encouraged to believe that communicating ("witnessing to") that truth is also a self-evident process. It is this misunderstanding of the natures of truth and persuasion, I believe, that not only has led to Operation Rescue's problematic conception of the public (discussed in chapter 8), but also has contributed significantly to Operation Rescue's failure to advance its cause meaningfully in the public arena.

Second, the rhetoric of Operation Rescue examined in this chapter also encourages particular views about Christian identity. Evangelical Christians are encouraged to see abortion as the paramount issue of importance to the Church. More important, though, evangelical Christians—specifically those active in Operation Rescue—are tempted to consider their Operation Rescue activism as the sole means by which they validate the authenticity of their faith. In the rhetoric of Operation Rescue examined here, boldness and courage in stopping the abortion "holocaust" (i.e., participating in "rescue" protests) are cast as essential and integral aspects of Christian identity, obedience, and maturity.

Finally, this powerful rhetorical connection between "rescuing" and the authentic expression of evangelical Christian faith is further strengthened by the function of testimony in this rhetoric. This testimony, as seen above, functions not only to legitimize Operation Rescue by suggesting a broad base of support, but also to make use of "conversion" as an insulating rhetorical strategy.

The most significant implications of the theological function of this rhetoric, though, are seen in how this rhetoric tempts identification with a particular representation of the evangelical Christian faith. To the degree that this rhetoric is able to advance a representation in which the entirety of the Christian faith is reduced merely to bold opposition to abortion in the form of Operation Rescue activism, it can function powerfully to constrain motivation and action in the enactment of one's Christian faith.

Rhetorical representation in this way certainly can strengthen commitment to Operation Rescue and to the pro-life cause, since it creates motives based not primarily on specific beliefs about abortion, but rather on fundamental reaffirmations of Christian identity. There is a significant downside, however. Such a representation can result not only in fundamental error in understanding, applying, and living out the Christian faith; but also in the creation of a mindset more favorable to incivility and violence. This final concern—the connection between the rhetoric of Operation Rescue and violence—is the subject of the next chapter.

Notes

1. *Operation Rescue*, Operation Rescue, 1989, videocassette.
2. J. Christopher Soper, *Evangelical Christianity in the United States and Great Britain: Religious Beliefs, Political Choices* (New York: New York University Press, 1994), x.
3. Dallas A. Blanchard, *The Anti-Abortion Movement and the Rise of the Religious Right: From Polite to Fiery Protest* (New York: Twayne Publishers, 1994), 46.
4. James Davison Hunter, *American Evangelicalism: Conservative Religion and the Quandary of Modernity* (New Brunswick, N.J.: Rutgers University Press, 1983), 9.
5. *Operation Rescue*, back cover of videocassette case.
6. Terry, quoted in Judy Lundstrom Thomas, "Terry and His Cause Allow No Neutrality," *Wichita Eagle*, August 25, 1991, VUTEXT database, document 238112, 16.
7. Timothy P. Weber, "The Two-Edged Sword: The Fundamentalist Use of the Bible," in *The Bible in America: Essays in Cultural History*, ed. Nathan O. Hatch and Mark A. Noll (New York: Oxford University Press, 1982), 111–12.
8. Ibid., 114, 117.
9. The jeremiad is a rhetorical form—named after the prophet Jeremiah—that creates a motivation for social change by positing a community "promise" or vision of the good life, the community's failure to live up to the terms of the promise, and the opportunity for the promise to be restored if the community again commits to the terms of the promise. For a classic book-length discussion of the jeremiad, particularly its pervasiveness in American political history, see Sacvan Bercovitch, *The American Jeremiad* (Madison: University of Wisconsin Press, 1978).
10. Randall A. Terry, *Operation Rescue* (Springdale, Pa.: Whitaker House, 1988), 146.
11. Ibid., 178.
12. Blanchard, *The Anti-Abortion Movement*, 49.
13. Christ said of his disciples, "You are the salt of the earth" (Matthew 5:13).
14. Keith Green was a prominent member of the Jesus Movement and a pioneer in Christian popular music. His name and his work are well known in evangelical circles.
15. Robert James Branham, "The Role of the Convert in *Eclipse of Reason* and *The Silent Scream*," *Quarterly Journal of Speech* 77 (1991): 410–12, 424.
16. Soper, *Evangelical Christianity in the United States and Great Britain*, 44.

6

THE RHETORICAL FOUNDATIONS OF PRO-LIFE VIOLENCE

(Mis)representation in the Rhetoric of Operation Rescue

Death opens her cavernous mouth before you. Thousands upon thousands of children are consumed by her every day. You have the ability to save some from being tossed into her gaping mouth. As hundreds are being rushed into eternity, other questions shrink in comparison to the weighty question, "Should we defend our born and unborn children with force?" Take defensive action!
—Paul J. Hill[1]

On July 29, 1994, outspoken pro-life activist Paul J. Hill became the second person to commit murder in the name of the pro-life cause. That morning, he shot Dr. John Bayard Britton and one of his clinic escorts with a shotgun at pointblank range just outside of a Pensacola, Florida, abortion clinic.[2] Writing an editorial about the incident a few days later, *New York Times* columnist Anthony Lewis clearly was not content with explanations that Hill was an isolated deviant in an essentially nonviolent pro-life movement, a "pariah" with "only a handful of supporters."[3] Rather, Lewis held pro-life rhetoric directly responsible for the violence. He wrote that "when you [pro-life activists] tell your followers that abortion is 'murder,' that doctors are 'baby-killers,' that America has an 'abortion Holocaust,' you cannot so neatly disavow responsibility once someone takes you at your word. The hysterical rhetoric of the anti-abortion movement in this country is an invitation to violence."[4]

This tendency to exaggerate the causal connection between rhetoric and violence is not limited to the abortion controversy. In the wake of the 1995 Oklahoma City bombing, President Clinton delivered a speech in Minneapolis in which he claimed that the airwaves are all too often used to keep people paranoid, spread hate, and give the impression that violence is acceptable. These comments then sparked renewed debate about the civility of public discourse and the limits of free speech.[5]

The concern over the relationship between rhetoric and violence has also appeared in scholarly discussions of both the "culture war" and the question of civil public discourse. One of sociologist James Davison Hunter's concerns, as outlined in his influential book, *Culture Wars*, is the manner in which conflict is handled in public discourse. While acknowledging that "the personal disagreements that fire the culture war are deep and perhaps unreconcilable," he laments that "these differences are often intensified and aggravated by the way they are presented in public."[6] The result, Hunter claims, is a public discourse that is "shallow and fragmentary," a polarizing discourse that silences moderating voices in an "eclipse of the middle."[7]

The ominous title of Hunter's follow-up volume, *Before the Shooting Begins*, makes clear his conviction that much more is at stake than just the quality of public discourse. Noting that "tension, conflict, and perhaps even violence are inevitable" when "cultural impulses this momentous vie against each other to dominate public life," and that "culture wars always precede shooting wars," Hunter strenuously advances the importance of the "democratic imperative" as a corrective to the trend toward authoritarianism and violence.[8] This imperative, further, is to be instantiated not as the "shallow democracy" that currently plagues the American polity, but instead as a "substantive democracy": a new dispensation of "modesty in politics" that would feature a broader redefinition of the "public," a revival of "the art of argumentation and persuasion," and a revitalization of "politics within its limits."[9]

The foundation of urgency for Hunter's democratic imperative, I would venture, is not that bellicose culture warfare rhetoric explicitly advocates violence, nor that it has no connection to the dangers of violence. Rather, Hunter's foundation appears to be the assumption that such rhetoric functions to create a public rhetorical climate in which violence can more easily be considered as an expedient solution, a justified solution, and/or the *only* solution for the meaningful, satisfactory resolution of public controversy. This chapter focuses on this subtle yet dangerous function of rhetoric.

The previous two chapters focus on how the rhetoric of Operation Rescue encourages identification with particular representations of the evangelical Christian faith. Chapter 4 examines how the rhetoric of Operation Rescue promotes a particular vision of history that can shape activists' connections between faith and action. Chapter 5 elaborates upon the relationship between rhetoric and these connections by examining how the rhetoric of Operation Rescue functions theologically. These rhetorical representations of the evangelical Christian faith have considerable persuasive power to generate and sustain commitment to Operation Rescue and to the pro-life movement more generally. Such rhetorical representations, however, also reproduce problematic aspects of the evangelical faith tradition—problematic in terms of both appropriating the faith as "equipment for living" and engaging in public dialogue.

In this chapter, I highlight the problematic features of representation in the rhetoric of Operation Rescue by focusing on how it creates a cultural climate among Operation Rescue activists that is more favorable to incivility and violence, and also how it contributes to the same climate in public discourse more generally. I also show how the creation of such a rhetorical climate can be tied to how the evangelical Christian faith is rhetorically represented, or, perhaps more accurately, *misrepresented*.

Accordingly, this chapter focuses on representation as a rhetorical phenomenon that, in this particular case, works to oversimplify the complexity of the evangelical Christian faith. In this oversimplification, the complexity of this faith is reduced to the simplicity of Operation Rescue activism or other confrontational pro-life activity. The chapter begins with a discussion of Kenneth Burke's ideas regarding rhetoric and representation, upon which the analysis of this chapter is based.

I then trace the existence and function of two representative themes in the rhetoric of Operation Rescue: "holy war" and "identification with the unborn." Both representative themes, I suggest, misrepresent the evangelical Christian faith simplistically and overreductionistically.

The analysis of these representative themes is focused specifically on an unpublished collection of "testimonies" written by Operation Rescue activists incarcerated during Operation Rescue's 1988 Atlanta campaigns. This sharper focus is advantageous for at least two reasons. First, it allows for a clearer elucidation of the attitudes of rank-and-file activists themselves, as opposed to the discourse of group leaders (e.g., rally speeches).[10] Second, it targets discourse that is produced within the specific context of direct activism and direct establishment response. From the testimonies one gets a better sense of how Operation Rescue activists perceived their "in the trenches" experiences, and how they made use of rhetoric to make sense of those experiences.

Following the analysis of Operation Rescue rhetoric, I turn to an examination of a position paper written by Paul Hill immediately following Michael Griffin's shooting of Dr. Gunn in 1993, in which Hill explicitly proclaims the justice of using deadly force to stop abortions. The presence of the same pattern of misrepresentation in Hill's rhetoric buttresses my claim of a connection between this pattern of rhetorical misrepresentation and violence.

Rhetoric and Representation

Rhetoric, as discussed in chapter 2, functions powerfully in a generative, perspective-shaping capacity. As "symbol-using animals," human beings use language and symbols to construct perspectives by which to make sense of reality.[11] Because these perspectives are but "approximation[s] to the truth,"[12] the issue of representation is important in discerning the usability, the depth, and the overall "accuracy" of the approximation. Does the perspective in question represent reality well enough to allow its adherents to function well, to get along with others, and to handle the ambiguities and complexities that exist in the real world? Or is the perspective in question so simplistic that its adherents end up approaching both the world and other people dysfunctionally?

Burke addresses this issue of representation in more depth in *A Grammar of Motives*, arguing that these symbolically constructed perspectives need to have suitable scope, appropriately balancing simplicity and complexity. In order to help people make sense of the sheer complexity of reality, all usable perspectives are at least somewhat reductive. However, great care must be taken to ensure that a given perspective is not so simplistic that it fundamentally miscalculates or misrepresents fundamental aspects of what it seeks to explain.

In order to help discern the difference between serviceable and oversimplistic representations, Burke distinguishes between *action* and *motion*, suggesting that oversimplistic representations tend to cast human motives and human behavior not as action (which involves volition, choice, and moral gravity), but rather as motion (i.e., the sort of behavior exhibited by inanimate objects acted upon by their environment, such as a rock rolling down a hill). For example, Burke criticizes behaviorism and other philosophies of materialism precisely because, in his view, they represent the human condition too simplistically—as motion instead of action. He also justifies his own key terms of *drama* and *dramatism* to represent the human condition by claiming that they avoid this sort of misrepresentation.[13]

Burke's concern with representation is also at the heart of this conceptualization of the "pentad": his breaking down of human motives into the key terms of act, scene, agent, agency, and purpose. While a significant number of rhetoric scholars have employed the pentad as a methodological scheme, Burke's use of the pentad seems to be more philosophical. His critique of the various "philosophic schools" (e.g., materialism, idealism, pragmatism, etc.), which spans much of the middle section of *A Grammar of Motives*, is based on his claim that each system of philosophy he discusses engages in oversimplistic misrepresentation—emphasizing one term of the pentad and neglecting the others. For example, philosophies of materialism (such as behaviorism) overemphasize *scene*. To avoid this problem, Burke argues, a perspective needs to account more broadly for all five terms of the pentad. The pentad, then, is best seen as a theoretical elaboration of this issue of rhetoric and representation.

This problem of oversimplistic representation has been noticed by other writers and thinkers as well. G. K. Chesterton, for instance, pinpointed this problem as the root of "maniacal" thinking. The insane mind, he writes, "moves in a perfect but narrow circle. A small circle is quite as infinite as a large circle; but, though it is quite as infinite, it is not so large. In the same way the insane explanation is quite as complete as the sane one, but it is not so large. . . . The lunatic's theory explains a large number of things, but it does not explain them in a large way."[14] Put another way, the lunatic's vocabulary offers a complete representation of the world and of human motives, but it lacks sufficient *scope*. The lunatic's vocabulary, with its excessive reductionism, fundamentally misrepresents reality.

These theoretical considerations can be applied readily to an at least partial explanation of how the rhetoric of Operation Rescue might function to construct an attitude in which violence can be considered to be more plausible. As with human motivation more generally, the striving "to know and live Christianity in its authentic and divinely intended manner"[15] corresponds with a broad pattern of experience that can be represented more suitably or less suitably. In the rhetoric of Operation Rescue examined here, two different representative themes can be seen: (1) holy war, and (2) identification with the unborn. Both of these representative themes, I suggest, represent the evangelical Christian faith less suitably and more dangerously.

Representative Theme #1: Holy War

Kenneth Burke not only posited an essential connection between language and perspective, but also accorded the trope of metaphor a significant role in this connection. "Every perspective," he states concisely, "requires a metaphor, implicit or explicit, for its organizational base."[16] In his earlier discussion of "recalcitrance," Burke emphasized the power of a metaphor not just in the origins of a perspective, but also in the face of challenges that are posed to it by other perspectives and by the non-symbolic world. In response to such resistance, it becomes increasingly tempting for the organizing metaphor to be taken as an immutable reality. Such a perspective, according to Burke, "would be so firmly established in our habits of thought that we could everywhere find it corroborated in 'hard fact,' particularly since the instruments of precision and thought by which we made our examinations were themselves shaped by this same point of view."[17] As rhetoric scholar Robert L. Ivie puts it, there is "the ever-present temptation of literalizing one metaphor to the exclusion of others."[18]

This literalizing process has received significant scholarly attention, particularly with respect to war metaphors. Rhetoric scholar David Zarefsky's study of President Lyndon B. Johnson's "War on Poverty" campaign, for example, highlights the recalcitrance created by the use of a war metaphor as a sweeping rhetorical strategy. When Johnson formally "declared war on poverty" in his January 8, 1964 State of the Union message, the resonance of the war metaphor helped to ensure speedy passage of the Economic Opportunity Act of 1964, as well as the speedy creation of the expansive Office of Economic Opportunity. In Zarefsky's view, the war metaphor characterized the Administration's anti-poverty efforts in a way that virtually guaranteed their at least short-term success. It made them vast, overarching, and uncompromising. It made them national in scope. It reduced the burden of proof for the persuasive advancement of these efforts. It took away moral legitimacy from political opponents. Finally, it served as a moral unifier for the country.[19] Unfortunately, the same metaphor virtually guaranteed "long-term rhetorical failure," in that the Administration's anti-poverty efforts naturally failed to live up to the totalized expectations created by the war metaphor. "To define one's goals in the loftiest of terms," Zarefsky states, "is to arouse expectations and to court disappointment when the tangible benefits fall short of its avowed goals, as inevitably they will."[20] The war metaphor, as the conceptual foundation for Johnson's anti-poverty efforts, did just that. Inevitable political compromise, placed in the context of war, became unavoidably characterized as *defeat*.

While Zarefsky's study focuses more narrowly on the use of the war metaphor in a persuasive public policy campaign, historian Michael S. Sherry has taken a broader view. In his book, *In the Shadow of War*, he put forward a history of the United States in the twentieth century in which *militarism* has been an important shaping influence. In Sherry's view, it is an influence in which "war and national security became consuming anxieties and provided the memories, models, and metaphors that shaped broad areas of national life."[21] This influence of militarism "reshaped every realm of American life—politics and foreign policy, economics and technology, culture and social relations—making America a profoundly different nation."[22]

The articulation of a more explicitly rhetorical account of the war metaphor's broader social influence has been the concern motivating much of Ivie's work.[23] In his more recent work, he has explored how the Cold War rhetoric of militarization has hampered the United States' ability to gauge adequately its challenges and responsibilities in the post–Cold War era. These "rhetorical habits," in Ivie's words, have produced an "addiction to tragic fear" that "prods us as a people to continue the fateful struggle against international chaos as if one nation might control the world sufficiently by itself to achieve a lasting and just peace," and "perpetuates a futile quest for security through global hegemony."[24] In the wake of the terrorist attacks of September 11, 2001, Ivie has argued, the United States has only become more addicted to these rhetorical habits in conceptualizing and executing its foreign policy.[25]

As the analysis below will illustrate, the discourse of Operation Rescue reflects the internalization of the war metaphor. But war alone does not capture the metaphoric grounding of this discourse, as there is also an overtly religious dimension that results in a "holy war" representation. This combination of war and religious metaphors has been explicitly investigated by rhetorician Suzanne Daughton, who examined the presence of this metaphoric combination in President Franklin Roosevelt's first inaugural address. This combination, which "asks listeners for unquestioning obedience and inspired, committed action for a morally satisfying victory over evil," is shown by Daughton to be a uniquely "powerful"—yet also dangerous—source of "rhetorical energy."[26]

Metaphor, then, can function powerfully in a representative capacity. In the remainder of this section, I show how the metaphor of "holy war," functioning as a representative theme, structures both the experiences of Operation Rescue activists and their appropriation of the evangelical Christian faith. I focus on three general characterizations evident in the testimonies of Operation Rescue activists: (1) characterization of the protest scene, (2) characterization of those opposed to the protesters, and (3) characterization of the protesters themselves.

Characterization of Scene

Throughout the testimonies examined here, Operation Rescue activism is explicitly characterized as waging war. One activist explained her absence from Operation Rescue and pro-life activism by writing that "I was sick and so was out of the war for a while"; she then described her return as "[c]oming back on duty."[27] "I am glad God called me as one of His soldiers," another activist proclaimed. "Every time I pack," she continued, "I feel like I am going to war.... The troops have landed, the fight has begun."[28] "I pray for new fruitful people to hear the battle cry of the Lord," wrote Baby Jane Doe #2443.[29] "Come join us in God's great army. He has given us the victory!"[30]

This war is also one in which the stakes are apocalyptically high and profoundly moral—holy—in nature. "These truly are the last days," declared one activist, and "sides are being drawn up." Because of this, "Christians must take a stand for righteousness. It may be our last chance!" she exclaimed.[31] "When the Lord impressed on my heart that abortion is human sacrifices to Satan," declared Baby Jane Doe #915, "suddenly the war between good and evil became very real."[32] In the same vein, another activist made clear that this war is "the war against the devil."[33]

The image of the "holy war" is also reflected in the testimonies by the comparison between abortion and the Nazi Holocaust. Baby Jane Doe #2403 wrote that "I feel a great many things about the Rescues, but an overriding thought has been: I cannot [act] as the 'good Germans' who stood by and did nothing."[34] Baby Jane Doe #741 related that "[t]he girls trying to enter the clinic were in obvious fear and distress—the abortionists said 'Come on in and we'll take care of your "problem."' It was like watching people going to the gas chambers in Nazi Germany."[35]

Protest scenes, further, are characterized as battlefields. Operation Rescue activist Brenda Taber described the early stages of one particular protest. Noting that "[t]he police officers had already place[d] barricades up and down the streets," Taber declared that "[w]hile on hands and knees, the inches gained in attempt[ing] to rescue babies were not [many] before the police began to take people into custody."[36] Protester John Arena stated that "[a]fter the rough treatment" the activists received at the hands of the police, "the police guarded the death centers like it [*sic*] was Fort Knox."[37]

Characterization of Those Opposed to Protesters

The holy war representation, as evident in the testimonies, extends beyond the protest scene to include a consistent characterization of those opposed to the protesters. Explicit characterizations in the testimonies can be seen of the police, of pro-choice activists, and of those working at abortion clinics.

Characterizations of the police focus mainly on their cruelty to the protesters. Relating her account of arrests at one particular protest, activist Brenda Taber began by summarizing that the arrests were "done in the most aggressive manner ever to be seen by my eyes except on war movies." She then related her account of cruelty: "My heart and eyes cried while I watched these people, helpless on all fours, being lifted up by iron grips around the back of the neck from ear to ear. I saw a young man, maybe 20 or so, being told 'WALK, WALK!' The officer had this 'iron grip' around his neck, dragging him along. The young man was standing up but unable to walk.... [H]is arms were outstretched in a backaward [*sic*] fashion." Aside from the "iron grip," she continued, "the police used other techniques as well, such as pulling bodies by the hair, bending or twisting arms and wrists. They would drag them on the ground by one foot. One lady had her blouse up around her shoulders while being dragged." In her account, further, the scene reflected the acts of the police. "I saw blood stains on the pavement," she declared, "after arrestes [*sic*] were completed."[38]

The testimonies of other activists present similar accounts of police cruelty. "I've never had to suffer physically," related Baby Jane Doe #2191, but "[t]he indescribable anguish came when watching the others being painfully dragged away."[39] "At times," recounted Operation Rescue activist Myrna J. Shaneyfelt, "because of the cruelty that I saw, I couldn't watch and closed my eyes and prayed for the officers that were so cruel and for all of us to have the strength to be strong when it was our turn." She then described some of what she saw. "After I was seated in the back of the bus," she recalled, "my heart broke again as I watched a different officer pull and drag a young lady through the aisle, banging her along on the seats as she was crying out in obvious pain.... One of the officers had his foot on her buttocks and was pushing her with his foot, while the other officer dragged her." After the police brought more protesters onto the bus, she stated that "[a]ll were laying on a heap, weeping and injured on the floor of the bus. As they were lying there, one officer reached over and started yanking on their arms as they were stuck in this jammed position." He grabbed another protester's arm "and jerked her up half-way onto the body of the man, and in doing so knocked the breath out of her and caused her to groan in deeper pain."[40]

In addition to being described as inflictors of "totally unnecessary cruelty," the police are characterized in other negative ways in keeping with their position as the "enemy." They are characterized as unfair. "I observed cruelty by the Atlanta police," declared activist Marilyn Matheny. "I was sometimes treated like sentenced inmates although one is supposed to be considered innocent until proven guilty."[41] They are characterized as deceptive. "In order for the rescuers to appear to be struggling" while being arrested, according to Taber, "the officers would jerk their heads around before taking their photos."[42] And they are characterized as complicitous with pro-choice activists and clinic workers. "I later returned with a camera," stated Taber, and two officers "pulled a deathscort [clinic escort worker] between them with proud smiles, posing."[43]

Although most of the descriptions here of those opposed to Operation Rescue activists are of the police, pro-choice activists and those working at abortion clinics are also commented on in a similar manner. Pro-choice activists, for instance, are explicitly characterized as evil. "It was while picketing," related Baby Jane Doe #7141, "that the Lord opened my eyes to the reality of the satanic deception and its power over people. I could feel the evil as I marched by the pro-choicers' barricades and looked into their laughing, mocking eyes."[44]

Characterization of Protesters

Compared with the characterizations of the scene and of the "enemy," more extensive space in the testimonies is given to the characterization of the protagonists in this holy war. As seen above, Operation Rescue activists characterize themselves as participants in a war, as warriors. The characterization of the protesters themselves speaks much more to the kind of warriors they are. The exhaustive connections between their work and God serve both to proclaim the moral legitimacy of their role in the war, and to magnify the stakes of the struggle as a holy war. A number of consistent themes in this regard can be discerned.

First, those activists offering these testimonies consistently characterize Operation Rescue activists as *obedient to God*. This characterization presumes that God has commanded them to undertake this work. After attending her first Operation Rescue rally, testified one activist, "God started working in my heart." After she had gone home and "prayed about" what she had heard, "God wouldn't let me sleep—I was obsessed with concern over this and realized that even tomorrow mothers would be going to kill their babies—for convenience!" She related that after her first "rescue," "I told the Lord I would get my affairs in order and be arrested, if necessary, the next week. He soon said, 'No, I want you to go now!'"[45] "When I heard Randy [Terry] on Focus on the Family," shared activist Caroline Yeoman, "the Holy Spirit got 'a hold' of me and I was convinced I had to go."[46] "There was never a question in my mind," related activist Valerie Yates, "that God intended me to, for once, take an active stand against the murder of the innocent."[47]

Correspondingly, Operation Rescue activists are portrayed as obedient to these commands from God. "I was arrested August 10 [1988]," stated one activist, "and plan to stay in prison indefinitely—till the *Lord* releases me."[48] "God seems to gently push at times," said Baby Jane Doe #2403, "and here I am."[49] Baby Jane Doe #2443 related her obedience to God's command a bit more personally: "My heart cried to the child lost to abortion, for a nation, a church that allows the killing. Suddenly, tremendous grief struck me and I wept. I cried from the depth of my spirit, 'Here I am, Lord.' He said, 'Go to Atlanta.' I replied through the tears, 'But what can I do? You know how many times I've failed you.' He replied, 'Pick up my cross and carry it for the children.' Within days, I left for Atlanta."[50]

Second, the testimonies advance a consistent characterization of Operation Rescue activists as *displaying the love of God*—both to other prison inmates and to each other. "The inmates are a great mission [field]," stated one activist. "We were only at the farm three days but the change in the inmates was amazing just because we gave them love and compassion and the word of God."[51] Writing of fellow incarcerated activists, Valerie Yates testified that "[t]he caring and comfort of the women lock[ed] up here is beyond description. There is a bonding. We are all in different places in our spiritual growth, and we all learn from one another."[52] "There has been such unity and peace among all of us women here at Key Road Church (prison farm)," wrote activist Patti Dale. "There has not been one instance of arguing or division or selfishness among the 150 plus women of all ages and faiths."[53]

Third, there is the characterization of Operation Rescue activists as *doing God's work*. "I also feel privileged," one activist shared, "that my God has allowed me to aid Him here on earth in saving His and our pre-born children."[54] Recounting how she felt during a protest, another activist wrote, "I prayed and knew that God brought me to this city and this is God's battle. You see the world still does not understand; we're not following the commands of a man, but of a higher law of God."[55] Part of doing God's work, moreover, is communicating truth to the world. "I'm not here to punish myself," wrote one activist of her activism and subsequent incarceration, "but to try to help others understand what a serious, irreversible decision abortion is," as well as "to help bring the truth to the general public through the usually biased media."[56]

Finally, the testimonies exhibit a consistent characterization of Operation Rescue activists as *being blessed by God*. Activist Jeff Lind testified, "God has taught me a lot through this past week"—"new dimensions in humility, meekness, and repentance," as well as "the importance of trials in the growth ... of Christians."[57] "There's so much to tell," wrote another activist, "about what I have experienced of God's grace and mercy in the past week. He has taken care of us in every way; in suffering, He has given us protection, comfort and Joy! He has given us strength and prophecy, victory. I've seen healing here, ministry among the Body. I could go on and on."[58] "The Lord has blessed me much," activist Gloria Harley related, "by allowing me to be here in jail with these wonderful ladies of many faiths. And it has helped me to renew my life as a Christian as well as re-entering the pro-life movement."[59] In sum, these testimonies of Operation Rescue activists show holy war to be an organizing metaphor that shapes how Operation Rescue activists make sense of their experiences and share them with others. How they see themselves, how they see their task, how they see those opposed to their task—all are shaped by the generative power of this organizing metaphor.

As seen above, the rigidity of a particular organizing metaphor, particularly that of the holy war metaphor, shapes how Operation Rescue activists make sense of their religious faith. The rhetoric of these testimonies constructs and reinforces a representation of the "authentic" Christian faith that is encompassed almost entirely by the boundary of "fighting the good fight" at abortion clinics. This, unfortunately, is an oversimplistic misrepresentation, one that draws the Chestertonian "circle" too narrowly to include aspects of the evangelical Christian faith that are not overtly militaristic and not overtly associated with the abortion issue.

In what immediately follows, I also explore the existence and function of a second representative theme: identification with the unborn. This second representative theme, unfortunately, is as misrepresentative as the first.

Representative Theme #2: Identification with the Unborn

To be sure, the theme of identification with the unborn is by no means unique to Operation Rescue. Before Operation Rescue's rise to prominence, the most conspicuous proclamation of this theme was done by Joan Andrews, a Catholic pro-life protester who in 1986 was sentenced to a multi-year prison term for dismantling an abortion suction machine and subsequently engaging in "noncooperation."[60] In a letter written around the time of her initial sentencing, Andrews advanced a radical, exclusive identification with the unborn:

> The closer we are to the preborn children ... the more faithful we are, then the more identically aligned we become with them. This is our aim, and goal, to wipe out the line of distinction between the preborn and their born friends, becoming ourselves discriminated against.... The rougher it gets for us ... the more we can rejoice that we are succeeding; no longer are we being treated so much as the privileged born, but as the discriminated against preborn. We must become aligned with them completely and totally or else the double standard separating the preborn from the rest of humanity will never be eliminated. I don't want to be treated any differently than my brother, my sister. You reject them, you reject me.[61]

This type of identification—between the "rescuer" and the unborn—can easily become representative of the centrality of the Christian experience. Pro-life writer Mark Belz observes, "Such an identification of interests can, for the Christian, be a powerful illustration of the solidaric relationship between Christ and the sinner, and is in turn a witness to that greater truth."[62]

"Rescuers" represented in the testimonies, as seen in some of the above examples, commonly identified themselves as "Baby Jane Doe" or "Baby John Doe." Following arrest during the 1988 Atlanta protests, protesters withheld their real names from police, using only these pseudonyms. "Their anonymity was not intended as a gimmick," Belz argues, but was "an attempt to identify fully with the unnamed unborn. By refusing to give authorities their names, the Atlanta rescuers recognized that they would continue to be held in jail pending trial." However, "in this forfeiture of personal rights, they participated in the anonymity of the unborn who, for lack of proper identity and recognition, had lost an incredibly higher right than freedom from jail: the right to live."[63]

In the testimonies of incarcerated Operation Rescue activists examined here, this type of identification with the unborn can be seen in three different ways: in obedience, in suffering, and in the experience of God's blessing.

In Obedience

Some of the references in the testimonies to identification with the unborn are in the context of obedience to God. This identification is pursued and embraced because this is what God requires. One activist cast such identification in Jesus' command in the parable of the sheep and the goats, to "do for the least of these" as "you would do for me."[64] "I say my name is Baby Jane Doe," she wrote, "nameless, faceless, unwanted child who died—perhaps today she died. I say this in her memory, and in solidarity with her brothers and sisters who have also died. I say this with my hands and heart raised to Heaven in the name of he who said that whatever I do the least of these, I do to Him."[65]

Another activist connected such identification with obedience to God by making reference to Jesus' repeated commands in the Gospels to "take up the cross" and "follow Him."[66] "And as Jesus silently went to the cross to die and bear our sins," wrote Baby Jane Doe #2443, "I knew that rescuing is what I must do to help save the lives of the unborn. Now I know why the Lord had me go to Atlanta. I saw that literally standing in the gap for the voiceless, defenseless little baby was His call for me to be obedient and pick up the cross and follow Him."[67]

In Suffering

Identification with the unborn is also brought up in the testimonies as a way of explaining and/or dealing with the suffering faced by the "rescuers." The unearned suffering is therefore redemptive because, among other things, that suffering is interpreted as the essence of how the unborn are treated—having no rights and being discriminated against.

"Eight days in jail," wrote activist Marilyn Matheny, "was small compared to the cutting and slicing and vacuuming that goes on with real Baby Janes all across America."[68] "I wanted to fly over everyone to rescue the person the police were 'taking care of,'" wrote one activist who had been witnessing what she characterized as brutal treatment at the hands of the police. "But something inside of me kept me in my spot," she continued, "knowing each of us is here because we CHOSE to take the place of the babies who have no choice."[69] In a written prayer to God, activist Debra Newson related the unearned physical suffering of the activists as part of this identification with the unborn as well. "Father," she wrote, "help me to know when I see the injustice and brutality that I have seen, when I've seen elderly, grandmothers dragged across the streets, priests beaten, pastors knocked unconscious, pregnant women thrown into buses, the lady in the wheel chair forced out of her chair by the arms and dragged into the bus, when I've heard the screams of the people being picked up by their ears and throats, help me to remember that no one has had their arms and legs torn off, no one was burned to death like our unborn brothers and sisters." The endurance of suffering on behalf of the unborn, moreover, is really for the activists' ultimate benefit: identification with God. "I thank you," she continued with her written prayer, "that you have allowed me to suffer with you. My suffering is so small, my reward is so great."[70]

In Experience of God's Blessing

Finally, some of the activists connected identification with the unborn as the way they experience blessing from the God they serve. One activist explicitly connected obedience and blessing in this identification: "Just imagine if each of us took on just one voice of one baby, the grace Our Father wants to bless each of us with. He waits for us to make our tiny sacrifice for His babies. He wants to bless us desperately. Let us pray, we can hear their screams and respond."[71]

Relating her feelings at the end of her time in jail, another activist wrote: "Exhausted, we were still full of holy joy, for that is what sustained all of us during those grace-filled, yet fatiguing days. May Jesus Christ be praised!" She then linked that blessing back with the fundamental commitment to the plight of the unborn. "All for the greater glory of God," she went on, "may our 'little inconveniences' bring about the restoration of the hearts of mankind to God and end this attack against Him and His creation, the lives of these holy innocents. Thank you, Lord, for letting me hear your voice and giving me the strength to follow."[72]

In these testimonies, then, the vibrancy and vitality of one's Christian faith is represented in terms of one's response to the unborn. Repentance, suffering, obedience, blessing, victory—all of these elements of living out the "authentic" Christian faith are tied inextricably to the unborn, and, therefore, to the abortion issue. Again, the Chestertonian "circle" is drawn narrowly around just the abortion issue.

Both of these representations of the evangelical Christian faith—engagement in a holy war and identification with the unborn—represent an oversimplification of that faith. In short, both representations lack sufficient scope for activists to use the evangelical Christian faith to engage the complexity of life's experiences, particularly social protest experiences. The lack of scope involved with these representations, further, can truncate the possible range of motivation and action for these activists. In the case of

Christians operating under a literalized metaphor of spiritual warfare, for instance, the grand scope of human motivation, human history, and the human condition are seen exclusively in "spiritual warfare" terms. The faithful are cast as "warriors" whose primary purpose is to *defeat* the enemies of God. The unfaithful are cast as either complicitous with Satan, profoundly duped, or both. The faithful can be courageous. They can be compromised. They can be victorious. They can be cowards. They can even be AWOL. They cannot, however, be merciful. They cannot be charitable. They cannot be compassionate. They cannot find significant common ground with their adversaries, or even with people who do not entirely agree with them.

Similarly, with both representations the "part" of Operation Rescue activism (or other confrontational pro-life activism) can rigidly and monolithically stand for the "whole" of the Christian experience. This disallows the full complexity of motivational resources of the evangelical Christian tradition in dealing with an undeniably difficult, contentious issue. Without these other motivational resources, such as humility, compassion, and trust in God's sovereignty, a rhetorical climate is created that makes more likely desperation, incivility, and ultimately violence.

The discussions of (mis)representation above are, in sum, part of a rhetorical explanation of how violence can subtly and implicitly be encouraged in particular discourse communities—specifically social protest communities such as Operation Rescue. Is there an actual connection, however, between these rhetorical phenomena and actual violence? Although a comprehensive answer to this question is one that would involve more sustained investigation than this chapter will allow, I present two lines of support for the existence of this connection.

First, others investigating the radical fringes of the pro-life movement have suggested such a connection, specifically with regard to those Operation Rescue activists whose rhetoric I have investigated here. In their account of the militarism of the pro-life movement, journalists James Risen and Judy L. Thomas have drawn explicit connections between activists' incarceration in the 1988 Atlanta protests and some of the activists' fuller embrace of extremism. "For at least a few," they observe, "jail in Atlanta became not only a searing experience but an addictive one, transforming them into full-time activists, regulars who would ultimately develop their own floating subculture of anti-abortion militancy and extremism."[73] The authors then elaborate upon this connection specifically with respect to violence: "Many of those who later became prominent in the extremist fringe of the anti-abortion movement first came together in jail in Atlanta in 1988:

Shelley Shannon, an Oregon housewife later convicted of shooting an abortion doctor in Wichita, Kansas; John Arena, an upstate New York activist later imprisoned for acid attacks against clinics; . . . and James Kopp, who was nicknamed 'Atomic Dog' in jail in Atlanta, a nickname later mentioned prominently in the anonymously written Army of God manual, which shows extremists how to make bombs."[74] The preface to this manual is "so full of inside jokes, nicknames, and coded references to people and events known only to those intimately involved in Operation Rescue's Atlanta campaign that it seems almost certain that its author was one of those arrested with Operation Rescue in Atlanta in July 1988."[75]

Another way in which this alleged connection between this type of rhetoric and violence can be supported is to examine briefly the rhetoric of a pro-life activist who has explicitly advocated violence to stop abortions. A brief examination of an essay written by Paul Hill—a man who not only advocated violence but also took the lives of a doctor and one of his clinic escorts—will show that these same representations exist in an even more calcified, literalized form. This, in turn, lends further support to the claim that these vocabularies of misrepresentation are significant in creating a rhetorical climate favorable to violence.

Calcified Oversimplification: The Rhetoric of Paul Hill

Within five days following Michael Griffin's slaying of Dr. David Gunn in 1993, Paul Hill appeared on the *Donahue* program to proclaim, in the words of Risen and Thomas, his "pro-Griffin zeal."[76] "It's not too strong to say," they write, "that *Donahue* created Paul Hill as a national symbol of anti-abortion extremism."[77] After this appearance, and after his subsequent excommunication from the Orthodox Presbyterian Church, Hill began to circulate his first paper titled "Should We Defend Born and Unborn Children with Force?" It is this text, a position paper explicitly supporting violence (including homicide) to stop abortion, that I now examine.

Manifestations of the Holy War (Mis)representation

As with the testimonies of the incarcerated Operation Rescue activists examined earlier, Hill's position paper is thorough in its characterization of the abortion issue as the fighting of a holy war. As with the Operation Rescue testimonies, Hill's essay is replete with congruent characterizations of the *scene*. The term *defense* is consistently used throughout the essay, suggesting morally justified militarism. Violence undertaken on behalf of the pro-life cause, including homicide, is consistently labeled as "defensive action." In fact, Hill's organization was named "Defensive Action," and he describes it as "a pro-life organization proclaiming the justice of using all action necessary to protect innocent life."[78] In organizing his apologia for violence, Hill uses such headings as "The Biblical Basis for Defensive Action," "Ethical Basis for Defensive Action," and "Theological Basis for Defensive Action."[79]

Elaborating on this notion of "defense," Hill speaks specifically of waging a "defensive war" against a government that "defends with the sword the killing of approximately 4,100 innocent people every day."[80] After briefly reviewing one treatment of just war principles, Hill declares bluntly that "[c]onsidering the pressing urgency of the cause and the lack of any other justifiable course of action *our duty is to pursue a defensive war if possible.*"[81]

Further, this "defensive" war against abortion is characterized as of a comparable and even higher moral order than the Civil War. Hill states, "The resources we have garnered since the Civil War have caused us to become lazy and apathetic to the issues of freedom and justice over which the Civil War was waged. This is the time for us once again to expend our energies, resources and lives in defense of life, liberty and the pursuit of happiness."[82] The higher moral order of this "war" is made clear in another comparison. "The concept of a just cause urged both sides into the conflict in the Civil War," Hill declares. "If their motives were mixed and their cause unclear, ours need not be. Our motive is love to our unseen neighbor and our cause is just."[83] A bit earlier in the essay he is even more blunt: "Thousands died in violent action during the Civil War for a lesser cause."[84] Hill's characterization of the abortion conflict as a holy war also extends to his depiction of the protagonists. Hill celebrates "violent zeal" as the preferred motivation for those fighting his holy war. He discusses the biblical figure of Phinehas,[85] a priest who drove a spear through two people who had been using God's tabernacle for "immoral purposes." Hill states, "This violently zealous act made atonement for the sons of Israel. *Though sin had fanned God's righteous anger to a searing blaze, the shedding of guilty blood had cooled the flame and saved the people from destruction.*"[86] Hill further celebrates "violent zeal" near the end of his essay. After declaring the purity of the cause, Hill exhorts: "*Should we not therefore with zeal fired to a stead white glow, go forth to show God's righteous indignation upon those who defile with gruesome death children made in His image and likeness?*"[87]

This zeal is also explicitly described as holy: "Our zeal will be from God Himself. He will cause us to 'mount up with wings like eagles.' He will make us 'run and not get tired.' By His strength we will 'walk and not become weary.' He will give us strength and joy in defending the innocent that we have never dreamed of before."[88]

Hill also celebrated the "Christian soldier." "Biblical Christianity," he declares, "has always held in highest esteem the true Christian soldier," one who "self-sacrificially respond[s] to a call of duty to protect life, liberty and the pursuit of happiness. The Christian soldier may . . . with love and humility, take guilty life to defend innocent life from unjust harm."[89] Michael Griffin, Hill makes clear, is one such person. Far from being a callous murderer, Griffin "took the defensive posture and with apparent self-sacrifice killed the guilty to defend the innocent from a horrid death." Griffin, according to Hill, "was defending your neighbor's children at great personal cost."[90]

Interestingly, Hill uses Christ's sacrifice not as a model for humility and self-sacrifice,[91] but rather implicitly as support for this violent zeal. Answering an anticipated objection that "Christ is to be our example and He did not resist the government that put Him to death," Hill declares: "Christ had a direct command from God that He should offer His life as an atoning sacrifice. His case was unique. We have no such command."[92] To Hill, Christ's superlative example of humility, self-sacrifice, and non-violence is to be interpreted quite narrowly, not broadly.

Finally, Hill's systematic characterization includes a congruent depiction of the antagonists. His description of Dr. David Gunn figures prominently here. In a short section entitled, "Who Was the Real Aggressor?" Hill answers this question unequivocally. "Rather than accepting the common portrayal of a gentle hardworking doctor being chased down and shot in the back by a murderous lunatic," he argues, "consider the facts. *A brutal paid killer of hundreds of innocent unborn children was deterred by deadly force as he approached his latest victims.* The fact that the government describes what Dr. Gunn was about to do as abortion does not change the fact that it was the bloody slaughter of people made in God's image. The fact that Dr. Gunn killed the innocent in the white garb of the doctor with government approval does not justify his killings. His killing was no more justified than a man entering a school and personally killing school age children."[93] To add to the portrayal of the sheer moral turpitude of Gunn's acts, Hill compares him directly to Dr. Mengele, the Nazi "doctor" who ran torturous "medical experiments" on Jews at Auschwitz.[94]

Hill's portrayal of the antagonists in this holy war, further, extends beyond just Dr. Gunn. Hill characterizes the United States government as essentially oppressive and totalitarian. Responding to the anticipated objection that church leaders oppose "defensive action," Hill implicitly equated

THE RHETORICAL FOUNDATIONS OF PRO-LIFE VIOLENCE

the contemporary United States government with the World War II Nazi government. "We should not be surprised," he explains, "to encounter opposition to these truths from the church. Before World War II the church in Germany also shrank from resisting the evils of an unjust, oppressive government."[95] Hill also suggests that the current United States government should be overthrown. Noting that "[j]ust wars are . . . usually considered unwise until there are enough men and resources available to offer a reasonable hope that the effort to overthrow the existing government will be successful,"[96] Hill devotes most of the remainder of his essay to explaining how such men and resources might be gained in this particular "war."

Regarding those who oppose the idea of "defensive action" as "religious fanaticism," Hill offers another insulating explanation. "Their mockings," he bluntly explains, "are ultimately directed at God. Their hatred of their Creator reaches its most blasphemous height when they kill the unborn made in His image and when they vilify us for protecting them."[97] Clearly, then, those opposed to Hill's position are characterized both as evil and as in rebellion against God.

Manifestations of Reductionistic Focus on the Unborn

Throughout his position paper, Hill maintains a focus on the unborn as the foundation for his reductionistic portrayal of the evangelical Christian faith. Authenticity as a Christian, in this position paper, is consistently equated with a concern for and identification with the unborn. As one subtitle reads, Hill's concern is that we "don't forget the babies."[98]

Hill's initial statement about the moral justification of violence, not surprisingly, depends upon such an identification. "The *justice* of using force to defend the unborn is apparent," he states, "if we don't forget that the object is to defend unborn babies from violent death. The justice of using force to protect children from deadly force would be easy for you to affirm if your life had been spared by the use of defensive force."[99] Thus begins a consistent pattern of appeal for readers to put themselves in the position of the unborn. Another such appeal occurs with Hill's invocation of the "golden rule." "If someone was about to tear your limbs from your body," Hill asks, "what would you do? If you could defend yourself with force, would you? If you couldn't defend yourself with effective force, would you want someone else to? If so, Christ teaches that you should treat others similarly."[100]

Hill also makes use of descriptive language to help the reader visualize the unborn, making identification with them easier. Early in the essay Hill states, "If next to Dr. Gunn's dead body were to be spread the gruesome remains of the thousands he killed, the mere space needed would be staggering."[101] At the end of his essay, Hill says, "Death opens her cavernous mouth before you. Thousands upon thousands of children are consumed by her every day. You have the ability to save some from being tossed into her gaping mouth."[102] He then reminds the reader of the centrality of this "war" to defend the unborn, declaring that "[a]s hundreds are being rushed into eternity, other questions shrink in comparison to the weighty question, 'Should we defend our unborn children with force?'"[103]

The reminder of the centrality of the unborn to the evangelical Christian faith also takes place near the end of Hill's essay, in which he asks a series of questions of the reader: "Will you remain at home while your neighbors respond to a call from the womb? *Will you continue to build bigger barns while your little neighbors are being abruptly decapitated?* Will you be like the priest and the Levite who passed by on the other side of the way to pursue their own interests? Or will you be like the good Samaritan who gave of his time and property and risked his very life because he realized that his fellow men are his neighbors?"[104]

Manifestations of Calcified Rigidity

I would like to close this section on Hill by briefly considering what I believe to be a fairly significant difference between the Operation Rescue testimonies and Hill's essay. While both samples of discourse reflect the misrepresentation I have described, Hill's essay appears to do so in a more rigid, more closed, more calcified, more literalized way. While the incarcerated activists of Operation Rescue expressed their simplistically reductionistic worldview by relating their own personal and emotional experiences, Hill did so coldly, impersonally, logically.

While the Operation Rescue activists advanced their truth claims primarily in the context of experience, Hill merely advances his with the assumption that they are patently self-evident, obvious. Hill described them, for instance, as "common sense." The whole of Hill's position is referred to at one point as "[t]he common sense principles contained in this pamphlet."[105] Writing against the "spiritual" solution of prayer and fasting to the abortion problem, he declares later in his essay that "[c]ommon sense clearly condemns the 'piety' that would respond to the mugging of a helpless victim with prayer without defensive action."[106]

In like manner, Hill also makes use of the term *right understanding* to characterize his "self-evidently truthful" position. At the outset of his essay, he states that "[t]wo distinctions must be made in order to rightly understand the issues surrounding the death of Dr. Gunn."[107] To preface his initial discussions of wisdom and justice this way gives the not-so-subtle suggestion that to approach the "issues" in any other way is to be mired in error and falsehood. Similarly, elsewhere Hill directs the reader to "[o]ne of the rules for the right understanding of the Ten Commandments" as a way of framing his own position.[108]

In answer to the anticipated objection, "Many people oppose defensive action," Hill again takes the opportunity to claim rationality for his point of view:

> The beliefs and duties outlined in this pamphlet are so entirely contrary to popular opinion and practice that opposition is to be expected. Our reaction to opposition must be one of understanding and patience. We must respond to severe criticism and searching questions with solid answers and winning persuasion. As people grasp at any straw of objection to deny these truths, we must recognize what they are doing and be patient.[109]

In this portrayal, the truth (which nicely corresponds with Hill's position) is self-evident; accepting or refusing to accept the obvious becomes almost exclusively a matter of will. Hill can support his position with "solid answers" and "winning persuasion"; those opposed merely "grasp at straws." I mention this final point on calcification because it helps to explain why Paul Hill, and not most others, ended up actually using deadly force against a doctor who performs abortions. The oversimplified representations present in both samples of discourse are nonetheless more completely calcified, more completely literalized in the case of Paul Hill. Hill's "vocabulary" of the evangelical Christian faith is so unreflexive, so closed to question, so closed to moderation that it deterministically pushed Hill to the logical conclusion of violence. Hill's vocabulary of the Christian faith was indeed comprehensive in its accounting of the "signs" of the world, but it was also most certainly "narrow" in the Chestertonian sense. And it was violent.

Conclusion

This chapter on the relationship between the rhetoric of Operation Rescue and violence showcases the most explicit and damaging implications of rhetorical misrepresentation. As the previous chapters have shown, though, the misrepresentation that encourages incivility and violence is very much rooted in the peculiarities of the relationship between the rhetoric of

Operation Rescue and the evangelical Christian faith tradition. The rhetorical appeal of the two simplistic and constraining representative themes discussed in this chapter, in other words, would not be so strong but for certain predispositions toward the understanding and appropriation of the evangelical Christian faith.

Such predispositions, unfortunately, grow out of and reinforce recurring yet problematic aspects of the evangelical Christian faith tradition, as described in chapter 3. In an important sense, then, the influences on the part of the rhetoric of Operation Rescue to encourage attitudes of incivility and violence should not be seen primarily and generically as arising from its capacity as social protest rhetoric. Rather, these influences should be seen in the context of evangelical Christian rhetoric, though certainly not in that faith tradition's more noble nor its most suitably representative manifestations.

Nonetheless, I trust that the foregoing analysis has suggested a more nuanced, more balanced explanation of the connections that exist between "confrontational" rhetoric and violence. Individuals with a public voice, such as Anthony Lewis, apparently see the importance of rhetoric well enough that they advance their own implicit and thoroughly causal theories concerning the relationship between rhetoric and violence, even if those theories are overtly partisan and decidedly simplistic. Such simplistic, causal accountings of this relationship can serve political ends in the designs of less noble individuals, as the push to pass overly broad "hate speech codes" on college and university campuses might suggest. On the other hand, it is important to recognize that a significant—even if not tidily articulated—relationship indeed exists. It is important, therefore, to be alarmed at the presence of hate speech and at the increasing paucity of civil public discourse in the United States and elsewhere.

Building upon the discussions of how the evangelical Christian faith is represented in the rhetoric of Operation Rescue, the following three chapters examine the implications of the group's rhetoric regarding public discourse. We shall see not only how the rhetoric of Operation Rescue affected the group's prospects of accomplishing its preferred version of social change, but also how that rhetoric has reflected and helped to shape the climate of contemporary public discourse.

Notes

1. Paul J. Hill, "Should We Defend Born and Unborn Children with Force?" unpublished essay (Pensacola, Fla.: Defensive Action, [1993]), 13.
2. Tony Freemantle, "Abortion Clinic Shotgun Attack Leaves 2 Dead: Suspect Urged Violent Acts," *Houston Chronicle,* August 2, 1994, 21A.
3. Rev. Patrick Mahoney, quoted in Patrick Rogers and Spencer Reiss, "Is Murder 'Justifiable Homicide'?" *Newsweek,* August 8, 1994, 22.
4. Anthony Lewis, "What Is It about America that Nourishes Extremism over Abortion Issue?" *Houston Chronicle,* August 2, 1994, 21A.
5. See, for instance, William F. Buckley, Jr., "What Does Clinton Have in Mind?" *National Review,* May 29, 1995, 70–71; Steven V. Roberts, "After the Heartbreak," *U.S. News and World Report,* May 8, 1995, 46; Cass R. Sunstein, "What to Do with G. Gordon Liddy: Is Violent Speech a Right?" *Current,* November 1995, 21–23.
6. James Davison Hunter, *Culture Wars: The Struggle to Define America* (New York: Basic Books, 1991), 34.
7. Ibid., 318, 159–60.
8. James Davison Hunter, *Before the Shooting Begins: Searching for Democracy in America's Culture War* (New York: Free Press, 1994), 4, 13.
9. For the discussion of "substantive democracy," see Hunter, *Before the Shooting Begins,* 227–44.
10. Sociologists Rhys H. Williams and Jeffrey Blackburn have made the same point in urging more stress on individual "rank-and-file" group members in order to gain a more complex account of Operation Rescue's ideology. See Williams and Blackburn, "Many are Called but Few Obey: Ideological Commitment and Activism in Operation Rescue," in *Disruptive Religion: The Force of Faith in Social Movement Activism,* ed. Christian Smith (New York: Routledge, 1996), 167–85.
11. Kenneth Burke, "Definition of Man," in *Language as Symbolic Action: Essays on Life, Literature, and Method* (Berkeley: University of California Press, 1966), 3.
12. Kenneth Burke, "The Philosophy of Literary Form," in *The Philosophy of Literary Form: Studies in Symbolic Action,* 3rd ed. (Berkeley: University of California Press, 1973), 6.
13. See, specifically, Kenneth Burke, *A Grammar of Motives* (1945; reprint, Berkeley: University of California Press, 1969), 61; "Terministic Screens," in *Language as Symbolic Action: Essays on Life, Literature, and Method* (Berkeley: University of California Press, 1966), 52–54.
14. G. K. Chesterton, *Orthodoxy: The Romance of Faith* (1908; reprint, New York: Image Books, 1990), 20.
15. James Davison Hunter, *American Evangelicalism: Conservative Religion and the Quandary of Modernity* (New Brunswick, N. J.: Rutgers University Press, 1983), 9.
16. Kenneth Burke, "Semantic and Poetic Meaning," in *The Philosophy of Literary Form: Studies in Symbolic Action,* 3rd ed. (Berkeley: University of California Press, 1973), 152n.
17. Kenneth Burke, *Permanence and Change: An Anatomy of Purpose,* 3rd ed. (Berkeley: University of California Press, 1984), 258.
18. Robert L. Ivie, "The Metaphor of Force in Prowar Discourse: The Case of 1812," *Quarterly Journal of Speech* 68 (1982): 240.

19. David Zarefsky, *President Johnson's War on Poverty: Rhetoric and History* (Tuscaloosa, Ala.: University of Alabama Press, 1986), 36.
20. Ibid., 205.
21. Michael S. Sherry, *In the Shadow of War: The United States since the 1930s* (New Haven, Conn.: Yale University Press, 1995), xi.
22. Ibid., x.
23. See, for instance, Robert L. Ivie, "Images of Savagery in American Justifications for War," *Communication Monographs* 17 (1980): 279–94; "The Metaphor of Force in Prowar Discourse"; "Speaking 'Common Sense' about the Soviet Threat: Reagan's Rhetorical Stance," *Western Journal of Speech Communication* 48 (1984): 39–50; "Literalizing the Metaphor of Soviet Strategy: President Truman's Plain Style," *Southern Speech Communication Journal* 51 (1986): 91–105; "Metaphor and the Rhetorical Invention of Cold War 'Idealists,'" *Communication Monographs* 54 (1987): 165–82; "Metaphor and Motive in the Johnson Administration's Vietnam War Rhetoric," in *Texts in Context: Critical Dialogues on Significant Episodes in American Political Rhetoric*, ed. Michael Leff and Fred Kauffeld (Davis, Calif.: Hermagoras Press, 1989), 121–41; "Eisenhower as Cold Warrior," in *Eisenhower's War of Words: Rhetoric and Leadership*, ed. Martin J. Medhurst (East Lansing: Michigan State University Press, 1994), 7–25.
24. Robert L. Ivie, "Tragic Fear and the Rhetorical Presidency: Combating Evil in the Persian Gulf," in *Beyond the Rhetorical Presidency*, ed. Martin J. Medhurst (College Station: Texas A&M University Press, 1996), 176.
25. See, in particular, Robert L. Ivie, "May We Act Wisely," public statement, September 15, 2001, August 1, 2003, http://www.indiana.edu/~ivieweb/wisely.htm; "This So-Called War," public statement, October 16, 2001, August 1, 2003, http://www.indiana.edu/~ivieweb/so-called.htm; "The Presumption of War," public statement, December 10, 2002, August 1, 2003, http://www.indiana.edu/~ivieweb/warpresumption.htm.
26. Suzanne Daughton, "Metaphorical Transcendence: Images of the Holy War in Franklin Roosevelt's First Inaugural," *Quarterly Journal of Speech* 79 (1993): 436, 440.
27. "Testimonies from Jailed Rescuers," unpublished collection, Josephine County [Oregon] Right to Life, [1988], 11.
28. Ibid., 15.
29. "Baby Jane Doe" and "Baby John Doe" were pseudonyms used by Operation Rescue activists who had been arrested during the 1988 Atlanta Protests.
30. "Testimonies," 19.
31. Ibid., 2.
32. Ibid.
33. Ibid., 15.
34. Ibid.
35. Ibid., 1.
36. Ibid., 7.
37. Ibid., 20.
38. Ibid., 7.
39. Ibid., 10.
40. Ibid., 39–40.
41. Ibid., 12.
42. Ibid., 7.

43. Ibid.
44. Ibid., 1.
45. Ibid..
46. Ibid., 11.
47. Ibid., 17.
48. Ibid., 1.
49. Ibid., 15.
50. Ibid., 18.
51. Ibid., 3.
52. Ibid., 17.
53. Ibid., 13.
54. Ibid., 14.
55. Ibid., 18.
56. Ibid., 10.
57. Ibid., 8.
58. Ibid., 13.
59. Ibid., 19.
60. See, for instance, Barbara Hinkson Craig and David M. O'Brien, *Abortion and American Politics* (Chatham: N.J.: Chatham House Publishers, 1993), 58; Richard Cowden-Guido, "Introduction," in *You Reject Them, You Reject Me: The Prison Letters of Joan Andrews*, ed. Richard Cowden-Guido (Manassas, Va.: Trinity Communications, 1988), 16–18.
61. Joan Andrews, quoted in Cowden-Guido, *You Reject Them, You Reject Me*, 21.
62. Mark Belz, *Suffer the Little Children: Christians, Abortion, and Civil Disobedience* (Westchester, Ill.: Crossway Books, 1988), 118–19.
63. Ibid., 118.
64. See Matthew 25:31–46.
65. "Testimonies," 15.
66. See, for instance, Matthew 10:38, 16:24; Mark 8:34; Luke 9:23.
67. "Testimonies," 18.
68. Ibid., 12.
69. Ibid., 10.
70. Ibid., 14.
71. Ibid., 33.
72. Ibid., 42.
73. James Risen and Judy L. Thomas, *Wrath of Angels: The American Abortion War* (New York: Basic Books, 1998), 274–75.
74. In May 2003, James Kopp was also convicted and sentenced for the 1998 murder of Dr. Barnett Slepian. See "Abortion Doc's Killer Gets 25 to Life," CBSNews.com, May 9, 2003, August 2, 2003, http://www.cbsnews.com/stories/2002/06/05/national/main511121.shtml.
75. Risen and Thomas, *Wrath of Angels*, 275.
76. Ibid., 345.
77. Ibid., 346.
78. Hill, "Should We Defend Born and Unborn Children with Force?" 14.
79. Ibid., 2, 3, 4.
80. Ibid., 10.
81. Ibid.

82. Ibid., 13.
83. Ibid.
84. Ibid., 12.
85. See the biblical text of Numbers 25.
86. Hill, "Should We Defend Born and Unborn Children with Force?" 3.
87. Ibid., 13.
88. Ibid., 12.
89. Ibid., 8.
90. Ibid., 6.
91. See, for instance, Philippians 2.
92. Hill, "Should We Defend Born and Unborn Children with Force?" 7.
93. Ibid., 6.
94. Ibid., 9.
95. Ibid., 8.
96. Ibid., 11.
97. Ibid., 10.
98. Ibid., 1.
99. Ibid.
100. Ibid., 3.
101. Ibid., 1.
102. Ibid., 13.
103. Ibid.
104. Ibid.
105. Ibid., 5.
106. Ibid., 8.
107. Ibid., 1.
108. Ibid., 9.
109. Ibid.

Part Four

Public Dialogue

7

COUNTER-CHARACTERIZATIONS OF OPERATION RESCUE

Oppositional Rhetoric, 1988–91

I just wanted to make the point that I believe that the violence will continue. I've seen some of this violence firsthand at clinics around the area and have seen some of these people go to jail. And what they want to continue to do is, I believe it's like the Inquisition where, if you won't convert and believe what we believe, then we are going to systematically make you suffer. And we're going to do as many underhanded and subversive things as we can to allow our position to grow.... And they're going to, I believe, murder as many people as they can who don't agree with what they believe.

—A Pennsylvania man, calling in on CNN's March 8, 1994, *Sonya Live* program on abortion and violence.[1]

Dr. Gunn, who was a loving man, who had children, who was a person who worked very hard serving poor women and provided medical services is dead, murdered in cold blood. And not only is he a victim, but other doctors, Dr. George Tiller has been shot, other doctors have been tormented. The doctor right in [Operation Rescue National director] Flip Benham's home area, a doctor there is being followed, stalked. His wife is being followed and stalked. It's been on television. The death threats [are] pouring in.

—Eleanor Smeal, president of the Feminist Majority Foundation, speaking on the same program.[2]

COUNTER-CHARACTERIZATIONS OF OPERATION RESCUE

"I have a question for Ms. Wattleton," a caller posed to the president of Planned Parenthood during the September 6, 1991 airing of the *Donahue* talk show from Wichita, Kansas. "What happens to the baby that was aborted and lives?" "I do not accept that a fetus is a baby," Faye Wattleton replied. "It is a fetus." Operation Rescue founder Randall Terry, also a guest on the *Donahue* program, retorted, "Even if it lives, it's not a baby! It's a post-partum fetus."[3]

This contentious exchange between Terry and Wattleton provides an important reminder of the power of language to shape perceptions and to characterize situations. "Truly," declares rhetoric scholar Andrew King, "the maker of a definition is more like a god than a human being."[4] This power of language, as discussed in chapter 2, comports nicely with the broad, generative conception of rhetoric used in this book.

This conception of rhetoric, as seen in the previous three chapters, is useful in explaining how Operation Rescue is seen both by its members and in the context of the evangelical Christian faith tradition. We have seen how the rhetoric of Operation Rescue offers to its adherents particular representations of the Christian faith. These representations serve as "equipment for living" by which activists can affirm their identity as evangelical Christians, and by which activists are afforded a relatively unambiguous guide to the integration of faith and action. We have seen not only some of the ways in which this representation occurs, but also some of the important consequences.

This chapter focuses on still other consequences stemming from the rhetoric of Operation Rescue. In particular, I am concerned with how the rhetoric of Operation Rescue has shaped its participation and its fortunes in national public dialogue. Before investigating the rhetoric of Operation Rescue, though, it is necessary to place Operation Rescue's public rhetorical efforts in context with the public rhetorical efforts of the group's opponents. This chapter provides this context.

Operation Rescue held numerous protests all over the United States in its years of growth and vitality. As mentioned in chapter 1, though, two particular protest campaigns stand out not only because of their size and length, but also because of their pivotal roles in the group's history. These are the 1988 "Siege of Atlanta" and the 1991 "Summer of Mercy" in Wichita, Kansas.

During these campaigns, Operation Rescue worked long and hard to "witness" to America about the "truth." At the same time, opponents of Operation Rescue began offering a consistent rhetorical "vocabulary" by which one understands and characterizes the group—and its particular brand of protest—in decidedly unflattering, malevolent, and delegitimizing ways. The public emergence of this counter-characterizing vocabulary is the subject of this chapter.

The notion of "public vocabulary" suggests the importance of rhetoric not only in helping to provide a broader explanation of social protest outcomes, but also in helping to shed light on the problems of public discourse more generally. It is easy, though, to adopt a more narrow view of rhetoric when discussing social protest campaigns, subsequently underestimating the influence of rhetoric in such campaigns.

Concluding their case study of the "Summer of Mercy" campaign, communication scholars John W. Bowers, Donovan J. Ochs, and Richard J. Jensen observe that the abortion issue "will undoubtedly divide groups for generations. Only the strategies employed by the two groups will change—depending on who has access to the power of the establishment."[5] Such a conclusion follows logically from a social movement perspective that places much stock in the actions of the establishment and the material resources at the establishment's disposal. Yet it is easy, perhaps too easy, to think of social movements and social protest strictly in terms of size and material resources. This is not to say, of course, that such resource considerations are unimportant. Noting that "the establishment was able to keep the clinics open in Wichita," Bowers, Ochs, and Jensen explain that "[t]he establishment had the power and was willing to use it to gain control of the situation . . . injunctions and the arrest of movement leaders had a significant impact on the dissent."[6] The authors' methodological perspective of "agitation and control" indeed works well to explain how rhetoric works in the dynamics of specific and localized social protest. Nonetheless, that perspective does not account as well for more long-term and more fundamental, pre-inventional (that is, prior to the development of argument) rhetorical influences. This book—focusing on these more fundamental matters of rhetoric and representation—targets such rhetorical influences much more explicitly.

By looking at public discourse regarding two prominent Operation Rescue campaigns, then, this chapter considers a more expressly and uniquely discursive matter. I am concerned here not with how rhetoric functions tactically in specific acts of social protest, nor with the "persuasive" rhetorical strategies of specific social movements. Rather, my concern is with how rhetoric works to negotiate the *legitimacy* of social protest forms themselves. In a society like ours, what types of social protest are allowed and which are not? Further, how might rhetorical discourse work to reinforce or subvert the legitimacy of a particular protest form, or at least the practice of the form by certain groups? My larger claim is that the pro-choice movement has been successful in incorporating into the public vocabulary an unflattering and delegitimizing lexicon of terms with respect to the pro-life movement and particularly Operation Rescue. Such a lexicon of terms supports an interpretation of pro-life activists, and particularly Operation Rescue activists, not as legitimate social protesters forcibly calling attention to an important issue, but rather as base, intolerant, insensitive, fanatical, violent individuals who should not be accorded the status of legitimate social protesters.

To advance this larger claim, I must first show that such a vocabulary has been consistently articulated in the public sphere. To do this, I examine samples of public discourse surrounding Operation Rescue's 1988 "Siege of Atlanta" and 1991 "Summer of Mercy" campaigns. For the 1988 "Siege of Atlanta" campaign I collected, via online search on the Internet, every article and editorial printed by the *Atlanta Journal and Constitution* between September 19, 1988 and March 19, 1989 in which Operation Rescue is mentioned. This collection totals 147 documents. Likewise, for the 1991 "Summer of Mercy" campaign I collected, via database with the cooperation of the *Wichita Eagle* library staff, every article and editorial printed by the *Wichita Eagle* between June 2, 1991 and September 25, 1991 in which Operation Rescue is mentioned. This collection totals 166 documents.

To be sure, a significant portion of this discourse reflects support for Operation Rescue and for the pro-life movement more generally. A significant portion of this discourse also reflects the ambiguity and angst typical of what sociologist James Davison Hunter has called the "Muddled Middle."[7] Yet, a significant portion of this discourse features the essential terms of a coherent rhetorical vocabulary, a vocabulary that supports a decisively unflattering and delegitimizing understanding of Operation Rescue.

In what follows, I frame the discussion by exploring in a bit more detail the theoretical concepts of "public vocabulary" and "vilification," particularly as they relate to the broader, generative conception of rhetoric with which I have been working. I then turn directly to the texts themselves, illuminating key features of this delegitimizing vocabulary as seen in this sample of discourse.

Rhetoric and Public Vocabulary

While the subject of the "public" has received considerable attention from rhetoric and communication scholars, there is no broad agreement on what the "public" is. The differing conceptions range from the public as objectively meaningful and empirically verifiable to the public as sheer rhetorical fiction.[8] To whatever degree the "public" is rhetorical, though, rhetoric is fundamentally involved in the identity and the negotiation of public issues—the stuff of public dialogue. Rhetoric is employed not only in actual public deliberation (e.g., audience analysis, argument selection, and so on), but also in the formulation and use of terms and understandings that make engaged deliberation possible. The concept of "public vocabulary" helps to explore this second and more foundational public role of rhetoric.

In her book-length study of the American abortion controversy, rhetoric scholar Celeste Michelle Condit makes use of the term *public vocabulary* to explain how rhetoric functions in this second role. To Condit, the "public vocabulary" is best described as "[t]he acceptable words, myths, and characterizations used for warranting social behavior in a community."[9] The "words," "myths," and "characterizations" that comprise the public vocabulary are the sanctioned, common symbolic tokens employed in public dialogue. They have that same *naturalized* quality that linguist and philosopher Roland Barthes attributed to myth, a quality that "transforms history into nature."[10] Thus, the partisan, perspective-shaping meanings implied by terms in the public vocabulary are seen not as partisan or ideological—which is what they really are—but instead as assumed, as taken-for-granted, as beyond the realm of reflectivity.

When discussing the "illegal abortion" narratives put forward in the early 1960s as an impetus to abortion reform, Condit underscores the importance of the public vocabulary. The narratives, she points out, "had to *use* rather than *confront* the beliefs and social conditions in the existing American repertoire," and "did so by respecting the crucial values and characterizations of the culture while redefining the act of abortion itself."[11] Narratives such as Sherry Finkbine's were powerful in advancing the case for abortion reform because they attacked "only criminal abortion, not families, healthy fetuses, children, or mothering."[12] In other words, such persuasive abortion reform efforts were effective because they worked within the public vocabulary with respect to abortion at that time. Later, those supporting the repeal of restrictive abortion laws were able to articulate new terms to compete for prominent inclusion in the vocabulary—terms such as *equality*, *choice*, and *reproductive freedom*. It was in large part the articulation of these "ultimate terms"[13] that set the stage for *Roe v. Wade* and subsequent judicial victories for the pro-choice movement. With respect to this judicial power in the 1970s, Condit writes that "[t]he pro-Choice vocabulary was adopted as a legitimate component of the national repertoire; the coercive power of the state was no longer to be employed to prevent women's choices."[14]

The notion of public vocabulary provides further evidence of how language functions in a broadly rhetorical, generative capacity. As seen in what immediately follows, it shapes visions of the bad as well as visions of the good.

Rhetoric and Delegitimizing Discourse

The generative power of rhetoric also illumines how discourse can function to delegitimize adversaries. In the context of war, religion scholar Sam Keen demonstrates how symbols can function powerfully and dangerously to delegitimize and dehumanize people. Declaring that "[i]n the beginning we create the enemy,"[15] Keen argues that before a nation or culture mobilizes for war against an enemy, a common cluster of images is employed to characterize the enemy in ways that render them inhuman and therefore easier to kill with impunity or without revulsion. To advance this argument, Keen examines a comprehensive and cross-cultural collection of war posters and other public visual images relating to warfare. The grotesque nature of many of the images provides a disturbing lesson of how dehumanizing symbolic representations can function to encourage not only war, but also genocide in the service of an ideology.[16]

In an earlier study of how adversaries are characterized in intergroup conflict, communication scholar Bonnie Johnson has shown how the dehumanization of adversaries takes place more subtly by denying them agency, by reducing, in Kenneth Burke's words, their "action" to "motion."[17] In Johnson's analysis, adversaries are represented in terms of "mindless metaphors," including mechanical and organismic metaphors. The communication and persuasive efforts of adversaries, likewise, are represented in ways that deny agency: as brainwashing, as "poison," and as "magic."[18]

In her case study of pro-life and pro-choice rhetoric, communication scholar Marsha Vanderford examines how vilification functions to rob opponents perhaps not of their humanity, but most certainly of their legitimacy. "Vilification," she suggests, "is a rhetorical strategy that discredits adversaries by characterizing them as ungenuine and malevolent advocates. Rather than differentiating opponents as good people with a difference of opinion, vilification delegitimizes them through characterizations of intentions, actions, purposes, and identities."[19] This strategy, pervasive in social movements, functions not just to deny legitimacy to opponents, but also to "encourage, shape, and sustain activism." It does so by presenting a consistent image of opponents, characterizing them as "simultaneously powerful and vulnerable," as "violat[ing] democratic principles," and as having purposes that are "unjust and dictatorial."[20]

These delegitimizing functions of discourse can be observed readily in the pro-choice rhetorical responses to Operation Rescue. In what follows, I detail some of the important ways in which pro-choice rhetoric, as articulated publicly during Operation Rescue's "Siege of Atlanta" and "Summer of Mercy" campaigns, functioned to subvert Operation Rescue's practice of civil disobedience as a legitimate form of social protest. If this delegitimizing vocabulary is accepted—if it becomes ensconced in the public vocabulary—then Operation Rescue's activities at abortion clinics might be considered a number of different things. It will not, however, be considered legitimate social protest.

Pro-Choice Delegitimizing Discourse

Dissociation of Operation Rescue and the Civil Rights Movement

Operation Rescue's identification with the civil rights movement of the 1960s is quite important from a rhetorical point of view. It legitimizes the form of social protest practiced by Operation Rescue by linking it with the form of social protest practiced by those who protested against segregated businesses by blocking access to them. It also enables Operation Rescue to borrow from the ethos of the civil rights movement, insofar as they have sought to characterize their activism in terms of saving human lives and extending human rights to the "pre-born."

Not surprisingly, this connection between Operation Rescue and the civil rights movement was vehemently resisted. The issue of this connection was more prominent in the 1988 Atlanta protests, since Atlanta was Martin Luther King's hometown. Operation Rescue, doubtless aware of this fact, sought to emphasize those connections, with the group's leaders declaring their intentions to make Atlanta "the Selma of the anti-abortion movement."[21]

A number of editorials appeared in the *Atlanta Journal and Constitution* regarding this comparison; the majority of them asserted that Operation Rescue and the civil rights movement are dissimilar. The argument is spelled out clearly in the first such editorial. The editorial first acknowledges the comparison, stating that "[t]he choice of Atlanta, hometown of the late Dr. Martin Luther King Jr., may be no accident. Even the language [of Operation Rescue] comes right out of the civil rights movement. But there the similarity ends."[22]

This argument for dissociation, as with almost all the others, is grounded in "rights" but centers on the "right" to abortion and ignores Operation Rescue's claims regarding the "rights" of the "pre-born."[23] The editorial declares, "Civil rights demonstrators fought for rights—access to jobs, housing, voting booths, schools and public facilities—that were unconstitutionally denied them." Operation Rescue's goal, however, is much less noble, seeking "to deny women their right to a legal medical procedure of the most personal sort," as well as to "impose a minority religious belief on the majority." "The closer one looks," then, "the more insulting the attempt to relate the two 'peaceful' protests becomes. Officials had it in their power in the 1960s to correct racial injustices; no federal law or Supreme Court ruling prevented it. That is not the case with abortion, a constitutional right."[24] Then comes the peroration of the editorial. "Abortion foes," the editorial states, "are entitled to express their views and to work to change the law, but they are not free to deny the rights of others." "No staged arrests and allusions to the civil rights movement," the editorial concludes, "can obscure that."[25]

This essential stance underlies all of the other articulations of dissociation as well, though other grounds are offered. "I don't think it's a legitimate comparison," related Rev. Joseph Lowery, president of the Southern Christian Leadership Conference. "One of the basic tenets of civil disobedience is you openly and willingly submit to the punishment."[26] An editorial letter to the *Atlanta Journal and Constitution* states that "[u]nlike men who were active in civil rights demonstrations, the men leading and joining in Operation Rescue demonstrations can't possibly believe they are protesting an act that infringes upon their constitutional rights."[27] To this writer, then, civil disobedience worthy of comparison to the civil rights movement requires that one be fighting for one's own rights. Since Operation Rescue claimed to be fighting for the rights of others—the "pre-born"—the comparison is illegitimate.

The dissociation theme was also apparent throughout the 1991 "Summer of Mercy" campaign. Ann Baker, president of the 80 Percent Majority Campaign, protested: "I resent that comparison [between Operation Rescue and the civil rights movement]. [Randall Terry] is not at all like Martin Luther King. Theirs is not civil disobedience, because they are depriving rights rather than working to extend those rights."[28] Kate Michelman, executive director of the National Abortion Rights Action League, echoed this sentiment in declaring that "[t]his action [of Operation Rescue] is not about civil disobedience. It is about violating the civil rights of women to obtain health care."[29] Noting that "[i]t seems contradictory that liberals are demanding law and order and conservatives are justifying protests," Anna Quindlen wrote that this "is no more contradictory than the rest of this sorry [Wichita] episode, in which... those who march beneath the banners that say 'Choose Life' deny others their choice and disrupt the lives of thousands."[30]

This overall theme of dissociation is perhaps observed best in Michelman's contentious observation that "[l]ike the segregationists who blocked the doors of schools to keep out people of color, Randall Terry and Operation Rescue violate the civil rights of women."[31] This rhetoric suggests that the social protest form employed by Operation Rescue should not be considered "civil disobedience." In so doing, the position suggested in this rhetoric seems to be that the legitimacy of a particular protest *form*, particularly when that form goes beyond the boundaries of legally acceptable protest, is directly related to the *content* of that form.[32] A style of protest that involves blocking access to an establishment or impeding that establishment's normal function (e.g., sitting down in front of the entrances to an abortion clinic or a segregated diner, chaining oneself to a front gate of a nuclear power plant or to a tree about to be cut down), according to this position, seems to be acceptable only when applied to certain causes (e.g., civil rights social protest). Yet this same style, this same form, is considered unacceptable when applied to other specific causes (e.g., pro-life social protest). The key seems to be whether or not "rights" are being advanced, a criterion that makes claims on the *content* of the social protest, not the *form*. This is an important implication of the dissociation of Operation Rescue and the civil rights movement, as seen in pro-choice response rhetoric.

Operation Rescue Activists as Fanatics

Michelman's comparison of Operation Rescue activists with the segregationists of the South implies another feature of pro-choice response rhetoric. Operation Rescue activists are systematically portrayed not as men and women of conviction, urging change on an important and divisive issue, but rather as fanatics that have no regard whatsoever for the rights and the well-being of others.

The image of fanaticism is one that sociologist Eric Hoffer uses in his classic study of mass movements. Arguing that mass movements are maintained by a core of activists he terms "true believers," Hoffer articulates a primarily psychological—and certainly unflattering—explanation both of their motives and of their role in the creation and maintenance of mass movements. True believers, he claims, are "[p]eople who see their lives as irremediably spoiled" and "cannot find a worth-while purpose in self-advancement. Their innermost craving is for a new life—a rebirth—or, failing this, a chance to acquire new elements of pride, confidence, hope, a sense of purpose and worth by an identification with a holy cause."[33]

Interestingly, Hoffer interchanges the terms "true believer" and "fanatic" in his discussion of these psychological deficients. "It is doubtful," Hoffer claims, "whether the fanatic who deserts his holy cause or is suddenly left without one can ever adjust himself to an autonomous individual existence," for "[a]n individual existence, even when purposeful, seems to him trivial, futile and sinful." In Hoffer's view, such people are not motivated by truth, nor ideology, nor the inherent worthiness of the movement. "What matters," he explains, "is not the contents of the cause but the total dedication and the communion with a congregation. He is even ready to join in a holy crusade against his former holy cause, but it must be a genuine crusade—uncompromising, intolerant, proclaiming the one and only truth."[34]

The recurrent image of fanaticism, then, is delegitimizing not only in its declaration of moral turpitude, but also in its characterizations of people portrayed as lacking certain essential features of well-adjusted human beings. In either case, though, the image serves an important delegitimizing function. People seen as fanatics are not to be listened to nor taken seriously, but rather opposed and silenced with moral impunity. Therein lies the power of this pro-choice characterization to delegitimize Operation Rescue and other pro-life groups.

Comparisons of Operation Rescue to other groups widely seen as fanatical or morally bankrupt are common. Atlanta Police Sergeant Carl S. Pyrdum, for instance, declared that Operation Rescue's "terroristic acts" are "in the same category as cross-burning or anti-Semitic actions, where the very act itself frightens persons targeted specifically."[35]

Others made more specific use of white supremacists and the Ku Klux Klan to make delegitimizing comparisons. Referring to Operation Rescue, *Los Angeles Times* writer Carol Sobel declared that "[t]he group's organized campaign, like the activities of the Ku Klux Klan, seeks by force to prevent women from exercising their constitutional rights to travel to obtain medical care, including the right to decide whether and when to terminate a pregnancy."[36] Speaking early in 1989, the leader of Coalition Opposing Operation Rescue (COOR) denounced Jerry Falwell and his endorsement of Operation Rescue. "Today is the 60th birthday of Martin Luther King," he exclaimed, "and we have this white supremacist leader preaching here who's anti-woman and-black [sic] and anti-gay."[37] Some went further than just making the comparison known. Referring specifically to Operation Rescue's 1988 Atlanta protests, Plano [Texas] resident Alexander D. Bell declared in an editorial letter that "[t]he Ku Klux Klan appears to be a more socially responsible group than the pro-life advocates."[38]

Comparison of Operation Rescue with other groups perceived as morally bankrupt is but one way rhetorically to attach to Operation Rescue a persistent image of fanaticism. Feudal images that support this image of fanaticism are also seen in pro-choice characterizations of Operation Rescue. The Reverend George T. Gardner, pastor of College Hill United Methodist Church in Wichita, evoked the Crusades. "In 1096," he stated, "Pope Urban II, in a stirring sermon, asked the synod at Clermont, France, to rescue the Eastern Christians from the infidels.... [T]he congregation, deeply moved, boomed out 'Deus vult' ('God wills it'). Thus began a century of Christian crusades."[39] Gardner then made the explicit connection between Operation Rescue and the "destructive zeal" of the Crusades.[40] "This same 'God wills it' banner," he declared, "has been flying over Wichita. Under the siege mentality of Operation Rescue, we have seen not civil disobedience but a re-enactment of religious crusades. And, like the crusaders of yesterday, the rescuers have exploited our community and left us with serious division."[41] Gardner further wrote that while "the anti-abortion crusaders ... have every right to express and practice their religious faith," they "have no right to impose it on our community. They do not define religion in Wichita."[42]

Gardner's suggestion, then, is that Operation Rescue protesters do not respect the rights of others in a democratic society, and that makes their protest illegitimate and destructive. Claiming that "anti-abortion crusaders wave the banner of simplicity," Gardner wrote that "[u]nder the banner of 'loving children' the anti-abortion crusaders have as their agenda the assassination of character. Anyone who opposes them is 'of the devil' or as I have been called, 'the anti-Christ.'"[43]

Feudal images, furthermore, are not limited just to the Crusades. Denise Betty Bruce, a Wichita resident, wrote that "[Wichita mayor] Knight, and others who seek to impose their religious and moral beliefs on this city, must occasionally be reminded that Wichita is not their personal fiefdom."[44] Wichita YWCA director Jane Gilchrist alluded to past religious injustices on Phil Donahue's talk show by exclaiming, "And Mr. Terry, I say to you, you and Operation Rescue are the poison of the past. You are not the voice of the future!"[45] Bruce's editorial also articulated the image of fanaticism more directly. Describing Mayor Knight and his "happy band" of supporters as "would-be moral dictators," she wrote that "[f]or two weeks, Knight and his underling allowed a mob of religious zealots to prevent patients of Dr. George Tiller from receiving medical services."[46]

The feudal image suggests another important feature of the characterization of Operation Rescue activists as fanatics. Put simply, Operation Rescue activists are uncivil and anti-democratic, implying that they and their brand of protest should not be tolerated because social change should be based on "persuasion." Their protests in 1988 were referred to as "anti-democratic" and as an "anti-abortion temper tantrum."[47] Exclaiming that "[t]hey're b-a-a-a-c-k" following a brief attempt by Operation Rescue activists to revitalize the protests in early 1989, an *Atlanta Journal and Constitution* editorial states that "[i]nstead of trusting their case to be strong enough that they could prevail with persuasion, anti-abortion demonstrators are back trying to intimidate and harass women who disagree with them." In so doing, they "not only break the law" but also "mock morality, civility and common sense." The editorial concludes, "Enough has long since been enough in this matter."[48]

These accusations of incivility and coercion also surrounded the 1991 "Summer of Mercy" campaign. Mary Tush of Wichita declared that "I am tired of being beaten over the head by the anti-choice groups.... I am tired of fanatics trying to force their opinions upon me and the other women of this community."[49] Speaking at a pro-choice rally in Wichita, abortion counselor Fran Belden thundered, "How dare they tell [a 15-year-old girl] that she has to follow their beliefs. How dare they invade our town and assault our neighbors.... To Operation Rescue I say, 'You cannot bully us. You cannot force your religious views on me or on this community.'"[50] In decrying the law enforcement burden the then-upcoming protests would create, Wichita resident Viva Lu Thompson characterized Operation Rescue activists not only as "anti-choice," but also as "compulsory-pregnancy zealots" who will "deliberately create expensive havoc."[51]

Jesse E. Todd, Jr., not wanting "to live in a society where the ultimate authority over social conflict is God's law as interpreted by the Randall Terrys of the world," provides a fitting summary of this characterization. "Operation Rescue," he stated, "is unhappy with [the current societal views on abortion] now, and some of its members are not content to rely just on persuasion to change it. Essentially they want to use physical intimidation and harassment to impose their religious conviction on people who believe differently."[52]

Fanatics, of course, are characterized not only by their disdain for civility and their disregard for the rights of others, but also by their relentlessness.

Declaring that Operation Rescue activists "are not your run-of-the-mill demonstrators," Betty Grant, president of the Georgia chapter of the National Organization for Women, said of Operation Rescue tactics: "It just indicates to me further proof that they will stop at nothing.... I think it's despicable."[53] Urging pro-choice groups to take a tougher stance in dealing with Operation Rescue, Michelman commented, "the lessons that pro-choice people all across the country have learned is that anti-choice people will go to every length they can to take away the right. They will stop at nothing to achieve their goal."[54] Valerie Berman, director of the Clinic Defense Alliance, agreed. "Nothing," she declared, "has convinced me more than Wichita that you must defend your clinics. Whenever Operation Rescue chooses to harass or intimidate women, we need to be out there."[55]

Fanatics can be characterized further by their ignorance and their simple-mindedness—a characterization that is also routinely applied to Operation Rescue and other pro-life activists. In an editorial letter to the *Wichita Eagle*, Wichita resident Jeff Fast offered a portrait of fear and intellectual backwardness. "[T]he anti-abortion movement," he claimed, "is all about limiting speech, expression, and rights." The current pro-life movement, in Fast's view, "has gone into a frenzy that hides behind 'traditional family values' and 'fetuses' because its followers are people afraid of sex, feminism and progressive ideas." "In conclusion," he declared, "I ask the anti-abortionists to go hide in their corner and play with their outmoded thinking, because they only have the quacks on their side."[56] Condordia [Kansas] resident Ralph Chubbuck, also writing to the *Wichita Eagle*, conveyed a representation of the pro-life "creed" in a manner that emphasizes narrow-mindedness and authoritarianism: "I am representative of God, and if anyone else sees things differently, of course, they are wrong. There is no place in my thinking for any belief other than my own, and I shall do my best to force other people to think as I think. If they do not see as I see, they are wrong; and I shall use strong methods to force them to follow my beliefs, because I believe that my view of God's will is the only one that can be right. There is no room for beliefs that disagree with mine. They must be evil!"[57]

This characterization of Operation Rescue activists as small-minded fanatics can also be seen in the public discourse surrounding the 1988 protests. After a priest urged abortion rights activist Bill Baird "to love God and love the Operation Rescue demonstrators," Baird declared: "I will never love a bigot. I understand bigotry, wherever it goes. We're not going to run from you. Never again will you turn this into a nation where you can decide our morality."[58]

Operation Rescue Activists as Violent

Already hinted at in some examples above is the view that Operation Rescue activists are not only intolerably intolerant and closed-minded, but also violent in the pursuit of their goals. Characterizing given instances of social protest as violent, of course, carries obvious implications regarding that protest's acceptability in a democratic society.

Writing for the *Wichita Eagle*, Buzz Merritt related that "what began as peaceful protest turned first to physical obstruction and, this week, has become outright assault on law enforcement people charged with maintaining access to the legal clinics."[59] Relating that "[o]ne man reportedly left a message on [Judge Kelly's][60] home answering machine, describing how his body would be dismembered after he was killed," Anna Quindlen exclaimed, "Now let me get this straight: It's wrong to destroy an embryo, but it's OK to kill a full-grown federal judge."[61] In an editorial letter, Rachel Hamman of Toronto [Kansas] declared of Operation Rescue tactics that "not only are these terroristic acts illegal, they are dangerous. Seems to me the only people these women need saving from is you."[62] On a somewhat more humorous note, Judge Kelly referred to Operation Rescue lieutenant Patrick Mahoney as "Monihan," suggesting a violent vigilantism characteristic of "Dirty Harry" Callahan.[63]

Voices from Atlanta in 1988 also articulated this general characterization of Operation Rescue activists as violent. Following an incident in which a woman trying to enter an abortion clinic tripped over a protester, the clinic director exclaimed that the Operation Rescue protesters "were brutal to that woman. They showed no compassion and no respect for her.... These people are vicious."[64] Speaking also from Atlanta, National Organization for Women president Molly Yard declared that while Operation Rescue activists "purport to save lives, they are endangering the lives of women."[65]

Others giving voice to the oppositional view support a characterization of Operation Rescue as violent by emphasizing the criminality of the group. With respect to Operation Rescue leaders, Great Bend resident Laleta Houser compared the protests with organized crime and violence by referring to them as "gang leaders" and "hoodlums."[66] Commenting on the practice of "baby steps" that protesters were allowed to take to prolong arrest time, Dr. Tiller's spokeswoman Peggy Jarman thundered, "It is inexcusable, absolutely inexcusable, that [the police] let people who are breaking the law take baby steps. This is totally unacceptable. It is complete anarchy with a bunch of hoodlums and terrorists running this town."[67] Urging Operation Rescue to "repent," Katherine Hancock Ragsdale of the Episcopal Women's

Caucus bluntly described Operation Rescue as "an act of terrorism" and "a blot on our nation's conscience."[68] One letter to the *Atlanta Journal and Constitution* characterized Operation Rescue activists bluntly as "criminals" who "promote their 'cause' by intimidating and verbally and physically abusing the women residents of Atlanta who choose to go to an abortion facility, which is these women's right."[69] "If the police and courts are not treating [Operation Rescue activists] with deference," noted an *Atlanta Journal and Constitution* editorial, "it is because they have demonstrated no more respect for the law and those administering it than any other scofflaws or repeat offenders."[70] In these examples, then, the proclamation of Operation Rescue's criminality—especially in an organized, "terroristic" form—seeks to emphasize Operation Rescue activists' proclivity to violence.

Others do not draw any kind of distinction between the practice of blocking abortion clinics and the practice of violence. *Wichita Eagle* editorial writer W. Davis Merritt wrote that "it is not a peaceful tactic to physically occupy space to which someone else has a legal right. It is intimidation.... If violence occurs, understand what started it."[71]

Violence is not necessarily practiced in a purely physical way, either, according to pro-choice characterizations. Seeing violence also as a verbal and emotional matter, Mary Tush expressed herself a bit more passionately. "Anti-choice groups say they are non-violent," she declared. "I'm sorry, I must disagree. Women trying to get past the pickets are yelled at and called terrible names by the anti-choice people. I consider that mental abuse. Is that not a form of violence? They must be very small-minded individuals to think that they practice non-violence."[72] "They tell you all this stuff about non-violence," declared Ann Baker during the 1988 Atlanta protests, "but they say the most offensive things to people entering the clinic. I have also stood and listened to them pray, calling down God's wrath on pro-choice people. I think that's very violent."[73]

Conclusion

The 1993 shooting of Dr. Gunn by a pro-life activist provided an important opportunity for the renewed and forceful public articulation of the delegitimizing characterizations described in this chapter. While such characterizations were articulated with renewed zeal from 1993 forward, they stemmed from a delegitimizing vocabulary that was already in existence. As suggested by the above exploration of public discourse during the 1988 "Siege of Atlanta" and the 1991 "Summer of Mercy" campaigns, this delegitimizing vocabulary was already articulated well before the first homicide by a pro-life activist took place.

This specific vocabulary frames Operation Rescue activists (and pro-life activists more generally) in ways that delegitimize their status as social protesters, negatively shaping attitudes and actions toward Operation Rescue and pro-life social protest. "Non-violent civil disobedience," associated with Martin Luther King Jr. and the 1960s civil rights movement commands respect, even devotion. "Terrorism" and "fanaticism," on the other hand, call for suppression with moral impunity, even moral zeal.

The counter-characterizing vocabulary detailed in this chapter represented a significant rhetorical challenge for Operation Rescue. If this vocabulary were to become the common rhetorical currency by which the public discusses abortion, the pro-life movement, Operation Rescue, and pro-life social protest, then the effect on Operation Rescue—and the pro-life movement more generally—would be cataclysmic. Yet, Operation Rescue utterly failed to meet or even essentially acknowledge this critical rhetorical challenge. The next chapter helps to explain why.

Notes

1. "Abortion and Violence," transcript of *Sonya Live*, narrated by Sonya Friedman, Cable News Network, March 8, 1994, 3.
2. Ibid.
3. "War in Wichita: Pro-Life Versus Pro-Choice," transcript of *Donahue*, narrated by Phil Donahue, KSNW, Wichita [Kansas], September 6, 1991, 15.
4. Andrew King, *Power and Communication* (Prospect Heights, Ill.: Waveland Press, 1987), 60.
5. John W. Bowers, Donovan J. Ochs, and Richard J. Jensen, *The Rhetoric of Agitation and Control*, 2nd ed. (Prospect Heights, Ill.: Waveland Press, 1993), 139.
6. Ibid., 138.
7. James Davison Hunter, *Before the Shooting Begins: Searching for Democracy in America's Culture War* (New York: Free Press, 1994), 106.
8. For a representative example of the former view, see Lloyd Bitzer, "Rhetoric and Public Knowledge," in *Rhetoric, Philosophy, and Literature: An Exploration*, ed. Don M. Burks (West Lafayette, Ind.: Purdue University Press, 1978), 67–93. For representative examples of the latter view, see Michael Calvin McGee, "In Search of 'The People': A Rhetorical Alternative," *Quarterly Journal of Speech* 61 (1975): 235–49; Michael Calvin McGee and Martha Anne Martin, "Public Knowledge and Ideological Argumentation," *Communication Monographs* 50 (1983): 47–65.
9. Celeste Michelle Condit, *Decoding Abortion Rhetoric: Communicating Social Change* (Urbana: University of Illinois Press, 1990), 228.

10. Roland Barthes, *Mythologies*, trans. Annette Lavers (1957; reprint, New York: Hill and Wang, 1972), 129.
11. Condit, *Decoding Abortion Rhetoric*, 25.
12. Ibid., 29.
13. For a substantial discussion of "ultimate terms," see Richard M. Weaver, *The Ethics of Rhetoric* (1953; reprint, Davis, Calif.: Hermagoras Press, 1985), 211–32.
14. Condit, *Decoding Abortion Rhetoric*, 116.
15. Sam Keen, *Faces of the Enemy: Reflections of the Hostile Imagination* (San Francisco: Harper and Row, 1986), 10.
16. See, for instance, Steven Perry, "Rhetorical Functions of the Infestation Metaphor in Hitler's Rhetoric," *Central States Speech Journal* 34 (1983): 229–35.
17. For the distinction between "action" and "motion," see Kenneth Burke, "Terministic Screens," in *Language as Symbolic Action: Essays on Life, Literature, and Method* (Berkeley: University of California Press, 1966), 53.
18. Bonnie McD. Johnson, "Images of the Enemy in Intergroup Conflict," *Central States Speech Journal* 26 (1975): 87–89.
19. Marsha L. Vanderford, "Vilification and Social Movements: A Case Study of Pro-Life and Pro-Choice Rhetoric," *Quarterly Journal of Speech* 75 (1989): 166.
20. Ibid., 179.
21. Mark Sherman and Lorri Denise Booker, "Falwell Wants Bush to Back Abortion Foes," *Atlanta Journal and Constitution*, August 10, 1998, April 16, 1999, http://stacks.ajc.com.
22. "Abortion Foes Would Deny Women's Rights," *Atlanta Journal and Constitution*, August 1, 1988, April 19, 1999, http://stacks.ajc.com.
23. To be sure, the question of "rights" has been a key tension between the pro-life and pro-choice movements. In their contrast of the pro-life and pro-choice movements, communication scholars Charles J. Stewart, Craig Allen Smith, and Robert E. Denton, Jr., fruitfully examine this tension in terms of "transcendence." See Stewart, Smith, and Denton, *Persuasion and Social Movements*, 3rd ed. (Prospect Heights, Ill.: Waveland Press, 1994), 263–82.
24. "Abortion Foes Would Deny Women's Rights."
25. Ibid.
26. Lowery, quoted in Sherman and Booker, "Falwell Wants Bush to Back Abortion Foes."
27. "Letters to the Editor: Trapped Whales Received More Concern than American Hostages Held in Beirut," *Atlanta Journal and Constitution*, November 2, 1988, November 27, 1998, http://stacks.ajc.com.
28. Baker, quoted in Judy Lundstrom Thomas, "Terry and His Cause Allow No Neutrality," *Wichita Eagle*, August 25, 1991, VUTEXT database, document 238112, 4.
29. Michelman, quoted in Ellen Warren, "Bush Urges Protesters to End Clinic Blockade," *Wichita Eagle*, August 19, 1991, VUTEXT database, document 232001, 3.
30. "Spotlight on Wichita: What the Commentators Are Saying," *Wichita Eagle*, August 15, 1991, VUTEXT database, document 228081, 5.
31. Michelman, quoted in Tamar Lewin, "With Thin Staff and Thick Debt, Anti-Abortion Group Faces Struggle," *New York Times*, June 11, 1990, A16.
32. The distinction between *form* and *content* is arguable. I do realize that there is usually interplay between the two, but I still maintain that essential protest forms can exist with different contents or ideologies. Support for this position can be found in

William Chaloupka's discussion of the *kynical* protest form. See Chaloupka, "Suppose Kuwait's Main Product Was Broccoli? The Street Demonstration in U.S. Politics," in *Rhetorical Republic: Governing Representations in American Politics*, ed. Frederick M. Dolan and Thomas L. Dumm (Amherst: University of Massachusetts Press, 1993), 143–66.

33. Eric Hoffer, *The True Believer: Thoughts on the Nature of Mass Movements* (1951; reprint, New York: Harper and Row, 1989), 12–13.

34. Ibid., 87.

35. Pyrdum, quoted in Mark Sherman and Michelle Hiskey, "26 More Protesters Arrested at Clinic, Including 4 Drivers," *Atlanta Journal and Constitution*, August 12, 1988, April 16, 1999, http://stacks.ajc.com.

36. Sobel, quoted in "Spotlight on Wichita," 2.

37. Jack Pelham, quoted in Ben Smith, III, "Falwell Predicts an End to Legal Abortions," *Atlanta Journal and Constitution*, January 17, 1989, September 17, 1998, http://stacks.ajc.com.

38. "Letter to the Editor: Abortion Endangers a Woman's Health and Well-Being," *Atlanta Journal and Constitution*, August 24, 1988, November 6, 1998, http://stacks.ajc.com.

39. George T. Gardner, "Crusade Won't Solve Issues Surrounding Pregnancy," *Wichita Eagle*, September 1, 1991, VUTEXT database, document 245146, 1.

40. Ibid., 4.

41. Ibid., 1.

42. Ibid., 2.

43. Ibid., 3, 4.

44. Bruce, quoted in "The Law Must Prevail over Knight's Politics," *Wichita Eagle*, August 3, 1991, VUTEXT database, document 216128, 3.

45. "War in Wichita," 4.

46. Bruce, quoted in "The Law Must Prevail over Knight's Politics," 2.

47. "Letters to the Editor: New Definition of 'Rights,'" *Atlanta Journal and Constitution*, October 24, 1988, October 27, 1998, http://stacks.ajc.com; Tom Teepen, "Tantrums of Anti-Abortionists Fail to Dislodge Pro-Choice Majority," *Atlanta Journal and Constitution*, October 11, 1988, October 27, 1998, http://stacks.ajc.com.

48. "Immoral, Uncivil, Illegal," *Atlanta Journal and Constitution*, March 18, 1989, September 17, 1998, http://stacks.ajc.com.

49. "Operation Rescue Railing, Rallying," *Wichita Eagle*, July 25, 1991, VUTEXT database, document 207131, 3–4.

50. Belden, quoted in Hurst Laviana and Bud Norman, "Abortion-Rights Rally Sends a Loud Message," *Wichita Eagle*, August 25, 1991, VUTEXT database, document 238110, 4.

51. "Fears, Hopes on Abortion Protests," *Wichita Eagle*, June 17, 1991, VUTEXT database, document 169058, 4.

52. Jesse E. Todd, Jr., "Fears a Society Where Randall Terry Is Law," *Wichita Eagle*, August 12, 1991, VUTEXT database, document 225095, 2, 4.

53. Grant, quoted in Lorri Denise Booker, "Anti-Abortionists Drive Point Home to Residences: Activists Are Targeting M.D.'s Where They Live," *Atlanta Journal and Constitution*, March 18, 1989, September 17, 1998, http://stacks.ajc.com.

54. Michelman, quoted in Judy Lundstrom Thomas, "Lessons of Wichita Will Echo for Years: Abortion-Rights Forces Rethinking Strategy," *Wichita Eagle*, August 25, 1991, VUTEXT database, document 238111, 4.

55. Berman, quoted in Thomas, "Lessons of Wichita Will Echo for Years," 1.

56. "More Voices on Abortion Protests," *Wichita Eagle*, June 19, 1991, VUTEXT database, document 171114, 4–5.

57. "Abortion, Laws, Coverage," *Wichita Eagle*, August 24, 1991, VUTEXT database, document 237120, 7.

58. Baird, quoted in Lorri Denise Booker and Gayle White, "350 Protesters Arrested at 3 Abortion Clinics," *Atlanta Journal and Constitution*, October 4, 1988, November 5, 1998, http://stacks.ajc.com.

59. Buzz Merritt, "Stop Now! Leaders Should Move to Calm Clinic Protests," *Wichita Eagle*, August 22, 1991, VUTEXT database, document 235166, 1.

60. United States District Judge Patrick Kelly, having jurisdiction over the Wichita area, issued an injunction prohibiting a restriction of access to Wichita's abortion clinics, and later called in federal marshals to help local police enforce the injunction. See Bowers, Ochs, and Jensen, *The Rhetoric of Agitation and Control*, 129.

61. "Spotlight on Wichita," 4.

62. "Rights, Morality on Abortion Issue," *Wichita Eagle*, July 24, 1991, VUTEXT database, document 206098, 2.

63. Kelly, quoted in Bud Norman, "Judge, Protest Leaders Volley," *Wichita Eagle*, August 15, 1991, VUTEXT database, document 228041, 2.

64. Lynn Randall, quoted in Lorri Denise Booker and Scott Bronstein, "3 Face Charges of Assault in Abortion Protest: Teen Entering Clinic Trips, 13 Are Arrested," *Atlanta Journal and Constitution*, October 6, 1988, October 29, 1998, http://stacks.ajc.com, ellipsis in original.

65. Yard, quoted in Booker and White, "350 Protesters Arrested at 3 Abortion Clinics."

66. "More Heat on the Abortion Issue," *Wichita Eagle*, August 3, 1991, VUTEXT database, document 216129, 3.

67. Jarman, quoted in Hurst Laviana, "Police Doing All They Can, City Officials Say," *Wichita Eagle*, August 3, 1991, VUTEXT database, document 216105, 2.

68. Ragsdale, quoted in "Digest: Presbyterians to Dedicate New Offices in Kentucky," *Atlanta Journal and Constitution*, October 29, 1988, October 27, 1998, http://stacks.ajc.com.

69. "Letters to the Editor: Adoption Alternative Isn't Viable for Non-White Babies," *Atlanta Journal and Constitution*, October 21, 1988, October 27, 1998, http://stacks.ajc.com.

70. "Jail for Offenders: It's No Holiday," *Atlanta Journal and Constitution*, October 10, 1988, October 29, 1998, http://stacks.ajc.com.

71. W. Davis Merritt, "Escalation: As Abortion Protests Peak Rights Need to be Protected," *Wichita Eagle*, August 20, 1991, VUTEXT database, document 233082, 2.

72. "Operation Rescue Railing, Rallying," 4.

73. Baker, quoted in Mark Sherman, "Abortion Protests Put Little-Known Leader in a Starring Role," *Atlanta Journal and Constitution*, August 12, 1988, April 16, 1999, http://stacks.ajc.com.

8

THE LIMITS OF RADICAL RHETORIC

Portraits of the Public in the Rhetoric of Operation Rescue

I may be a fool, but I still believe that grassroots America, and especially grassroots Kansans and grassroots Wichitans, are pro-life when they know the truth.
—Rev. Richard Exley, speaking at a 1992 Operation Rescue rally[1]

"You're going to have to sacrifice everything," the Reverend Patrick Mahoney exhorted to those attending a rally during Operation Rescue's 1992 Wichita "Summer of Love" campaign. "There's [sic] going to be people wounded," he warned. "There are going to be casualties. I'm telling you that now. I'm not going to whip you up and get you into a frenzy, and march you out into bullets. I'm telling you what's happening." Mahoney described the "battle" joined by Operation Rescue activists as one "against the forces of death killing God's beautiful children," forces that are "really spitting in the face of God." "It's not about children," Mahoney declared, making clear that more is at stake than just the abortion issue. Rather, "it's about whose will" shall "rule on this planet, God's or man's."[2]

At a rally one day earlier, the Reverend Richard Exley articulated similarly steep implications of this "battle." "Abortion," Exley declared, "is part of a moral malaise which threatens our traditional concept of the inherent value of human life, and is potentially shattering to the foundations of Western civilization." Because of this, "we're not only fighting for babies when we lay down our lives to blockade those doorways to death, but we are fighting for our nation, we are fighting for the American future, and we are fighting for decency and goodness and life."[3]

During a tent rally near the close of the "Summer of Love" campaign, prominent Chicago pro-life activist Joseph Scheidler described the abortion controversy as a "holy war." "Those of you," he continued, "who have been out at the clinics and have seen the deathscorts, and Queer Nation, and these other funny people, know that this is not simply a battle against a social issue. It is a battle between good and evil. It is a battle between God and Satan."[4]

These examples from the rhetoric of Operation Rescue exemplify what sociologist James Davison Hunter has called the "contemporary culture war."[5] Hunter has claimed that a fundamental cleavage exists between two "polarizing impulses" in American culture—impulses rooted in opposing and incommensurable moral visions. Both of these impulses, the "orthodox" and the "progressive,"[6] claim to "represent the interests of the majority" and struggle to "monopolize the symbols of legitimacy." Both also portray the opposition as "extremist" and "intolerant" through a hyperbolic discourse of "sensationalism."[7]

As discussed in chapter 6, Hunter has further argued that this bellicose climate of public discourse results not only in a degraded ability to arrive at meaningful solutions to the prevailing social and political problems, but also in an increased temptation to engage in coercion and violence to achieve goals. Such rhetoric is not only discomforting and dangerous, according to Hunter, but also reflective of problematic views of both the ends of political activism and democracy more generally.[8]

The rhetoric mentioned above also exemplifies what rhetorician James Darsey has called "radical rhetoric."[9] Unlike Hunter and other advocates of "civil" public discourse, however, Darsey is essentially sympathetic to this type of discourse, as well as its wellspring in what he claims is the American "prophetic tradition." In Darsey's view, the future of democracy depends not upon the cultivation of civility, but instead upon the cultivation of a particular *incivility*—in his words, "meaningful incivility."[10] "The fate of democracy," he states, "if not to fertilize its roots every fifteen years with the blood of revolution as Jefferson believed, is at least to engage in serious acts of redefinition based on radical principles. The goal cannot and should not be a state of restfulness. Quite the contrary, the goal must be endlessly competing zealotries."[11]

To achieve this goal, Darsey has urged the fuller appreciation and revival of the currently slighted tradition of historical American social reform rhetoric. That tradition, he has argued, is based most substantially upon the "fire and strength" of Hebraism.[12] This "fire and strength" affirms "sacred principle" that is "immutable," "beyond the reach of humankind," and "uncompromisable"; this "fire and strength" also entails "mystery and transcendence."[13] The "radical" rhetoric of that tradition, further, employs not a language of "reason" characteristic of Hellenistic "sweetness and light," but rather languages of "righteousness" and "judgment."

Darsey's advocacy of this rhetorical form emerges most forcefully in his criticism of contemporary gay rights rhetoric. In employing a language of "economics" instead of a language of "righteousness," the gay rights movement, in Darsey's view, has mired itself in "rhetorical poverty."[14] Gay rights rhetoric is a rhetoric of "disengagement," a rhetoric of "nonjudgment," a rhetoric in which "there is no potential for radical commitment."[15] Having abandoned transcendental ideals altogether," he suggests a bit later, "gay liberationists have no faith in their own righteousness."[16]

On the face of it, Hunter and Darsey offer two competing visions with respect to the role of rhetorical discourse in achieving—or at least managing—a sense of national community that maintains essential plurality, yet avoids the sort of balkanization that ultimately fosters coercion and violence. Hunter's hope for the amicable resolution—or at least negotiation—of the contemporary cultural conflict lies in a "context of public discourse" that "sustain[s] a genuine and peaceful pluralism."[17] This context would arise from a consensus over "*how* to contend over the moral differences that divide . . . *how* to publicly disagree."[18] To achieve this more modest consensus, Hunter has suggested "changing the environment of public discourse" to encourage "genuine debate" involving "direct and immediate exchange." He has also suggested (1) an implicit rejection of the "impulse of public quiescence"; (2) the "recognition of the 'sacred' within different moral communities"; and (3) a recognition by all parties of "the inherent weaknesses, even dangers, in their own moral commitments."[19] Hunter's vision appears to call for more civility, not less.

Darsey, on the other hand, appears to have located the problems of public discourse not in unreflectively fervent moral vision, but in no moral vision at all. This, according to Darsey, is

> the failing of so many current prescriptions for the national malaise. On the one hand, those on the right would retreat to rigid orthodoxies as sources of order. On the other hand, those who count themselves liberals place their faith in the processes of reason without content. Both responses embrace an

idea of civility, but neither comprehends the role of continuing radical opposition in maintaining cultural definition, the need to aerate the roots of society by means that involve some violence to the soil. [By contrast, Darsey has urged] the recovery of . . . this native radicalism [as a necessary condition to] the revival of a compelling social vision.[20]

Darsey's vision of vibrant public discourse appears to call for more zeal, not less.

The differences between Darsey and Hunter on the preferred nature of public dialogue are significant here in that they put into sharper relief both (1) the specific issues involved with the rhetorical practices of Operation Rescue, and (2) the more general issues implicated in the relationship between religion and politics. The general issues brought up by these differences illumine both the ineffectiveness of Operation Rescue's public rhetorical efforts and the broader consequences of these public rhetorical efforts for the quality of public dialogue. An important purpose of this chapter is to document these connections more clearly.

I will examine the rhetoric of Operation Rescue in terms of particular views of the "public" that the rhetoric encourages its adherents to adopt. As mentioned in the previous chapter, there is no uniform agreement on what exactly the "public" is. Whether or not the "public" is in actuality a distinct empirical phenomenon, though, it is more agreed upon that *particular visions* of the public's identity are indeed rhetorical constructions. As rhetoric scholar Edwin Black has noted, any given body of rhetorical discourse implies an audience to which that discourse would appeal.[21] That implied audience can then be seen as the reasonable standard to which that discourse is geared. If a particular rhetor (in this case, Operation Rescue) is attempting public persuasion, then the particular features of the rhetoric that is generated would depend upon how the group conceptualizes the public they are trying to persuade. If that conceptualization of the public is untenable or problematic, then the rhetoric is much more likely to be ineffective.

In this chapter, I claim that this is exactly what happened with Operation Rescue. More specifically, I claim that Operation Rescue held to a conception of the public that is essentially *passive*. In Operation Rescue's conception, the public has no agency in weighing truth claims and actively deciding what is right and wrong. The public, further, plays no active role in interpreting acts and truth claims; rather, the public can respond or not respond to acts and truth claims that are self-evident, obvious. This problematic view of the public is significant in that it not only provides further insight into the failure of Operation Rescue's public rhetorical efforts, but also suggests some significant limits of radical rhetoric as Darsey conceptualizes it.

To advance these larger claims, I examine portraits of the public in the rhetoric of Operation Rescue, using as a text sample a series of addresses given at rallies during the group's 1992 "Summer of Love" campaign in Wichita, Kansas. I argue that the public is portrayed in two distinct ways in this rhetoric. The first portrait characterizes the public as *virtuous but deceived*. In other words, the American people possess good moral sense and would oppose abortion if they knew the truth about it. In this way, Operation Rescue positions itself as representing the real interests of the majority. The general public is not aware of this, however, because they are being deceived by an extreme "pro-abortion" minority. The second portrait, on the other hand, characterizes the public as *complicitous in the evil of abortion*. In this portrait, the American people partake in a culture that is morally and spiritually bankrupt. The men and women of Operation Rescue, "citizens of conscience,"[22] are accordingly portrayed as a prophetic minority that confronts and warns against this ubiquitous spirit of the age.

Both of these portraits reinforce a conception of the public as passive by overemphasizing the agency of Operation Rescue activists and underemphasizing the agency of the public. In both portraits I examine, the agency of Operation Rescue activists is overemphasized in that the activists' "acts" are seen as self-evident. Whether as "education" or as "prophecy," acts of "rescuing" are seen as communicating truth unhindered and without consideration of how such acts are to be interpreted. Accordingly, the agency of the public is effectively discounted. In both portraits of the public, the public is seen as not doing any interpretive work in the process of persuasion, whether about abortion or whether about truth more generally.

Portraits of the Public

The Public Is Virtuous but Deceived

With this portrait, the public is characterized as endowed generally with good common and moral sense; with this sense the public would surely oppose abortion if only they knew the truth about the different procedures involved. During his June 5, 1992 pre-rescue rally address, Exley exhorted those in attendance to make sure they get a copy of a particular issue of the *Pentecostal Evangel*, which contains an article Exley described as "an exposé" on Wichita's "most famous citizen, the abortionist George Tiller." "I would like you to have as many of these," Exley declared, "and feel free . . . to use

Xerox machines and copy this article over and over, and paper the streets of Wichita with this information." Why should they do this? Exley quickly provided the answer: "I may be a fool, but I still believe that grassroots America, and especially grassroots Kansans and grassroots Wichitans, are pro-life when they know the truth." That is why "it's up to you and I [sic] to tell them the truth of what goes on behind closed and locked and guarded doors in the sanctuary of death on Kellogg Street," referring to Dr. Tiller's abortion clinic.[23]

During his July 11, 1992 tent rally address, prominent Chicago pro-life activist Joseph Scheidler reinforced this portrait of the American public as essentially pro-life when they know all the facts. "I think we have not made our own judgments," he declared. "Oh, you and I have, but the American people have not. The American people were handed *Roe v. Wade*." To support this assertion, and thus to suggest that the public is even now generally sympathetic to the pro-life position, Scheidler related that "polls show that 77% of the American people still believe that abortion is a form of murder.... Most people do not like abortions after the first twelve weeks. Very few people accept abortion . . . for sex selection."[24]

Scheidler then summarized by declaring that "the American people are not, from the little knowledge they have, pro-abortion." Even though the public does not know the real "truth" about abortion, in other words, they are surprisingly reserved about the practice of abortion. The implication, then, is that once the "truth" is out and the American people can make an informed decision, they will support the pro-life position more unequivocally and decisively. The implication is borne out with Scheidler's statement immediately afterward that the American people "still have not had an opportunity to make that decision, and I think they have to have that opportunity." That opportunity, again, presumes a full knowledge of what abortion is. "We have," he went on, "we've made our decision. George Tiller has made his decision. But Middle America has not."[25] According to Scheidler, then, the American people have not been able to make a "decision" because of limited knowledge.

Given that the public possesses moral and common sense, why do those constituting the public have limited knowledge, and why do they not see the truth? The simple and obvious answer, according to this particular portrait of the public, is that a determined and malevolent "pro-abortion" minority is determined to keep them in the dark. Exley brought up the desire for large profits as one motivation for deceiving the public. "Abortion," he declared, "is the largest unregulated industry in the United States of America, annually grossing between 500 million and one billion dollars.... Please hear me. Abortion mills do not employ counselors. Abortion mills employ salespersons under the guise of counseling." To support this claim, Exley quoted a former abortion clinic staff worker as saying that "I was given pages of information to read on how to be a good salesperson," and that in phone conversations with prospective patients, "we were told specifically to coax them by any verbal means outside of outright lies."[26] In characterizing abortion advocates as possessed by the profit motive, Exley implied that they are not concerned with public interests or the public welfare. They are not interested in representing the abortion issue truthfully because it would be bad for business.

Furthermore, the profit motive of the "pro-abortion" minority, as an impetus for deceiving the public about the truth concerning abortion, is just the tip of the proverbial iceberg. This determined minority is motivated by selfishness of a most reckless sort—a selfishness that explicitly justifies the killing of "unborn human beings." Following his discussion of the "scientific" development of "fetology," which has "documented life from the moment of conception to the moment of birth," Exley stated that "[n]o intelligent person any longer argues about whether or not the child in the womb is a living human being or not. In fact, the advocates of abortion are all too happy to say yes, it's a baby, and it's my baby, and if I want to kill it, I will."[27] In other words, pro-choice activists like these are not merely misguided or mistaken. Rather, they actually want to kill human beings, or at the very least are willing to exhibit flagrant disregard for the value of human life.

Pro-choice ("pro-abortion") activists are also portrayed as evil, or at least as expressly partaking in evil—a portrayal that explicitly emphasizes the perception of them as a malevolent minority. After describing an incident in which pro-choice activists left five defaced Bibles on his front porch, Scheidler declared that "[t]here's got to be some kind of exorcism over the evil in this country." Having described the general abortion struggle as "a holy war," "a battle between good and evil," and "a battle between God and Satan," Scheidler said simply of these activists: "They hate God. They hate the Word of God."[28] Speaking on the same day as Scheidler, Father Norman Weslin, leader of Operation Rescue-style group Lambs of Christ, preserved the evil component of "pro-abortion" motivation while also emphasizing the sheer aberration of this group of people. "There are," he declared, "four categories of people in those killing centers: drug addicts, homosexuals, Satan worshipers, all centering around a professional killer that pays them well." Weslin immediately reemphasized these categorizations to further make the contrast: "That's who the city escorts pompously into the killing center, when they escort with police escort, this man who's going to kill your Christian-American babies. Coming into the killing center with horns blowing and clapping by the homosexuals, the Satan worshipers, and the drug addicts. That's the reality of the situation that you have here."[29]

The portrait developed above, then, is of a public that is essentially sympathetic to the pro-life movement. Thus Operation Rescue is depicted as seeking to recover the majority interest by exposing the deception of an extreme "pro-abortion" minority. This is hardly the case, however, with the other portrait of the public in the rhetoric of Operation Rescue.

The Public Is Complicitous in the Evil of Abortion

The second portrait of the public, ostensibly inconsistent with the first, can be seen as following from the prophetic, polarizing stance of Operation Rescue on the subject of abortion. This portrait can also be seen as following from the central position accorded by Operation Rescue to the Judeo-Christian orientation, particularly as understood by conservative evangelicals and fundamentalists.

The proclaimed theme of Scheidler's address shows how this portrait of the public might come into play. Near the beginning of his address, Scheidler paraphrased John 15:18–21: "If the world hates you, you know that it hated me first. This is Jesus talking. If you belonged to the world, the world would love its own. But because you are not of the world, and I have selected you from the world, therefore the world hates you. Remember what I said to you. The servant is not greater than the master. If they persecuted me, they will persecute you." Scheidler continued, "Now I know you've heard that before, but we have to remind ourselves, we will be persecuted" because "Christ was persecuted by the world, by those who hated Him." Therefore, "if we're like Him, they'll hate us."[30] The repeated and central term *world*, here, means those who are not authentic Christians, which—at least according to the perspective of Operation Rescue activists generally—encompasses the majority of the American public. This language, especially in this context, implies that the vast majority of the American public is inherently opposed to the work of the pro-life movement—an implication quite consistent with Operation Rescue's notion of "bloodguiltiness," as discussed in chapter 5. Consequently, the American public is implicated in the evil of abortion.

Scheidler also spoke out about the moral turpitude of the American nation generally, reinforcing this portrait of the public as complicitous. In our society today, he explained, "we're being boiled alive in pornography, in accepting variant lifestyles, sexual lifestyles, homosexuality.... That's perversion. That's mortal sin." Declaring later that *Roe v. Wade* "has given us an outrageous attack on a whole class of people," Scheidler exclaimed that "other countries look at us with disgust.... We are sick. Our Court is sick. And this country is in the state of mortal sin, as long as we are allowed to murder five thousand children every day." This nationwide depravity stands in stark contrast with the moral virtue of that minority who "rescues" and performs other pro-life work. "And we are the ones," Scheidler declared, "this little group around the country, who are holding back God's wrath." This is so because "God is not mocked. God did not accept *Roe v. Wade* . . . He came first, and He has His laws. And when you disobey God's laws, you are in big trouble." Scheidler concluded, "This nation is in big trouble."[31]

Exley's address implied this public moral turpitude by mentioning the decline and collapse of public morality. He expounded:

In twenty short years we have witnessed the moral collapse of the American value. In 1973, the only way America could stomach the thought of abortion was when we believed the rhetoric which said it is not a child, it is not a human being, it is simply a mass of tissues. But now, now, in 1992, we sing 'It's my baby, and I'll abort if I want to.' Now we are saying it's a child, but if I don't want it, I'll kill it, and don't you stand in my way.[32]

Exley then continued his discussion of this collapse of public morality by describing Dr. Tiller's Fetal Indication and Termination of Pregnancy (FITOP) program. Exley explained:

Patients are encouraged to speak to their baby, if they wish, and finally to say goodbye. And the patient may elect to receive fetal ashes, conveniently supplied by the crematorium in his abortuary. Now do you understand the difference that has happened in twenty short years? Twenty years ago, no one would have thought of talking to their about-to-be-aborted baby, let alone telling that baby goodbye and then asking to receive fetal ashes. But the moral malaise, the decay, the erosion of values in our Western civilization now, now make it possible for a mother and father to speak to the child in the womb, perhaps to name it, to tell it goodbye, and then to kill it.[33]

Exley then went on to develop further the blasphemous effects of this decline in public morality by describing baptism services held in Wichita for aborted fetuses. "Now it's not only justified morally," he exclaimed, "but in a blasphemous act that is a desecration to the rite of holy baptism, they provide a false assurance of spiritual salvation for those parents, by performing a rite of baptism for the child they've just chosen to murder! What we have here is a microcosm of what abortion on demand is doing to America."[34] In short, abortion "on demand" has desensitized the American public to apathy in the face of great moral decay and turpitude, thereby putting them in a position of complicity.

Finally, the portrait of the public as complicitous is implied in one of Mahoney's addresses. In his June 5, 1992 kickoff rally address, Mahoney appealed to the people in his audience to participate in then-forthcoming "rescue" activities. He did this by laboring to establish the connection between the situation faced by Operation Rescue activists and the biblical situation faced by Shadrach, Mechach, and Abednego in the third chapter of the Old Testament book of Daniel. In this biblical situation, the three Hebrews were thrown into a furnace for defying Babylonian King Nebuchadnezzar's demand that they commit idolatry by bowing down and worshiping a golden image.[35]

The analogy is revealing. In the biblical situation, the Hebrews in Babylonian captivity, of which the three men are a part, are an orthodox remnant in the midst of a thoroughly decadent, pagan culture. The analogy, then, suggests that Operation Rescue activists, too, are a slim, orthodox minority in the midst of a decadent, pagan majority. The suggestion is made somewhat more explicitly by Mahoney himself. On the basis of that comparison, he declared, "You have a choice this evening. Your comfort, your security, your ease, or being a prophetic witness in standing up to this city."[36]

Mahoney's remark nicely captures the emphasis placed on Operation Rescue activists in this portrait of the public; those who "rescue" are characterized as prophets. With this portrait Operation Rescue and the pro-life movement are not acting in the majority interest, as would be the case in the first portrait of the public I have described. Rather, Operation Rescue and the pro-life movement are *confronting* the majority interest. With this portrait, moreover, the public is not merely duped by a depraved minority; rather, the public is complicitous with that depraved minority.

Public "Passivity" and the Self-Evident Nature of Truth

While the these two portraits of the public that exist in the rhetoric of Operation Rescue are strikingly different, they are alike in one important respect: both reinforce a notion of truth and persuasion that discounts the roles of interpretation and of interpretive frames. Both portraits of the public encourage the view that the acts and statements of Operation Rescue activists are self-evident. In the portrait of the public as virtuous but deceived, all that is needed from the vantage point of Operation Rescue is for the truth to be proclaimed, whether by word or by act. When this happens, the public will see through the deception and become more explicitly sympathetic to the pro-life cause. In the much different portrait of the public as complicitous in the evil of abortion, the response is essentially the same: relay self-evident truth prophetically by word or by act, hoping that conversion—to the pro-life cause and/or to the Christian faith—will take place. In the first portrait, the self-evident truth is conveyed in a spirit of hope; in the second portrait, the self-evident truth is conveyed in a spirit of confrontation. In both portraits, however, the truth is self-evident, not requiring any interpretive work on the part of the "speakers" or the "listeners."

In arguing for the essential connection between Operation Rescue and the success of the pro-life movement, Operation Rescue founder Randall Terry reveals this view of truth as self-evident. He does this by articulating a causal link between "rescuing" and social change. He urges the reader to "commit . . . to make this vision"—a vision of "defeat[ing] the abortion holocaust," of "restor[ing] religious and civil liberties to individuals," of "bring[ing] justice to our judicial system," and of "see[ing] common decency return"—a "reality while we still have time."[37] "We must," Terry insists to the reader, "take our bodies down to the abortion mill and peacefully and prayerfully place ourselves between the killer and his intended victims. This is the only way we can produce the social tension necessary to bring about social change."[38] In other words, the "act" of protesting at abortion clinics in this way is seen as conveying truth unassisted and directly to the general public. This assumption is also seen in Terry's maxim that "if you think abortion is murder, then act like it's murder."[39]

This assumption is seen as well in other apologia on behalf of Operation Rescue. Writing on behalf of Operation Rescue's brand of civil disobedience, Mark Belz also criticizes the apparent hypocrisy of pro-life activists, whom he believes leads the general public not to take the pro-life message seriously. "Does the world really hear what we [pro-lifers] are saying?" Belz asks the reader. "Is there reason for them to believe it? Or are actions—or lack of actions—speaking so loudly no one can hear what we are saying?"[40] Actions, then, "speak" unassisted and even better than words in communicating the truth about abortion. In complaining about lack of action on the part of pro-life activists, Belz is really claiming that there is a lack of *real* persuasion. Actions "persuade" by revealing self-evident truth, and in a way in which words do not. Scheidler reinforces the assumption of self-evident truth in his declaration that the American people "have to look at abortion." "You can read books about abortion. But you have to look at the baby that resulted from . . . an abortion to understand what abortion is."[41]

Scheidler's implicit claim—that images advance truth self-evidently—has been vigorously disputed by rhetorician Celeste Michelle Condit. In her study of abortion rhetoric, she claims that the persuasive power of fetal images—as seen in pictures, films, and lapel pins with tiny feet on them—arose from a skillful combination of "metonymic reduction" and metaphor. In Condit's view, the wide range of "developing human forms" are conflated "into a single entity—'the fetus as an unborn baby.'" She declares, "Instead of producing a clear, static image, multiple images of blastocyst/embryo/fetus at different stages would have emphasized development as a process. The pro-Life rhetors, however, wanted the American public to respond to the fetus as if it were one single distinct entity—a human baby; therefore, they worked to generate a *single* image of the fetus."[42] Combined with this metonymic reduction in the careful selection of fetal images has been a powerful metaphoric function. "Not only was a *single* image of 'the fetus' generated," Condit claims, "but that image was carefully selected to maximize the similarities between 'fetus' and 'human being.'"[43] This notion of the image as a rhetorical construction—not self-evident truth—is further supported by the verbal commentary that nearly always accompanies pro-life images. "Without verbal commentary," declares Condit, "pictures *DO NOT ARGUE* propositions. An image may suggest 'this looks like x,' but the assertion of identity, that 'this IS x,' must be verbally supplied." This is particularly true with the pro-life film *The Silent Scream*, in which the narrator continually guides and directs viewers verbally as to what they are "seeing."[44] Nonetheless, Scheidler maintained the "mystery" of self-evident truth in his confession that "I became active in the pro-life movement when I saw a picture of an aborted baby." "One picture," he added, "is worth a thousand words."[45]

This broader notion of truth as self-evident is also seen clearly in Mahoney's speaking. His analogy between Operation Rescue activists and the three Hebrews in the book of Daniel established a connection between faithfulness and "being a prophetic witness in standing up to this city." In this way, acts of "rescuing" work to "witness" to the truth. Near the end of that address, Mahoney declared bluntly that "[t]he nation is watching you.

The nation is watching what happens in Wichita."[46] The next day he echoed the same theme. "I want you to know," he declared, that "America . . . is looking at this city right now." He then elaborated: "Why do you think the network news has been here already? Last year we were four weeks into the event before we could get any kind of coverage. This week they are here ahead of time. Because they are looking to this city, God has touched the city" and has brought "rescuers" to the city "to preach and bring a powerful message to the nation and to the Christian community."[47] This depiction of the situation in Wichita not only underscores the sufficiency of "rescuing" to communicate self-evident truth—to "preach" and "bring a powerful message"—but also assumes that the public will automatically see the acts of "rescuing" as morally defined acts of conscience, and not merely as secularly defined political acts. "Rescuing" not only communicates truth, but also does it apart from any interpretive framework.

This notion of truth and persuasion as self-evident corresponds well with an image of the public common to the two divergent portraits: the public as passive. Whether essentially virtuous yet duped by the "lies" of an aberrant minority, or whether essentially complicitous to some degree in the maintenance of those "lies," the public is characterized as having no agency in the process of persuasion. If the public is virtuous but deceived, then a "priestly"[48] proclamation of the truth via "rescuing" will allow them to see through the lies and believe the truth. Likewise, if the public is complicitous in the evil of abortion, then a "prophetic" proclamation of the truth via "rescuing" will warn them and perhaps shock them into believing the truth, as the prophetic "watchman" of the third chapter of the Old Testament book of Ezekiel was to do. In either case, the public either believes the self-evident truth (about abortion, about God, and so on), or it does not. The truth speaks for itself; the public (or any specific interlocutor) does not engage in any interpretive negotiation in the process of persuasion.

This rhetoric of Operation Rescue, then, serves as significant evidence of how Operation Rescue conceptualized the public it was trying to persuade. Unfortunately for the group's prospects of success, Operation Rescue conceptualized the public in such a way as to deny it agency, to deny it significant and active choice in weighing the arguments, weighing the evidence, and coming to a responsible and moral decision about abortion. In Operation Rescue's view, truth is self-evident and obvious, leaving the response to it to be not a matter of significant moral casuistry, but instead sheer will.

While the failure of Operation Rescue's public rhetorical efforts will be shown more clearly in the next chapter, it is worth pointing out that this failure could be foreseen from Operation Rescue's conceptions of truth, of persuasion, and of the public. Operation Rescue, bluntly speaking, embraced notions of truth and persuasion that do not correspond well with the profound and rhetorical complexity that in actuality accompanies truth claims and attempts to persuade, and that helps to explain why its approach to argument and persuasion in the public sphere might not be effective. Similarly, Operation Rescue—in adapting its public persuasive approach to a public audience that arguably does not exist—failed to adapt its public persuasive approach to the public audience that actually does exist.

So while the issue of the "public" helps to explain why Operation Rescue failed in its attempts to influence public policy on abortion, the story does not end there. The issue of the "public" also provides a way of approaching the larger question of how public argument should work and, more specifically, a way of approaching the competing claims of Hunter and Darsey on the subject.

Operation Rescue and Darseyan "Radical Rhetoric"

Summarizing his exposition of the American prophetic tradition, Darsey explains that while the prophet "is somehow alienated from his audience, possessed of a message that is somehow exclusive," that person also "engages those premises that are central to the culture." The prophet "compels the audience, but only by use of those premises to which they have assented as a culture." The prophet "shares the ideas of his audience rather than the realities of its everyday life," reminding them "of that transcendental side of its culture that makes it larger than our individual wants or needs and aspirations." The prophet "sets himself apart from his audience," but also "depends on an understanding that they share the same world with him, thus making them the subject of his visions."[49] In short, the radical, "prophetic" rhetoric that Darsey celebrates requires a national community that shares together an essential, substantive vision. It requires an essential "mystery" that serves as the basis for the conceptualization of "virtue" and "righteousness." As Darsey puts it, such rhetoric grows from "a desire to bring the practice of the people into accord with a sacred principle."[50]

These characterizations of the prophetic tradition and of radical rhetoric are largely justified throughout Darsey's incisive, eloquently exposited account of the spirit and character of American historical social reform rhetoric. In fact, these characterizations are similar in purpose to Stephen Carter's characterizations of the proper role of religion in politics. Religion functions best, according to Carter, when it serves as a "prophetic" voice, "calling the world to account" and "pointing us in the direction of God's will."[51] In so doing, religion "subverts" the culture of which it is a part. It does so in that it "focuses the attention of the believer on a source of moral understanding that transcends both the authority of positive law and the authority of human moral systems," thereby "provid[ing] the believer with a transcendent reason to question the power of the state and the messages of the culture."[52]

Darsey's characterizations of the power and effectiveness of radical rhetoric become strained, however, when used as a more general descriptive and prescriptive model for contemporary American public discourse. The reason for this is simple. The contemporary, nationwide existence and power of an essential "mystery," required for the resonance of prophetic rhetoric, is at best questionable. As political scientists Frederick M. Dolan and Thomas L. Dumm have observed, the United States is no longer a "classical republic," but rather a "postmodern polity." "American politics," they state, "is shaped in a *plurality* of public spheres rather than by the grammar of a master discourse unquestioningly shared and respected by all."[53] Without such a master discourse—a discourse that articulates transcendent, sacred principle to which *all* are accountable—radical, prophetic rhetoric loses any hope of significant national resonance.

It is a significant degree of fragmentation, then, that makes the contemporary American national community dissimilar to the public communities examined by Darsey. The Old Testament prophets, for instance, operated within a national community that shared as sacred principle the worship of Yahweh, the authority of the Hebrew Scriptures, and observance of the Mosaic law. Likewise, the historical American social reformers of the nineteenth century—particularly abolitionists Wendell Phillips and William Lloyd Garrison—operated within a national community in which the Bible still held sway as an authoritative "grounding text"[54] in American political culture. "In the years between the American Revolution and the Civil War," suggests historian Mark A. Noll, "the Bible offered to many Americans the key for understanding not only private religious reality but also the public life of the country. The Scriptures were so widely used that it is not inaccurate to call the country a biblical nation during this period."[55] In both of these examples, then, there existed essential, perspectival commonalities—"sacred principle"—among a wide range of the national community that made possible the far-reaching resonance of prophetic discourse.

When operating in the context of transcendent and culturally binding principle, then, the radical rhetoric employed by the prophet brings only partial alienation. Perhaps it will provoke rejection, as was so frequent in the case of the Old Testament prophets; perhaps it will provoke subsequent repentance and commitment (or recommitment) to a "compelling social vision." In the absence of such principle, however, the radical rhetoric of the prophet merely reiterates the self-evident nature of an unaccepted truth and reinforces public quiescence. In such a situation, then, the prophet's alienation would be total. The prophetic discourse in question would stand little or no chance of resonating with the people, and the national community ultimately would fare no better, or perhaps would fare even worse.

The problem with Darsey's vision of continued social renewal through radical rhetoric, I believe, is that the current national situation is much closer to the latter characterization than to the former. This chapter's analysis of the rhetoric of Operation Rescue—and, more generally, the analyses of the book as a whole—suggest the ineffectiveness, or even danger, of Darseyan radical rhetoric in a national community in which a single "sacred principle" in large measure does not exist. Like the rhetoric of Operation Rescue, I strongly suspect that radical rhetoric, in the sense that Darsey understands it, speaks to an audience that already assents to the relevant "sacred principle" and that need only respond to its self-evident nature when proclaimed by the "prophet." That audience, unfortunately, scarcely exists.

Darsey is right about the importance in public dialogue of both conviction and the yearning after truth (or, as he might put it, "transcendent principle"). This importance is also reflected well in Hunter's model of public dialogue and public argument. Claiming that one of the most disturbing consequences of the "culture wars" has been apathy and quiescence among most of the public, Hunter affirms the importance of rejecting such impulses. "[W]ithout a common belief that public standards do exist and without a commitment to determine what they are," he declares, "there is no basis for making public compromises; there is not even the will to make the effort. We must avoid the temptation . . . to be 'idiots'—a word, which in one of its original meanings, described the totally private person who is oblivious to the importance of and the need for public-minded civility."[56] Without a general commitment to seek out as a national community what is true, what is fair, and what is just, the grounds for a truly civil and democratic society are fundamentally undermined. Without such a general commitment, ideas, arguments, and engagement no longer matter; instead, what matters is strictly how power—in its various forms—can be used coercively to advance one's own selfish and partisan interests. Conviction and the yearning for transcendent principles are indeed vital in a democratic culture.

Hunter's model departs from Darsey's, though, in its insistence on *humility* as well as *conviction* in public discourse. In *Culture Wars*, this notion of humility in public discourse is strongly implied in Hunter's admonition to public advocates that they recognize "the 'sacred' within different moral communities," and that they also recognize "the inherent weaknesses, even dangers, in their own moral commitments."[57]

In his follow-up volume, *Before the Shooting Begins*, Hunter makes this notion of humility—or "modesty," as he calls it—more explicit. According to Hunter, an important underlying feature of the bellicose public discourse marking the "culture wars" is a "perfectionism" akin to romantic notions of Puritan theocracy, an "underlying conviction that all institutions, and especially the state, can and should embody an idealized vision of social life in full historical measure."[58] This perfectionism, further, is not limited to religious or "orthodox" advocates, but broadly underlies all culture warfare rhetoric; as Hunter puts it, "Democrats, independents, and Republicans; conservatives, libertarians, and liberals; religionists and secularists—we all want America to be 'a city upon a hill.'"[59]

The problem with this "underlying utopianism," though, is that it easily leads to a practical ethics in which the ends justify the means, which then makes coercion or even violence both more acceptable and more rational. "Caught in the logic of this ethical perfectionism," Hunter declares, "it is easy to see how it is that liberals eventually become quite illiberal, Christians eventually act in quite un-Christian ways, humanists eventually behave inhumanely, conservatives eventually become insensitive to the traditions they espouse, champions of tolerance become intolerant, and so on."[60]

Hunter's call, therefore, is for "modesty" concerning political goals. He explains:

> For one, this means a recognition that America will never really be a city upon a hill, and if it is, it will be by necessity a city whose walls are crumbling and always in need of repair; America will never be a beacon, except one that is not so bright and that is periodically prone to go out. Modesty, then, means a recognition that America will always be flawed. For Christians and many Jews, this is not compromise but a frank recognition that the world will always be marred by sin, and that the believer's true citizenship is in heaven. For the secular humanist, this is not compromise but an honest

(perhaps even scientific) appreciation for the inherently frail nature of the human condition, and the fact that human progress is an extraordinarily long-term commitment."[61]

Hunter, then, has put forward a model of public dialogue that productively balances both conviction and humility. "[W]ithout abandoning one's ideals, the credo changes. No longer is it 'today, we will remake the world'; rather, it is 'today, we will try to make the world just a little bit better.'"[62]

While Darsey's model accounts well for the need for conviction in public dialogue, it does not account well for the reality of significant, even intractable moral difference in a pluralistic society. Without a clear and compelling sense of how to handle these sorts of differences in a way that respects convictions and respects the dignity of human beings who disagree, it seems too easy for prophets to become crusaders that employ coercion and perhaps violence in the name of righteousness. In this way, Darsey's model is significantly undertheorized.

Conclusion

"Fundamentalists," states anthropologist Susan Friend Harding, "do not simply *believe*, they *know*, that the Bible is true and is still coming true." "There is no gap," she continues, "between story and event, between Bible-based language and reality. Or, more accurately, like biblical realists before the coming of modernity, modern Bible believers effectively and perpetually close the gap and so generate a world in which their faith is obviously true."[63] It is such a lack of awareness of the complex relationship between language and reality that so accurately characterizes the rhetoric of Operation Rescue described in this chapter. The activists of Operation Rescue perceive biblical truth—and truth more generally—as transparent, clear, and self-evident. On the basis of this general view of truth, the public advocacy of Operation Rescue—in presenting visions of the public as both virtuous and depraved, as both uninformed and complicitous—presents a more unified vision of a public that is passive and lacking in agency. The public does not interpret. The public does not actively weigh truth claims and interpretations, making thoughtful and critical evaluations. The public has only to *respond*. The truth, in essence, is there: take it or leave it.

This underlying and unflattering view of the public helps to explain how the advocates of Operation Rescue might fail to make compelling rhetorical choices with the very people they were trying to persuade, as well as how the advocates of Operation Rescue might fail to respond well to the rhetorical choices of its adversaries. Making good choices in these matters requires a careful and thoughtful appreciation of the context(s) in which public persuasion occurs, as well as a careful and thoughtful appreciation of the relevant audience(s) whose adherence is necessary for success. Unfortunately, Operation Rescue's notions of truth and persuasion rendered such concerns unnecessary or, perhaps more accurately, defined such concerns out of existence entirely.

The rhetoric of Operation Rescue examined in this chapter, moreover, illumines more fundamental issues regarding notions of public persuasion and social change that emphasize conviction and "prophetic" discourse. The example of Operation Rescue, unfortunately, shows the enactment of prophetic rhetoric that lacks both broad resonance and the possibility for humble self-reflection. In short, it can be said that unlike the activists of the gay rights movement, whom Darsey has claimed have too little faith in their own righteousness, the activists of Operation Rescue had too much faith in theirs. This overconfidence is the core problem with radical rhetoric.

Notes

1. Richard Exley, address at June 5, 1992 Wichita "Summer of Love" (Operation Rescue) kickoff rally, *Wichita Summer of Love, Part I*, Christian American Family Life Association, 1992, videocassette.

2. Patrick Mahoney, address at June 6, 1992 Wichita "Summer of Love" (Operation Rescue) tent rally, *Wichita Summer of Love, Part II*, Christian American Family Life Association, 1992, videocassette.

3. Exley, *Wichita Summer of Love, Part I*.

4. Joseph Scheidler, address at July 11, 1992 Wichita "Summer of Love" (Operation Rescue) tent rally, *Wichita Summer of Love, Part III*, Christian American Family Life Association, 1992, videocassette.

5. James Davison Hunter, *Culture Wars: The Struggle to Define America* (New York: Basic Books, 1991).

6. Hunter defines *orthodoxy* as "the commitment on the part of adherents to external, definable, and transcendent authority," and *progressivism* as "the tendency to resymbolize historic faiths according to the prevailing assumptions of contemporary life." See Hunter, *Culture Wars*, 44–45.

7. Ibid., 146–48, 152.

8. Hunter develops his conception of "substantive democracy" (as opposed to the prevailing conception of "shallow democracy") in *Before the Shooting Begins: Searching for Democracy in America's Culture War* (New York: Free Press, 1994), 215–44.

9. James Darsey, *The Prophetic Tradition and Radical Rhetoric in America* (New York: New York University Press, 1997).

10. Ibid., x.
11. Ibid.
12. Ibid., 7.
13. Ibid., x.
14. Ibid., 176.
15. Ibid., 184.
16. Ibid., 206.
17. Hunter, *Culture Wars*, 307.
18. Ibid., 318.
19. Ibid., 320–22.
20. Darsey, *The Prophetic Tradition and Radical Rhetoric in America*, 209, 210.
21. Edwin Black, "The Second Persona," *Quarterly Journal of Speech* 56 (1970): 109–19.
22. Exley, *Wichita Summer of Love, Part I*.
23. Ibid.
24. Scheidler, *Wichita Summer of Love, Part III*.
25. Ibid.
26. Exley, *Wichita Summer of Love, Part I*.
27. Ibid.
28. Scheidler, *Wichita Summer of Love, Part III*.
29. Norman Weslin, address at July 11, 1992 Wichita "Summer of Love" (Operation Rescue) tent rally, *Wichita Summer of Love, Part I*.
30. Scheidler, *Wichita Summer of Love, Part III*.
31. Ibid.
32. Exley, *Wichita Summer of Love, Part I*.
33. Ibid.
34. Ibid.
35. Patrick Mahoney, address at June 5, 1992 Wichita "Summer of Love" (Operation Rescue) tent rally, *Wichita Summer of Love, Part I*, Christian American Family Life Association, 1992, video cassette.
36. Ibid.
37. Randall A. Terry, *Operation Rescue* (Springdale, Pa.: Whitaker House, 1988), 178.
38. Ibid., 27.
39. Terry, quoted in Judy Lundstrom Thomas, "Terry and His Cause Allow No Neutrality," *Wichita Eagle*, August 25, 1991, VUTEXT database, document 238112, 2.
40. Mark Belz, *Suffer the Little Children: Christians, Abortion, and Civil Disobedience* (Westchester, Ill.: Crossway Books, 1989), 30.
41. Scheidler, *Wichita Summer of Love, Part III*.
42. Celeste Michelle Condit, *Decoding Abortion Rhetoric: Communicating Social Change* (Urbana: University of Illinois Press, 1990), 82–83.
43. Ibid., 85.
44. Ibid., 85–87.
45. Scheidler, *Wichita Summer of Love, Part III*.
46. Mahoney, *Wichita Summer of Love, Part I*.
47. Mahoney, *Wichita Summer of Love, Part II*.
48. For a distinction between the "priestly" and "prophetic" rhetorical stances, see Kenneth Burke, *Permanence and Change: An Anatomy of Purpose*, 3rd ed. (Berkeley: University of California Press, 1984), 179–80.

49. Darsey, *The Prophetic Tradition and Radical Rhetoric in America*, 202.
50. Ibid., 16.
51. Stephen L. Carter, *God's Name in Vain: The Wrongs and Rights of Religion in Politics* (New York: Basic Books, 2000), 28.
52. Ibid., 30.
53. Frederick M. Dolan and Thomas L. Dumm, "Introduction: Inventing America," in *Rhetorical Republic: Governing Representations in American Politics*, ed. Frederick M. Dolan and Thomas L. Dumm (Amherst: University of Massachusetts Press, 1993), 6.
54. For a discussion of the notion of "grounding text," as used in apocalyptic rhetoric, see Barry Brummett, *Contemporary Apocalyptic Rhetoric* (New York: Praeger, 1991), 87–120.
55. Mark A. Noll, "The Image of the United States as a Biblical Nation," in *The Bible in America: Essays in Cultural History*, ed. Nathan O. Hatch and Mark A. Noll (New York: Oxford University Press, 1982), 51.
56. Hunter, *Culture Wars*, 321–22.
57. Ibid., 322.
58. Hunter, *Before the Shooting Begins*, 229.
59. Ibid.
60. Ibid., 230.
61. Ibid.
62. Ibid., 231.
63. Susan Friend Harding, *The Book of Jerry Falwell: Fundamentalist Language and Politics* (Princeton, N.J.: Princeton University Press, 2000), 272.

9

OPERATION RESCUE'S BITTER RHETORICAL HARVEST

Pro-Choice Vocabulary as Public Lexicon in the 1993 United States Senate Hearing on the Freedom of Access to Clinic Entrances Act

> *The FACE [Freedom of Access to Clinic Entrances] Act raises the stakes in abortion protest, muting by self-censorship America's prophetic voices of protest. To prevent this tragedy, the law must be challenged in courts until free speech is vindicated or Congress realizes what it hath wrought.*
> —Steven T. McFarland, director of the Center for Law and Religious Freedom, writing for *Christianity Today*[1]

"He shot two people in the head," said Bruce Barrett, son of a slain clinic escort. "It was cowardly and done because he thinks he has the right to interpret our lives and our relationships with God. I hope [the sentence] sends a clear message to others so they don't pull any triggers."[2] Barrett was referring to ex-Presbyterian minister Paul J. Hill, a pro-life activist who had long advocated and eventually used deadly force to stop abortions from taking place. His July 1994 crime represented the second murder incident firmly linked to abortion-related protest, but it was also seen as an alarming new trend in abortion-related violence. Between the March 1993 shooting death of Dr. David Gunn and Hill's crime, Dr. George Tiller was shot and injured in his car, and Dr. George Patterson, who owned four abortion clinics, was found dead of a gunshot wound.[3]

As noted in the first chapter of this book, the perceived escalation in abortion-related violence prompted new government action. A January 1994 U.S. Supreme Court ruling, for instance, permitted the application of the federal Racketeer Influenced and Corrupt Organizations (RICO) law to abortion protest. This application of the RICO law enables abortion clinic owners, in applicable cases, to collect triple damages from pro-life social protesters in civil lawsuits.

A critical turning point for Operation Rescue—and for pro-life social protest more generally—occurred just a few months later. In May 1994 President Clinton signed into law the Freedom of Access to Clinic Entrances (FACE) Act. This law renders a wide variety of pro-life social protest tactics, including blocking an entrance to an abortion clinic, federal crimes punishable by up to one year in prison and a fine of up to $10,000 for first offenses.[4] Steven T. McFarland observes that "[t]he shooting of abortionists in Florida and Kansas provided the necessary political cover for a far more ambitious project to silence all but the bravest in the pro-life movement."[5] Noting that the new law "promises severe penalties and civil penalties and civil liability judgments against anyone who (by force, threat of force, or physical obstruction) 'intentionally injures, intimidates, or interferes' with someone obtaining or providing an abortion," McFarland argues that the law permits its own application to an unduly "broad array of situations far removed from its alleged focus" of preventing violence. "Just about anything a pro-life protester might do on a sidewalk outside an abortion clinic," he exclaims, "could be construed as violating the act. Carrying a sign, trying to talk to a would-be patient or clinic worker, or even kneeling or pausing for prayer could 'interfere' by 'physical obstruction.'" "Similarly," he continues, "the very sight of protest is inherently intimidating for some. If the presence of peaceful demonstrators is emotionally disturbing to a patient outside the clinic, her mental distress could be sufficient 'intentional injury' on which to sue the protesters under the act."[6] A *Commonweal* editorial writer, observing that the FACE Act "highlights the dangers to liberty courted by the unrestrained political ambition the abortion question generates," is even more blunt: "The bill's disregard for constitutional guarantees of free speech and assembly should make every prochoice [sic] civil libertarian blush."[7]

This commentary suggests that there are considerable implications of this law on social protest and on constitutional free speech rights. Unlike the sit-ins and other acts of non-violent civil disobedience characteristic of the 1960s civil rights movement, similar acts of nonviolent civil disobedience protesting legalized abortion, as well as peaceful protest within normal legal dictates, would be subject to disproportionately severe federal criminal and civil penalties.[8] A *Washington Post* editorial reflected sensitivity to this danger. While freedom of access to abortion clinics must be maintained, in the editorial writer's view, "so must the constitutional rights of peaceful protesters, no matter how unpopular their cause." "Lawmakers with any concern for civil liberties," the writer concludes, "will proceed carefully in this area."[9]

Despite these concerns, the FACE Act received strong approval from the Senate Labor and Human Services Committee and was speedily enacted into law. In this chapter, I build upon the analysis of the previous two chapters by offering a rhetorical explanation of how these concerns failed to hinder or even temper the Act's appeal. My overall claim is that the public vocabulary with respect to the abortion issue has become dominated by *pro-choice* terms. These terms include the articulation of images and characterizations that delegitimize Operation Rescue and the pro-life movement more generally.

Chapter 7 explores how this particular lexicon of terms was articulated during Operation Rescue's 1988 "Siege of Atlanta" and 1991 "Summer of Mercy" campaigns. In this chapter, I explore how this delegitimizing lexicon was firmly ensconced in the public vocabulary used by the Senators as they debated the merits of the FACE Act. The ensconcement of such a lexicon in the public vocabulary does much, in my view, to explain why such an anti-protest measure would be passed specifically with respect to pro-life social protest, yet not with respect to similar social protest *forms* employed with respect to other issues and causes (e.g., labor, environment, and so on).

In this chapter, I proceed first by calling attention again to delegitimizing images of pro-life activists and pro-life social protest, which were articulated more vigorously following Dr. Gunn's death in 1993. From there, I move to an analysis of the Senate hearing itself, showing how the maintenance of these images, and consequently the perceived inherent public utility of the FACE Act, both legitimized the Act and delegitimized any meaningful critique of the Act.

Angling toward the FACE Act: Delegitimizing Images of Pro-Life Activists

In chapter 7, I develop in some detail the delegitimizing vocabulary that began to emerge in conjunction with Operation Rescue protests. In such a vocabulary, Operation Rescue activists—and, to some extent, pro-life activists in general—are seen as dissimilar to civil rights activists, as fanatical, and as violent.

Following the shooting of Dr. Gunn, many were quick to articulate the same delegitimizing images more generally with respect to pro-life activists and pro-life social protest. Writing for the *Washington Post*, Judy Mann declared that this "cold-blooded killing" brought to a head "the campaign of terrorism against these clinics."[10] Writing for the same newspaper less than two weeks later, U.S. Representative Constance A. Morella added parallels with racism. "They once came in the night," she declared, "wearing white hooded robes and brandishing fiery crosses, proclaiming that God was pro-white and on their side. Now they come in the morning, wearing suits and carrying incendiary posters, claiming that God is pro-life and on their side." To this characterization of racism and intolerance, Morella then added menace and fanaticism. "The election of a pro-choice president, the repeated refusals of the Supreme Court to strike down a woman's fundamental right to choose and the likely passage of the Freedom of Choice Act," she wrote, "have left antiabortion fanatics desperate and dangerous. Such fanatics should not be allowed to prevail."[11]

As seen in chapter 6, others went even further in suggesting that the rhetoric of the pro-life movement inherently promotes violence. During a CNN talk show on the topic of abortion-related violence, Feminist Majority Foundation president Eleanor Smeal argued that there is little difference between those pro-life activists who support violence and those who do not. "They both believe in a religious tyranny," she declared. "They are both talking about Christianity in a very rigid way, as if there's only one form of Christianity. . . . They have one way, and it's their way. And they are self-righteous. And, in my opinion, both are creating a climate that is causing people to be self-righteously harmful to others."[12] *New York Times* columnist Anthony Lewis, as seen in chapter 6, framed this connection between pro-life rhetoric and violence quite explicitly with his declaration that "[t]he hysterical rhetoric of the anti-abortion movement in this country is an invitation to violence."[13]

In sum, the pro-choice forces put forward a distinct and delegitimizing characterization of the pro-life movement. The pro-life movement, according to this perspective, is composed of religiously intolerant, zealous, terroristic, racist, sexist, violent, single-minded fanatics who have respect neither for democracy nor for the democratic process. They are characterized as, in Lewis's words, a "menace to civilized life."[14]

A closer look at the Senate hearing on the FACE Act provides a good illustration of the incorporation of these pro-choice terms into the public vocabulary. The use of these terms as the sanctioned symbolic tokens in this instance of public dialogue, as seen below, worked well to advance the case for passage of the Act while at the same time squelching legitimate critique of the Act.

The May 12, 1993, Senate Hearing

The one-day hearing took place before the Senate Labor and Human Resources committee. The hearing opened with a statement from the committee chairman, Senator Edward Kennedy, who described the purpose of the legislation. The prepared statements of Senators Harkin, Mikulski, and Pell also voiced support for the legislation. Also voicing support was Attorney General Janet Reno, who gave a prepared statement and then responded to questions.

The hearing then moved to the statements of Senators Kassebaum, Thurmond, Hatch, and Durenberger, who all expressed concern with the draft of the legislation under consideration. These statements were interspersed with interactions with Reno and the various Senators on the committee. Various witnesses were then called to present testimony: Constitutional experts as well as certain activists having a legitimate stake in the success or failure of the legislation. The testimony was also augmented by question-and-answer periods between the witnesses and the committee.

Senator Kennedy's opening statement did much to frame the debate in terms of the delegitimizing vocabulary under discussion. After calling the hearing to order, Kennedy immediately went to work in characterizing both the problem and those causing it. "Our hearing this morning," said Kennedy, "deals with the serious problem of access to medical clinics providing reproductive health services, including abortions. Across the country anti-abortion violence and intimidation are on the rise. Clinics are assaulted with human blockades and invasions. They are bombed, vandalized, and sometimes burned to the ground. The doctors and staff who work there and their families are assaulted and threatened."[15] Kennedy then contrasted the nature of the protest with the nature of the matter being protested. "Every woman in America," he declared, "has a constitutional right to decide for herself whether or not to terminate her pregnancy, and that fundamental right deserves the full protection of Federal, State, and local law." However, he continued, this "right" is being thwarted by a "nationwide campaign" of "violence."[16]

This depiction of the pro-life movement, at the hearing's beginning, displays marked similarity to the depiction offered by Kate Michelman and the Planned Parenthood organization, both established pro-choice partisans. Other Senators echoed this partisan depiction. Senator Harkin, while admitting his shock over "the assassination of Dr. David Gunn by antiabortion extremists," declared that this event "is only an escalation of the level of violence by radical anti-choice groups" opposed to "the rights of Americans . . . the fundamental right to privacy, and the right to choose." He further exhorted that "[t]his Congress should not stand idly by, while a determined, extreme minority uses intimidation, violence, and harassment to impose their will on women."[17] Senator Mikulski commented that "[w]hat we see every day is that terrorism, harassment, vandalism, and violence are taking place in the very place where people come to seek medical treatment and medical advice." While noting that she has "respect" for "people who have differing views," she also stated that "we should never block the barriers [sic] to providing health care."[18] Senator Pell stated his belief "that crime cannot masquerade as free speech or free expression," and that "people have a right to live their lives free of the fear, intimidation, and violence that has resulted in death, arson, stalking, and other heinous crimes against consumers and providers of many medical clinics."[19]

From the hearing's beginning, then, a partisan vision of abortion social protest was established. The very subject matter being disputed, legalized abortion, was cast in clear terms that place it beyond the province of debate. Legal abortion is described with approving and culturally powerful terms that include *choice, privacy, medical clinics,* and *health care.* In contrast, pro-life social protest is cast as essentially intimidating, terroristic, violent, and heinous.

Indeed, Janet Reno's statement went further than just validating this particular interpretive frame regarding the abortion controversy and pro-life social protest; it also set up the FACE Act as a clear solution to the problem. Reno summarized that "Federal legislation is necessary because the problem is national in scope, local law enforcement has been unable to deal effectively with it, and existing Federal law is inadequate to provide a complete response."[20] After describing the specific types of conduct prohibited by the Act—"(1) the use of force; (2) threats of force; (3) physical obstruction to injure, intimidate, or interfere with an individual seeking access to abortion services; and (4) destruction of the property of medical facilities"[21]—Reno explained the necessity of more severe civil and criminal penalties. "Some opponents of the right to choose," she expounded, "have escalated the level of their opposition in recent years to violent interference. They have demonstrated a willingness to break the law and to defy court injunctions." "Unfortunately," then, "criminal sanctions, including imprisonment, appear necessary to deter and punish unlawful conduct, as well as simply to incapacitate some of the more willful and persistent violators."[22]

This particular interpretive frame was also reinforced in the statements and responses of witnesses called to testify in support of the legislation. Those of Dr. Pablo Rodriguez, medical director of Planned Parenthood of Providence (Rhode Island), are the most exemplary. Characterizing his reason for attending the hearing as "shar[ing] ... my experiences as a physician who performs abortions, and as a father of two young children, ages 2 and 4,"[23] he related a number of narratives suggesting the malevolence of pro-life activists. "The day Dr. Gunn was shot," Rodriguez began one narrative, "I knew my life would irrevocably change. One week after his death, as I was driving my mother to the bus station, I realized that my car was steering poorly. Once I had dropped her off, I examined my tires and found that there were 45 nails deeply embedded in them—a fortunate finding considering that I was driving over 50 miles an hour on the highway. That evening when I returned home, still unaware of the location of this act of vandalism, my wife painfully discovered, with her foot, that my driveway was booby-trapped with roofing nails cleverly buried under the snow. An image of my young children running and skinning their knees on that same section of driveway has filled my heart with a fear that until this day I have not been able to shake off."[24]

Rodriguez then cemented the vision of his narrative by referring more directly to pro-life activists. "Well, I have small children," he continued, "and I can tell you that the hardest day of my life was the day that I had to explain to my son Kiko, now 4 years old, why someone put nails across the driveway for his mom and dad to step on. I also had to explain to him that someday he may hear bad people saying terrible things about his dad, and that we were not safe in our home because these bad people do not like the way his dad helps patients.... For Kiko Rodriguez, the end of innocence was forced upon him by these very 'responsible' people that claim to protect life."[25]

The question-and-answer period with Rodriguez then served, in accordance with the meanings of the prevailing frame, to contrast the motives of those who support abortion with those who protest it. Asked by Senator Kennedy why he continues to perform abortions, Rodriguez responded that although he is sometimes "overcome by fear that something might happen to me," he believes in the "constitutional right" of his patients. "I find myself as an instrument of the Constitution," he declared, "and as long as abortion is legal in this country and as long as I have a license to practice obstetrics and gynecology, I will continue to perform my duty as I was trained to do."[26] Again, the prevailing frame of interpretation was reinforced and personalized in Rodriguez's testimony. The danger created by these pro-life "terrorists" must be stopped; "helping patients" obtain "medical care" must be preserved. These two unstated propositions served as a powerful implicit argument for the need for federal legislation such as the FACE Act.

Challenges to this prevailing frame, as well as challenges to the merits of the legislation being discussed, were articulated during the hearing. A closer look at these challenges and the responses to them, however, shows the ease with which they were stifled.

The testimony of Joan Appleton, a registered nurse who then worked for Pro-Life Action Ministries, provided a competing interpretive frame by which pro-life activists and pro-life social protest can be viewed. Having worked at the Commonwealth Women's Clinic in Falls Church, Virginia from November 1984 to November 1989, she observed that "[d]uring my time there, the clinic endured daily pro-life picketing and sidewalk counseling as well as at least five Operation Rescue-type operations. At no time [did the clinic] experience any violence whatsoever during these rescues." She directly challenged the testimony of a previous witness at the hearing. "My recollection of the October 1988, December 1988 and August 1989 rescues," she stated, "are far different from Mr. Lasso's. I was there for all of them.... The demonstrators... were peaceful. They placed themselves at the entrances to the clinic, and they either sang or prayed until they were removed by the police."[27]

Appleton went on to suggest that the violence in abortion-related protests are caused mainly by pro-choice activists, not pro-life activists. Regarding the aforementioned "rescues," she observed that "[o]ne of the reasons why there was no violence at the clinic during these rescues was the fact that we did not allow counter-demonstrators or abortion advocates to be present." "The only violence I have ever witnessed at an abortion clinic," she then related, "was this past summer, at a clinic in the St. Paul-Minneapolis area, where there was a large number of pro-abortion demonstrators, invited by the director of the clinic." "I witnessed elderly pro-lifers," she continued, "being mocked and spat upon by the demonstrators while these elderly people were praying. I witnessed two young boys being sexually solicited by an adult pro-choice male demonstrator."[28]

In a written statement, witness Nikolas T. Nikas elaborated on the kind of conduct perpetrated against pro-life social protesters. "Often," Nikas declared, "radical pro-abortion activists and sympathizers have physically prevented the pro-lifers from walking up and down a public sidewalk, sometimes with their bodies, sometimes with large signs.... Sometimes, the pro-lifers have actually been hit by these signs or physically pushed away." The witness also claimed that vulgarity and intimidation are common with pro-choice counter-demonstrators. "[I]f pro-lifers attempt to exercise their fundamental First Amendment rights to speak to women entering a clinic," he wrote, "pro-abortion advocates will scream in an attempt to drown out the pro-life message being conveyed. Other methods that are not uncommon are placing radios within inches of the ears of pro-lifers and turning the volume to the maximum level. Sometimes portable cassette tapes with obscene or vulgar words or phrases repeated over and over are placed next to the ears of pro-lifers (for example, F— you! F— you! F— you! over and over again)." Other typical acts by pro-choice counter-demonstrators, as Nikas detailed, are specifically designed to provoke pro-life activists. Such acts include blasphemous statements—"your God rapes virgins"—and mockingly "praying" with a pro-life activist using vulgar words.[29]

Thus the typical scene at an abortion clinic, as related by Appleton and Nikas, is quite different from that depicted in accordance with the meanings of the prevailing interpretive frame. Within this competing frame, clinic staff and prospective patients are not abused and intimidated by pro-life activists; rather, pro-life activists are abused and intimidated by clinic staff and pro-choice activists.

Given this perspective, the ambiguously worded FACE Act would most certainly be used by abortion clinics to tyrannize peaceful pro-life social protesters. "This bill," Appleton declared, "puts sidewalk counselors at risk of arrest and incarceration for 1 year, not to mention a criminal fine and a civil penalty of up to $15,000.... All of these penalties could deter any peaceful sidewalk counselor from exercising his or her first amendment right to offer alternatives to women." "There is no doubt in my mind whatsoever," she continued, "that any sidewalk counselor standing on a public sidewalk can and will be accused by clinic personnel of physically obstructing or impeding access to a clinic with the intent of eliminating all pro-lifers from the vicinity of the clinic. I would have done it during my tenure at the Commonwealth clinic, and I have no doubt in my mind whatsoever that most clinics will also do this."[30]

Given the articulation of the two competing frames of interpretation, one particular question assumes significance. How is the tension between the two frames negotiated? An important clue is found at the end of Appleton's testimony:

> The CHAIRMAN: Would you like to make a concluding statement?
> Ms. APPLETON: Certainly. I presently work for Pro-Life Action Ministries in St. Paul, MN, where I exercise my first amendment right to protest the killing of innocent children and the psychological and physical destruction of women. I cannot in conscience allow the continuation of the pro-abortion lies without speaking out.
> You may pass laws to punish me for following my conscience because it leads me in a different direction from yours, but you cannot dictate my conscience. You do not have that power. In other words, all the laws in the world are not going to make the pro-life movement go away. As long as there are abortions, there will be someone who cares enough about the sanctity of human life to try to stop the holocaust.
> Thank you.
> The CHAIRMAN: Thank you very much. That really isn't what the legislation is about, but thank you.[31]

The significance of this closing comment by Senator Kennedy is worth noting. At first glance it may seem like a rational response, given the fact that Appleton was talking about peaceful pro-life protest, which ostensibly is disconnected from the stated goals of the FACE Act—curtailing abortion-related violence.

Yet this is precisely the point. Understanding pro-life protesters as essentially peaceful, understanding pro-choice counter-demonstrators as essentially abusive and intimidating, and understanding abortion clinics as essentially motivated by financial profit, as Appleton does, leads one to make a frightening connection between the FACE Act and its implications for nonviolent pro-life protest.

Kennedy did not see this connection because of the interpretive frame by which he reads the "signs" of the abortion controversy. It is not possible to see or appreciate such a connection when the pro-life movement is already characterized not as an essentially peaceful attempt to effect social change on a morally questionable issue, but rather as an essentially coercive, intimidating, violent enterprise designed to oppress women by robbing them of a basic right.

The case for the prevalence of the second interpretation at the hearing can be made by examining the responses to a specific and important critique of the FACE Act—that the broad, ambiguous definitions of the Act's operating terms will result in the eclipse of the pro-life protesters' First Amendment rights of free speech and free expression. A number of Senators at the hearing raised this critique. Having noted that "[t]he task that now confronts Congress is how to achieve a balance" between the right "to protest peacefully" and "the constitutional rights of others," Senator Kassebaum stated that "although overshadowed by the escalating number of violent acts associated with abortion protests, most clinic protests are peaceful in nature." "I question," she continued, "whether the current Senate bill is written so broadly that it could be used to prevent legitimate, peaceful protests against abortion."[32] "[M]any are concerned," Senator Hatch declared, "that S. 636 [the FACE Act] singles out the pro-life message for harsh penalties that do not apply to identical conduct on behalf of other causes." "The specter of viewpoint discrimination," he continued, "raises the question whether S. 636 violates the first amendment." Hatch then elaborated this critique with regard to civil disobedience. "Others," he said, "have raised a concern as to how S. 636 would treat purely peaceful civil disobedience that draws on the tradition of Gandhi and Martin Luther King Jr. Some say that S. 636 would subject peaceful civil disobedience in support of the pro-life cause to special penalties that do not apply to peaceful civil disobedience in support of such causes as pacifism, civil rights, or environmentalism. It also has been pointed out that S. 636 draws no distinction between violent lawlessness and peaceful civil disobedience."[33]

With the critiques of the legislation articulated, there are a number of rhetorical phenomena that, in my view, indicate that a commonly held, unflattering, and delegitimizing understanding of pro-life social protest worked to silence meaningful critique of the legislation. The following exchange between Senators Kennedy and Coats is illustrative:

The CHAIRMAN: I understand [Senator Coats's] opposition to this legislation but we will have an opportunity—
Senator COATS: Mr. Chairman, I am not opposed to this legislation. I made that statement very, very clear early on. I do not want it on the record that I am opposed to this legislation.
The CHAIRMAN: OK.
Senator COATS: Does this Senator have the right to ask a question as to whether this legislation is perfectly drafted or whether there ought to be some changes in it? When the Attorney General of the United States comes before this committee, do I have the right to do that?

The CHAIRMAN: You have it, and you have the right to it, and—
Senator COATS: Well, don't say that this Senator is opposed to the legislation.

. . .

Senator COATS: Well, will you please clarify the record?
The CHAIRMAN: I will correct the record. I am glad that the Senator supports the legislation.[34]

The considerable effort Senator Coats made to ensure his official support of the Act in principle is quite noteworthy. It is a testament to the collective understanding at the hearing—and most likely to perceived public understanding—of the FACE Act as a corrective to pro-life violence. This understanding follows from an interpretive frame that, as previously noted, casts pro-life protesters favorably and legalized abortion unfavorably.

The initial statement by Kennedy may well have been a strategic move to stop Coats's continued critique of the legislation, as it appeared following a lengthy exchange between Coats and Reno regarding the vagueness of the Act. Regardless of Kennedy's intent, though, Coats's response indicates that even though he may have wished to pursue further his critique of the Act's broad and ambiguous language—language that gives rise to the Act's potential for silencing peaceful pro-life social protest—he was trapped by the symbolic meaning of the Act as a corrective to violence. By suggesting Coats's opposition to the FACE Act, then, Kennedy was also suggesting (by design or by default) that Coats tacitly condones abortion-related violence. This equation of anti-Act and pro-violence would not have been rhetorically compelling were it not for acceptance of delegitimizing images of pro-life social protest, which characterize the FACE Act as a response to violence and nothing more.

The prevalence of such images in the public vocabulary enabled Reno to sidestep the critiques made by Coats and others. She did this by repeatedly invoking the term "fundamental right" to describe the practice of abortion. "Some have asked," Reno said near the beginning of the hearing, "whether there is a need for Federal legislation. My unequivocal answer is yes. A woman's right to choose whether to terminate a pregnancy is *fundamental*."[35] "I think it is critical that we leave the ultimate search for truth in the marketplace of ideas clearly expressed," she acknowledged a bit later. "At the same time, I don't think protection should go to physical conduct that obstructs and threatens and physically interferes with somebody exercising a *fundamental* right."[36] This term was also employed in Reno's direct responses to Senators' queries:

Senator KASSEBAUM: [T]his particular legislation identifies one particular viewpoint . . . and makes it a criminal act, while ignoring what perhaps has happened or could happen in other protests [of different subject matters]. . . . Is there any way we could take into consideration in [*sic*] other types of protests?
Attorney General RENO: . . . [W]e have carefully reviewed this. . . . First of all, you have a very *fundamental* right at stake here.[37]

. . .

Senator COATS: . . . My question is whether that is an appropriate penalty for an attempt to interfere.
Attorney General RENO: My understanding is that the penalties provided here are consistent with the general penalty and sentencing structure provided for similar activity against the exercise of *fundamental* constitutional rights.[38]

The use of this term *fundamental* suggests that the question of legalized abortion is a given, beyond debate. Yet Reno's use of the term is unclear. Is the "right" to abortion as fundamental as the right to free expression? Is it as fundamental as the right to life? Though the term is ambiguously applied, it is nonetheless used as an implicit justification for both the wording of the Act and the steep penalties to be imposed for violation of the Act.

In addition to invoking the term *fundamental* to impair critique of the FACE Act, Reno was able to table the critiques "for further consideration." One example of this move can be seen with regard to Coats's critique that the penalties would be unduly severe and unfairly applied across different types of conduct (e.g., violent vs. nonviolent):

Senator COATS: I think that is something we ought to investigate further. . . . I would like to see the evidence that it is the same and applied equally across the board for a similar act. And again, I'm not talking about a penalty for an act of violence. I'm talking about a penalty for an attempt to interfere, and given the vagueness of the term, it seems to me that that creates some problems here with the legislation.
Attorney General RENO: We are always happy to review any situation such as that.[39]

Coats raised an important question here. If the Act is targeted to violent protests, then how does it penalize nonviolent acts of civil disobedience ("interfering")? Reno, however, was not responsive. Another example

OPERATION RESCUE'S BITTER RHETORICAL HARVEST

appears in an exchange between Reno and Senator Gregg, in which he was pressing her on the ambiguity of the "force" and "intimidation" language in the Act.

> Senator GREGG: Yes, but the threat of force, if it is threat of force to attempt to intimidate, you have a whole series of language there that basically leads to an incredibly subjective determination... but the fact is there is no standard. It becomes totally subjective, this term "intimidation" and "attempt to interfere."
> Attorney General RENO: Senator, for 15 years, I construed what legislature [sic] said, and then some judges disagreed with what I did, and there is a process by which language is construed. I think this language has precedent, which can help construe it, and I feel very comfortable with it.
> Senator GREGG: I recognize that, but I am saying there are some problems with that.[40]

Again, Reno is essentially non-responsive. A bit later, Gregg got the same treatment when asking about similar enforcement for pro-life establishments (e.g., crisis pregnancy centers, headquarters, and so on) as for abortion clinics:

> Senator GREGG: You couldn't probably make a mirror of this bill, applying it to pro-life, if I understand your argument for this bill.
> Attorney General RENO: I haven't made an argument with respect to pro-life facilities.
> Senator GREGG: But I understand under your theory that you probably couldn't; that you couldn't apply this bill.
> Attorney General RENO: I haven't addressed the issue.
> Senator GREGG: Well, could you?
> Attorney General RENO: I would be happy to review the legislation that you proposed, as I indicated to Senator Coats.
> Senator GREGG: Would you be willing to draft legislation that would apply, as this legislation draft is applied to the pro-life situation?
> Attorney General RENO: I am happy to review it, just as we reviewed what the Chairman has proposed.
> The CHAIRMAN: Of course, has there been a national threat on the issues of pro-life? I mean, that, I understand, is the fundamental aspect of it.[41]

Again, Reno's responses to Gregg's inquiry were not substantive. In this way, she avoided dealing with the critiques and questions about the FACE

Act by merely responding along the lines of "We'll form a special committee to investigate that question." Her ability to do this can be explained at least partially by the prevalent understanding, during the hearing, of pro-life social protest—an understanding promoted by the incorporation of the delegitimizing lexicon. Kennedy's comment, if anything, supports this interpretation. Because the prevalent interpretive frame clearly set up pro-life violence as so flagrant, so widespread, and so out of control as to demand immediate and decisive redress, questions dealing with the niceties and the by-products of redress did not hold much significance. Thus Reno's polite dismissal of such questioning and critique did little to hinder the Act's appeal.

Implications

On the month following the Labor committee's hearing on the FACE Act, the legislation received the near-overwhelming backing of the committee.[42] One *New York Times* editorial celebrated the Act's passage nearly a year later, noting that the law is "firmly within that tradition" of Congressional duty "to protect [constitutional] rights with statutory law." "The Supreme Court recognized in 1973," the editorial writer declared, "that the Constitution protects Americans' privacy and that American women have a constitutional right to make the private decision to have an abortion. People who prevent women's access to the clinics that perform them—or who stop doctors from performing them—are depriving them of that right." "Making this sort of vigilantism a Federal crime," the writer continued, "is an appropriate way to attack a nationwide terror campaign waged by organizations that regularly cross state lines solely to interfere with women seeking abortions."[43]

Less clear, however, is the protection of the right of people in the United States to express themselves and to engage in peaceful social protest. The danger, though somewhat implicit in the fundamental stand of the law—affirming abortion as a "right" beyond any sort of meaningful critique—is exacerbated by the ambiguous phrasing of key terms. This phrasing might allow the stifling of expression and protest as clearly protected as picketing and talking with people.

In this chapter I have suggested that delegitimizing terms and images of pro-life activists and pro-life social protest played a significant role in the conception and passage of the FACE law. Such images and terms, ensconced in the public vocabulary, frame pro-life activists' identities, motives, and actions in ways that deprive them of legitimacy to speak or to act. By framing them in this way, the manner in which to deal with them also becomes clear. One respects the rights of social protesters, even civilly disobedient ones. However, one gives terrorists no quarter.

The writer of the same *New York Times* editorial declared that "[t]his law upholds the civility of American society, affirming that this is a country where persuasion, not coercion, is used to change people's minds."[44] Although this view certainly resonates with an idealistic view of the American political tradition, it also seems somewhat inconsistent and naïve. Certain social movements in American history have had to resort to means outside the law to make their message understood and to effect change—change that most now consider good and important. Would the editorial writer or the authors of the FACE law condemn the Underground Railroad of the abolitionist movement? Would they condemn the sit-ins of the civil rights movement? Both involved breaking laws ("criminal" activity). Both involved disrespect for the "rights" of others (e.g., the right to own a slave, the right of control over one's property). And both the abolitionist movement and the civil rights movement had their violent "fanatics" (e.g., John Brown, the Black Panthers). Would they be prepared to impose the equivalent of a FACE law on either of these two movements, had they the opportunity?

I suspect not. Therein, one might suggest, lies the arguable toleration of "viewpoint discrimination" that runs counter to the First Amendment. From this same suspicion, though, follows a less politically motivated but equally important point about the profound significance of rhetoric in public dialogue. It is here, with the passage of legislation that arguably precipitated the demise of Operation Rescue as a social and political force, that we can observe the group's bitter rhetorical harvest in the public sphere.

Operation Rescue's failures to contest meaningfully the pro-choice delegitimizing vocabulary, as well as to engage the public adequately with its own rhetorical vocabulary, can in part be located in the problematic features of the group's rhetorical approach. By conceptualizing truth and persuasion as self-evident, by denying the public agency in negotiating claims moral or otherwise, and by ignoring the role of interpretation, Operation Rescue effectively laid the interpretive "tools" at the proverbial door of their adversaries. In short, Operation Rescue failed to contend rhetorically for the *meaning* of its acts, and that failure provides an at least partial explanation of why Operation Rescue has suffered so consistently at the hands of the established order. Sociologist Hugh Dalziel Duncan has provided an important reminder of this connection between rhetoric and meaning: "Words are not merely 'signs,'" he states, but also "names whose 'attachment' to events, objects, persons, institutions, status groups, classes, and indeed any great or small collectivity, soon tends to determine what we do with regard to the bearer of the name."[45]

Operation Rescue largely failed to heed the essence of this important observation. Because it essentially surrendered in the *rhetorical* struggle over how to name its acts, it should come as little surprise that Operation Rescue has lost its *legal* struggle with its pro-choice adversaries. The character of the Senate hearings on the FACE Act, and the Act's subsequent passage, bear witness to the truth of this observation.

Notes

1. Steven T. McFarland, "Pro-Lifers' New Legal Nightmare," *Christianity Today*, August 15, 1994, 19.
2. Barrett, quoted in Diego Ribadeneira, "Killer of Abortion Doctor Sentenced to Electric Chair," *Indianapolis Star*, December 7, 1994, A1, A2.
3. "Suspect in Shooting Praised Accused Killer," *Bryan-College Station (Texas) Eagle*, August 22, 1993, A14; Sue Anne Pressley, "Was Doctor's Killing an Abortion Protest?" *Houston Chronicle*, November 17, 1993, 4A.
4. Paul Richter, "Clinton Signs Law Banning Abortion Clinic Blockade," *Los Angeles Times*, May 27, 1994, A20.
5. McFarland, "Pro-Lifers' New Legal Nightmare," 18.
6. Ibid.
7. "Unreasonable Ambitions," *Commonweal*, April 23, 1993, 3.
8. I am conceptualizing the term *civil disobedience* broadly here. My use of this term includes the violation of laws on behalf of conscience, even when the laws being violated are not the same laws being protested.
9. "Abortion and Clinics: Access and Speech," *Washington Post*, March 29, 1993, A18.
10. Judy Mann, "Terrorism at the Clinics," *Washington Post*, March 12, 1993, E3.
11. Constance A. Morella, "Clinics under Siege," *Washington Post*, March 23, 1993, A21.
12. "Abortion and Violence," transcript of *Sonya Live*, narrated by Sonya Friedman, Cable News Network, March 8, 1994, 7.
13. Anthony Lewis, "What Is It about America that Nourishes Extremism over Abortion Issue?" *Houston Chronicle*, August 2, 1994, 21A.
14. Ibid.
15. U.S. Senate Committee on Labor and Human Resources, *The Freedom of Access to Clinic Entrances Act of 1993*, 103rd Cong., 1st sess., May 12, 1993, 1.
16. Ibid.
17. Ibid., 2.
18. Ibid., 6.
19. Ibid., 8.
20. Ibid., 10.

21. Ibid., 11.
22. Ibid., 12.
23. Ibid., 48.
24. Ibid., 56.
25. Ibid., 57.
26. Ibid., 84.
27. Ibid., 108.
28. Ibid.
29. Ibid., 139–40.
30. Ibid., 109.
31. Ibid.
32. Ibid., 23.
33. Ibid., 24.
34. Ibid., 30.
35. Ibid., 9, emphasis added.
36. Ibid., 21, emphasis added.
37. Ibid., 25, emphasis added.
38. Ibid., 28, emphasis added.
39. Ibid., 29.
40. Ibid., 33.
41. Ibid., 34.
42. Adam Clymer, "Panel Backs Bill to Protect Clinics," *New York Times*, June 24, 1993, A18.
43. "A Victory for Abortion Rights," *New York Times*, May 14, 1994, 20.
44. Ibid.
45. Hugh Dalziel Duncan, introduction to *Permanence and Change, An Anatomy of Purpose*, 3rd ed., by Kenneth Burke (Berkeley: University of California Press, 1984), xv.

PART FIVE

Conclusion

10

THE LESSONS OF OPERATION RESCUE

Christians must always guard against letting their zeal turn them into zealots.
—Cal Thomas and Ed Dobson[1]

Since you [Christians] call on a Father who judges each man's work impartially, live your lives as strangers here in reverent fear.
—1 Peter 1:17 (NIV)

"The question," writes evangelical lay leader Jim Wallis, "is not *whether* religious faith should make a political contribution, but *how*." "If religious values are to influence the public arena," he continued, "they ought to make our political discourse more honest, moral, civil, and spiritually sensitive, especially to those without the voice and power to be fairly represented." In this sense, unfortunately, the political participation of conservative evangelical and fundamentalist Christians—particularly as seen in the Christian Right—has been a resounding failure. "Since the 1980s," Wallis declares, "the powerful influence of the Religious Right has helped make our political debate even more divisive, polarized, and less sensitive to the poor and dispossessed."[2]

Although Wallis speaks from a political position somewhat to the left of many conservative evangelicals, his concerns have been echoed by more conservative critics of contemporary Christian political activism in the United States. As discussed at the outset of this book, writers like Cal Thomas and Ed Dobson, Richard John Neuhaus, Os Guinness, and Stephen Carter have in various ways advanced a position similar to Wallis's (and mine). To be sure, many conservative evangelical and fundamentalist Christians who engage in public dialogue and political activism do so with good motives—with desires to bear witness to the God whom they serve, to impact lives for the better, and to make positive differences in the communities of which they are a part. Yet, their participation as a whole has been deeply problematic. They have been largely ineffective in their public persuasive goals, as writers like Thomas and Dobson, as well as Guinness, have pointed out. They have done the Christian message a profound disservice by failing to represent many of the core values of their faith tradition, as writers like Guinness, Carter, and Neuhaus have claimed. Finally, as writers like James Davison Hunter, Carter,[3] Neuhaus, and Wallis have pointed out, they have contributed to the further degradation of the quality of public discourse, reinforcing the bellicose rhetorical habits and practices that mark the contemporary "culture war." As such, they are contributing to a climate of public discourse in which it is increasingly difficult to engage and deal with profound moral differences without resorting to coercion and violence.

I have striven to demonstrate in this book that Operation Rescue's significance, to a profound degree, lies in its reflection of these larger problems. To be sure, Operation Rescue is significant as a social protest phenomenon in the late 1980s and early 1990s. Operation Rescue is also significant in that—even while it failed in reaching its primary goals and disintegrated as an organization—it arguably helped to maintain and reinforce the tide of conservative Christian activism in the United States.[4] Yet the greater value of studying Operation Rescue lies in gleaning more insight concerning how to diagnose more properly the glaring and discomforting problems in the relationships among religion, politics, and public dialogue in America.

This significance of Operation Rescue stems from its significance as an exemplar of the relationship between rhetoric and religious faith, particularly within the conservative evangelical and fundamentalist Christian faith traditions in the United States. Starting from the foundational notion of rhetoric as a generative, perspective-shaping force, the analyses of this book have explored the role of rhetoric in shaping particular understandings of religious faith—what it means, as well as how to live according to it faithfully and authentically. The analyses of this book have also explored how these particular understandings then shaped adherents' conceptions of how best to bear witness to that religious faith in public dialogue and political activism. In the particular case of Operation Rescue, this book has provided an account of how conservative evangelical and fundamentalist Christians *talk* about their faith, and how that specific talk has maintained and reinforced these larger problems regarding religion, politics, and public dialogue. The rhetoric of Operation Rescue, to put it another way, has done a profound disservice both to the Christian message and to society.

Operation Rescue's Representations of the Evangelical Faith

An important theme of this book is that the rhetoric of Operation Rescue has done a profound disservice to the evangelical Christian faith itself. As seen in chapter 3, there are recurring problematic features in the history of the evangelical faith tradition. These problematic features of anti-intellectualism and the impulse to hegemony do not represent the essence of this faith tradition; rather, they are part of the less noble and more human side of this faith tradition as it has been expressed rhetorically. Unfortunately, Operation Rescue built its rhetorical foundation by drawing upon the resources of these less noble features.

In so doing, the rhetoric of Operation Rescue tapped into the motivational power of the evangelical Christian faith while also misrepresenting that faith reductionistically. Chapters 4, 5, and 6 documents this rhetorical misrepresentation by showing how the rhetoric of Operation Rescue offers particular visions of history, of Christian obedience, of Bible interpretation, of the nature of truth and persuasion, and, ultimately, of the scope and character of the Christian faith.

In showing how the rhetoric of Operation Rescue represented the entirety of Christian faith as a holy war and as identifying with the "unborn" or "pre-born," the analysis in chapter 6 provides evidence for the relationship between rhetorical misrepresentation and violence. Kenneth Burke clearly recognized the risk inherent in this relationship. In a discussion on the relationship between metaphor and perspective, he observes that "characters possess *degrees of being* in proportion to the variety of perspectives from which they can with justice be perceived."[5] In this way, human beings have a much higher degree of being than plants, minerals, or inanimate objects because they can with justice be seen in so many different ways. To put it another way, human beings are complex enough, multifaceted enough, and sophisticated enough that representing them well in a perspective is difficult, even when that perspective is sophisticated and well rounded. Unfortunately, what happens all too often is that, particularly in perspectives that are oversimplistic and/or feature representations that are oversimplistic, human beings are represented as considerably—even dramatically—less than they are. Representing human beings, or at least certain types of human beings, in an oversimplistic way then facilitates a rationale for treating them in a manner considerably lower than their innate status as human beings deserves. Coercion or even violence employed against such beings can then be conceptualized as morally acceptable acts (i.e., it is good and right to do this to these beings) or as amoral acts (i.e., ethics and morality have no bearing on how these beings are treated, so their treatment can be evaluated on other grounds, such as its utility to achieve some other end).

In "Terministic Screens," Burke hints at this larger problem of rhetorical misrepresentation and dehumanization—and its connection with violence—in his discussion of *action* and *motion*.[6] As symbol-using beings, Burke claims, we have wills and can exert our wills in our environment, acting upon the world in which we live. Thus, we are capable of *action*. This stands in contrast with objects and beings being acted upon by their environment, which is more properly seen as *motion*. This distinction then leads to the explanation of this process of rhetorical misrepresentation as a portrayal of what should be rendered as action (e.g., human relations) as instead mere motion. "Often it is true," observes Burke, in calling attention to this rhetorical process, "that people can be feasibly reduced to terms of sheer motion."[7] As a particularly poignant example of this, Burke relates the process by which the German army captured a Belgian fortress during World War I. "The point," he states, "was simply this: The approach to the fortress was known to be mined. And the mines had to be exploded. So wave after wave of human flesh was sent forward, as conditioned cattle, to get blown up, until all the mines had been touched off. Then the next wave, or the next two or three waves thereafter, could take the fort."[8] The sheer carnage behind this military tactic was made possible through a rhetorical process by which soldiers were represented or conceptualized as considerably less than full human beings, and represented or conceptualized instead as motive objects, as disposable and expendable military assets.

The rhetoric of Operation Rescue suggests, then, that while there is not a direct, causal relationship between rhetoric and violence—as some have suggested—the rhetoric of reductionistic misrepresentation can help to create and reinforce attitudes in which the move to violence can be made more easily. So we should not harbor the mistaken belief that rhetoric deterministically transforms people into mindless purveyors of violence. But we should, however, be keenly concerned with how rhetoric shapes understandings of reality, motives, and the conceptualization of the "good life," particularly with respect to how obstacles to the vision are conceptualized. If adversaries or opponents are placed into a simplified and dualistic framework for dealing with reality, as they are in Operation Rescue's "holy war" representative theme, then the identity and motives of these adversaries are conceptualized in such a way as to render them less than fully human.

While the ability of rhetorical misrepresentation to create a more favorable climate for coercion and violence is perhaps the most important concern, it is certainly not the only one. The example of Operation Rescue also shows that rhetorical misrepresentation also functions to reinforce certain attitudes and expectations that not only increase the attraction of ineffective methods of public persuasion, but also help to make civility unattractive and incivility more attractive in publicly engaging people with significant moral differences.

Although writing from a theological position outside the boundaries of orthodox evangelical Christianity, Christopher Levan has illustrated well the more fundamental appeal of "fundamentalism," a mindset he has claimed encompasses self-identified fundamentalists as well as the Religious Right and conservative evangelicalism. To Levan, fundamentalism is a "psychological attitude" marked by an "unyielding determination to confer a transcendent ultimacy" on specific principles of eternal truth, as well as an "unwillingness to enter into any serious questioning of its own position." Further, the "self-assurance and undialectical flavor of religious fundamentalism . . . combines a demanding devotional life with simple rules, discourages debilitating anxiety, and offers, in return for spiritual obedience, a sense of enduring righteousness."[9] "In the face of so much ambiguity," Levan continues, pressing his point, "fundamentalism carries on the primitivism of revivalism in the adoration of uncomplicated ideas, self-reliance, plain talk, and moral living," yearning for "an older, better way of life, free of the doubts and uncertainties of the modern world."[10] One of the key features and attractions of fundamentalism, he went on to declare later, is "the reduction of life's complexity and ambiguity into a simple formula."[11]

Care must be taken to make sure that characterizations of fundamentalism are not themselves oversimplistic, unfairly unflattering, and potentially dehumanizing—as is potentially the case with Dallas Blanchard's "fundamentalist syndrome" and Eric Hoffer's "true believer."[12] Nonetheless, Levan's description of fundamentalism fits well with a perspective plagued by rhetorical misrepresentation. Simplicity and certainty are overwhelmingly prized. Good and evil must be clearly and easily identified. The purposes of life and the logic of history must be clear and easily ascertained. Ambiguity is abhorred. Tension and confusion are abhorred. Humility and the acknowledgment of limitations on human understanding and ability are not encouraged. The "mystery" of life and of a transcendent God is expunged. Doubt is erased. The Christian life becomes simple, and living it authentically becomes a matter of sheer will. Thinking is indeed "maniacal" in Chesterton's sense of the term.[13]

The example of Operation Rescue, as discussed in this book, shows how this problem is profoundly a *rhetorical* one, a problem that is reinforced and magnified in how conservative evangelical and fundamentalist Christians *talk* about what their faith is, what their faith means, and how to be faithful to it in how they live their lives, how they profess their faith publicly, and how they engage in social and political activism. Apart from the implications of this rhetorical misrepresentation for coercion and violence, this fundamental rhetorical problem also leads to faulty conceptions of their faith and their God, faulty conceptions about what goals can and should be achieved in temporal life, and faulty conceptions about the best means to employ to achieve those goals.

Seeing this problem as a profoundly rhetorical one fits well with evangelical historian Mark Noll's diagnosis of the political maladroitness of contemporary American evangelicals. Much, if not most, evangelical political engagement has been criticized by Noll as "anti-Christian" and "abandon[ing] Christ."[14] Much of the reason for this, according to Noll, is that evangelical political engagement emphasizes too strongly the role of Christ as "reigning King" and too thoroughly neglects the simultaneous and equally important role of Christ as "suffering Servant." Instead, a workable balance between these two roles is needed in conceptualizing both evangelical faith and evangelical politics—a distinctly *rhetorical* task. "Evangelical politics will be a Christian politics," he declares, "if we evangelicals follow the commanding Christ as he takes possession of the world, but it will be a fully Christian politics only if my fellow evangelicals and I recall the road to Calvary that the Lord Jesus took to win his place of command and never forget that the robes of the saints shine white only because they are washed in the blood of the Lamb."[15] "A proper Christian politics," then, "will display humility, a willingness to question one's own motives, and the expectation that reform of political vision will always be needed because even Christian politics is carried out by individuals who know they are still sinners, however glad they are to be sinners saved by grace."[16] These important features are glaringly lacking in the public discourse and political activism of conservative evangelicals and fundamentalists, then, in large part because of a rhetorical misrepresentation that prominently emphasizes certain features of their faith traditions and profoundly neglects other necessary and corrective features. Evangelicals do well to bring to bear the needed elements of truth, conviction, justice, and transcendence to the public sphere and to the political process. However, they also need to bring to bear humility, patience, compassion, long-suffering, respect for the dignity of other human beings, and recognition that the temporal world will always be marred by imperfection and sin. With the example of the rhetoric of Operation Rescue, it can be seen how *talk* about faith can reinforce these fundamental problems and make alternative, corrective thinking more difficult.

These problems with rhetorical misrepresentation of the evangelical Christian faith also help to make sense of the more specific problems with evangelical politics identified by other authors. As seen in chapter 1, Cal Thomas and Ed Dobson's critique of the Christian Right is grounded in its reduction of the *spiritual* (i.e., living out the Christian faith—both individually and communally—in the world) to the *political* (i.e., trying to effect specific changes in public policy on a narrow range of issues).

While bemoaning the lack of religious influence in American public life, Richard John Neuhaus has criticized the general contemporary approach to politics by conservative evangelical and fundamentalist Christians—which he refers to as the "religious new right"—as an unhelpful or even corrosive influence on American public life. A key aspect of the problem is vision, a deficient and simplistic understanding of the "big picture." The problem with the religious new right, declares Neuhaus, "is that there is no texture, no particularity, in their understanding of time and times.... History is flattened out, as it were."[17]

Evangelical writer Os Guinness has also grounded his critique of contemporary evangelical politics—which he has claimed is sectarian, partisan, mean-spirited, divisive, and inimical to the strengthening of democratic institutions—in a lack of vision. The evangelical Christian community, according to Guinness, lacks both "a public philosophy" and "any distinctively Christian thinking" in its approach to public dialogue and political activism.[18] As a result, politically active evangelicals have for the most part taken on the role of "cognitive bitter-enders." Cognitive bitter-enders, according to Guinness, are

> those who believe in a manner leading to contempt for the faith of others. When it comes to religion and politics, they so emphasize the logic of truth or of free exercise and integration that they refuse to be beguiled by civility, let alone surrender to relativism. Prizing truth instead of peace, they press everything and fight everything to the bitter end. By making absolutes even

where no absolutes exist, they achieve a ruthless, scorched-earth consistency, but at the expense of all civility.[19]

If it is true, as Guinness has claimed, that a constructive engagement with "the contentiousness of religion and politics" requires a "clear sense of perspective," a "healthy respect for the explosive power of religion in public life," and an ability to "grasp the complexity of the overlapping conflicts that make up . . . the ideological clash between fundamentalists and secularists,"[20] then the public discourse and political activism of conservative evangelical and fundamentalist Christians has not only failed but has made the problem noticeably worse. Observing that "[c]ivility is not an excuse for gutlessness or fence-sitting," Guinness claims that "when positions are chosen and stands made, these things must be undertaken in the best interests of all faiths and the nation at large if one or all of these is not to be the loser."[21] If this is indeed true, then the public discourse and political activism of conservative evangelical and fundamentalist Christians has in large measure not only failed but has made the problem noticeably worse.

The example of Operation Rescue, as suggested by the analyses of this book, has shown that rhetorical misrepresentation has not only encouraged a climate in which coercion and violence become more rational and more attractive, but has also encouraged and reinforced dysfunctional approaches to public dialogue and political activism. Thus, the contemporary problems at the intersection of American religion, American politics, and American public life are in large part *rhetorical* problems—problems rooted in how language and symbols are used to conceptualize both means and ends. Attention should be paid, then, not only to the specific rhetorical choices that advocates make as they try to make their voices heard and win others over to their visions, but also to the more subtle rhetorical choices that help advocates understand what their voices and visions are in the first place. This is one important lesson of the rhetoric of Operation Rescue.

Operation Rescue and Public Dialogue

The rhetoric of Operation Rescue, as shown in the analyses of this book, reveals not only how rhetoric can function more broadly to corrode the environment in which public discourse takes place—making incivility, naked partisanship, coercion, or even violence more rational and more attractive—but also how rhetoric can predispose advocates to make fundamentally ineffective choices in public persuasion. Operation Rescue's ultimate failure to achieve its goals, as described in the opening chapter, can also be seen in large measure as a consequence of its poor rhetorical choices.

As seen particularly in the previous chapter, stern government responses against "rescuing" as a form of pro-life social protest arose from a public understanding of an explicit, causal connection between this form of protest and violence. The equations in the public vocabulary between Operation Rescue activists (and, to a somewhat lesser extent, to pro-life activists more generally) and violence came about at least in part because of the success of the pro-choice movement in articulating these equations. Nonetheless, these unflattering and delegitimizing characterizations of pro-life activists and "rescuing" became ensconced in the public vocabulary, at least in part, because of Operation Rescue's public failures from a rhetorical point of view.

Operation Rescue's failure to contend *rhetorically* for the meaning of abortion, and for the characterizations of its activists and its acts, can be explained in part by its activists' particular understandings of truth and persuasion. As seen in chapter 5, the rhetoric of Operation Rescue encourages a view of truth—foundationally, truth gleaned from the Bible—as plain, self-evident, and not requiring any sort of interpretation. And as truth generally is seen as plain and self-evident, so also is the proclamation of it. This misunderstanding of persuasion corresponds well with the rhetorical construction of the public as passive, as documented in chapter 8. In overemphasizing the persuasive power of the context-less "act" and the "agency" of the protesters, the rhetoric of Operation Rescue either assumes a public audience that simply does not exist, or it essentially ignores the public audience altogether. Ultimately, the rhetoric of Operation Rescue spoke to few apart from the already committed.

This failure of the rhetoric of Operation Rescue to accord agency to the public audience ultimately entailed more than just unsuccessful persuasion. In clinging to the notion of truth as self-evident, the activists of Operation Rescue allowed the pro-choice movement essentially unfettered rein to shape the public vocabulary with respect to the characterizations of Operation Rescue and the pro-life movement more generally. Chapter 7 traces the articulation of a consistent and delegitimizing vocabulary in the public sphere to characterize Operation Rescue. As chapter 9's analysis of the United States Senate deliberations on the FACE Act makes clear, this delegitimizing vocabulary was firmly ensconced in the public vocabulary used by Senators and other public officials as they deliberated over the suitability of the Act as a corrective to abortion-related violence. The common understandings of Operation Rescue activists and pro-life activists as intolerant, as violent, and as generally inimical to the democratic process, worked to constrain the voices of those skeptical of or opposed to the legislation. These common understandings also reinforced a characterization of the legislation strictly as a corrective to violence, effectively preempting considerations of how the legislation might affect nonviolent pro-life social protest, or how it might affect social protest more generally.

While I am not suggesting that the failure of Operation Rescue's efforts at public persuasion are exclusively responsible for its legal and political failures, I am suggesting that the group's rhetorical insensitivity certainly contributed to the public's generally negative understanding of it and of "rescuing" as a form of pro-life social protest. Consequently, when doctors performing abortions were being shot and killed, the general public made an easy connection between confrontational pro-life social protest, such as Operation Rescue's, and deadly violence. Paul Hill's 1994 shootings, state Risen and Thomas, "provided the coup de grâce to anti-abortion activism." "The press and public," they continue, "no longer accepted the arguments of moderate activists like new Operation Rescue leader Flip Benham who tried to distance themselves from the violence; tarred with a broad brush, Operation Rescue was now publicly perceived as little more than a violence prone cult. America's tolerance for clinic blockades and other forms of anti-abortion civil disobedience abruptly ended."[22]

The ineffectiveness of Operation Rescue's efforts at public persuasion also provides an important reminder with respect to issues of social protest and social change. In his classic study on social movements, communication scholar Robert S. Cathcart argues convincingly that confrontation is an essential feature of social movement rhetoric.[23] Yet, it might be easy to forget that there must be more than just confrontation in the pursuit of the "dialectical enjoinment in the moral arena" that Cathcart has argued is so necessary to a social movement's long-term success.[24] In order to secure long-term "changes in societal norms and values," communication scholars Charles J. Stewart, Craig Allen Smith, and Robert E. Denton, Jr., explain, movements "must transform perceptions of reality, prescribe and sell courses of action, mobilize the disaffected, and sustain the movement over time."[25] The offensive use or misuse of symbols that are involved in a rhetorical strategy of confrontation is necessary, especially at the beginning of a social movement or social movement campaign. However, it must be part of a long-term rhetorical engagement with the general public. As studies like rhetoric scholar Celeste Condit's and sociologist Suzanne Staggenborg's show,[26] the pro-choice movement has enjoyed considerable success in this long-term rhetorical engagement. However, the rhetorical choices of Operation Rescue undercut its own ability to function in this way.

Evangelical Religion, Politics, and Public Discourse: Toward a "Rhetorical" Corrective

The problems with the rhetoric of Operation Rescue are significant and worthy of sustained attention for a variety of reasons: for what they reveal about the need for audience adaptation and audience engagement, for what they reveal about the sheer power and importance of rhetoric in shaping perspective and in furnishing human beings with what Kenneth Burke called "equipment for living,"[27] for what they reveal about the constraints faced by conservative social protest rhetoric and radical rhetoric more generally, and for what they reveal about more fundamental problems with how public discourse functions in a democratic and pluralistic society. What has ultimately compelled me to study the rhetoric of Operation Rescue over the past ten years, though, is how the group mirrored the broader rhetorical habits of American conservative evangelical and fundamentalist Christians. I have been keenly interested in knowing more about what these deficient rhetorical habits are. Beyond this, I have been keenly interested in knowing more about how these deficient rhetorical habits have distorted evangelicals' ability to understand the complexity and transcendent meaning of their religious faith. I have been keenly interested in how these rhetorical habits have in many ways led evangelicals to bring to public life a grossly distorted and unattractive caricature of their faith tradition. Finally, I have been keenly interested in how these rhetorical habits have functioned in many ways—for publicly minded and politically minded evangelicals—to rationalize and encourage attitudes and behavior that are inconsistent with the values of their faith tradition, that corrodes the environment in which public discourse takes place, and even that emotionally and physically harms others.

All of this brings up the question of what is to be done. While a full elaboration of a corrective to these deficient rhetorical practices could well (and perhaps should) take up an entire book in its own right, I would like to close this study on Operation Rescue by offering some tentative musings about what I think such a corrective for conservative evangelical and fundamentalist Christians might look like. As a conservative evangelical Christian myself, and as someone who cares deeply about having a discursive environment in our social and political culture that maximizes our ability to handle pluralism and fundamental moral differences in productive, dignifying, and non-coercive ways, I find the articulation of such a corrective to have great appeal. I also believe, though, that such a corrective should be of considerable appeal to evangelicals and non-evangelicals alike.

For evangelicals, such a corrective would enable them to accomplish their purposes with greater efficacy. At the core of evangelical Christian culture is the conviction that Christians have a responsibility to share the truth they have found with the world, and to live life and engage in service to others in such a way as to represent well to the world what God is like. Political scientist J. Christopher Soper notes that evangelicals place considerable emphasis on "integrating religious beliefs and personal conduct" and on "activism in the world," which, according to Soper, "assumes a religious significance for evangelicals."[28] In defining evangelicalism, likewise, Noll points to "activism," or "a concern for sharing the faith," as one of its distinctive features.[29] Evangelicals Cal Thomas and Ed Dobson emphasize both the importance of public witness and cultural influence in their critique of evangelical approaches to political activism. "The faith about which Jesus spoke," they state, "was to shine like a light before men and women." In addition, according to Thomas and Dobson, the more general and "all-important mission" of evangelicals is "to change the world from the inside-out."[30]

There is evidence, however, that the American evangelical Christian community in these respects—representing their faith authentically and convincingly, as well as having a distinct and positive impact on the larger culture of which they are a part—has been markedly less than successful. One relatively recent sociological study has suggested that while contemporary American evangelicalism has been robust and thriving in the sense of nurturing a meaningful identity while also avoiding the problems of isolation and non-engagement, it has nonetheless had very limited effectiveness in achieving social change.[31] In addition, evangelicals have been significantly misunderstood by American social and cultural elites, as well as by mainstream non-evangelical culture. Noting that "American evangelicalism needs a good dose of demythologizing," sociologist Christian Smith observes that "American evangelicals remain one of the last social groups in the United States that people can speak disparagingly about in public and get away with it."[32] As I have suggested throughout this study of Operation Rescue, these problems exist in large part because of how evangelicals use rhetoric in problematic ways to conceptualize matters of faith, practice, and public participation. Presumably, using rhetoric in more holistic and healthy ways to conceptualize these things might help evangelicals to overcome these problems and represent their faith—to others and to the surrounding culture—more authentically.

For non-evangelicals (those who identify themselves as Christians but not as evangelicals, as well as those who do not identify with the Christian faith), a corrective to these deficient rhetorical practices of evangelicals will be of benefit by helping to strengthen and reinvigorate the quality of public discourse in a pluralistic, democratic society. In making tentative suggestions for the reform of evangelicals' rhetorical practices, I am starting with the premise that religious voices are good and necessary for a robust, vibrant, healthy, and productive public discourse.[33] This premise is argued for by a number of other authors, including Guinness, Neuhaus, and Carter. The utility of religious voices in public dialogue, these authors suggest in various ways, lies to a great extent in their largely unique abilities to critique dominant moral and value assumptions in culture and in society, to offer checks against the control of the state and the cultural status quo over fundamental meanings, to offer vision and transcendence, to call us—individually and collectively—to live according to the more noble aspect of our natures, and to call us to account when we fail to do so. The public discourse and political activism of American conservative evangelical and fundamentalist Christians, unfortunately, have for the most part taken the lower road of partisan cultural warfare, and has done so to the detriment of all. If it is true, as I have suggested in this study, that this debased state of evangelical public discourse and political activism is in large part a *rhetorical* problem, then a corrective to the rhetorical practices of evangelicals might do much to help them—in their public engagement with culture and in their political activism—realize the good and helpful role they can play in a democratic, pluralistic polity.

A substantial and productive reform of evangelicals' rhetorical practices, to my mind, would involve the following broad and interrelated imperatives. First, evangelicals need to *be more sensitive to audience and context*. Audience sensitivity is a basic theme in almost any public speaking course, yet most of the public persuasion by politically involved evangelicals—as with the public persuasion attempted by Operation Rescue—appears to speak to few apart from the already committed. Evangelicals need to learn to acknowledge the diverse ideas, values, experiences, and moral commitments held by those whom they seek to influence. More important, though, they need to engage these particulars in a charitable and sufficiently nuanced way, which is what sociologist James Davison Hunter was getting at with his imperative that those engaging in public dialogue recognize "the 'sacred' in different moral communities."[34] Moreover, evangelicals need to give more sustained attention to the credibility they have (or do not have) with those whom they are trying to influence, and they need to give more sustained attention to how they can build credibility in ways consistent with the values of their faith tradition.

Likewise, evangelicals need to be more sensitive to the cultural and historical contexts surrounding their public engagement and political activism. They need to be more attentive to the values and norms of popular culture. They also need to be more aware of the social, political, and religious history of their polity, and they need to be more reflective about their own history, which is both more complex and more relevant than I suspect they imagine.

Second, evangelicals need to *cultivate the life of the mind and critical thinking as values*. Care must be taken not to characterize evangelicals as wholly anti-intellectual, as some scholars have been tempted to do.[35] Nonetheless, the life of the mind and critical thinking as values have not been sufficiently cultivated within the evangelical Christian community, as scholars like Noll and theologians like Wells have insightfully pointed out.[36] This poses a specific problem for evangelicals in that this inattention goes fundamentally against the biblical imperative for Christians to love God with all of their minds. As Noll put it, "fidelity to Jesus Christ demands from evangelicals a more responsible intellectual existence than we have practiced throughout much of our history."[37] This inattention also poses a more general problem for evangelicals in that it facilitates the reification and rigidification of potentially flawed perspectives—as seen in the specific case of Paul Hill discussed in chapter 6—and makes the conceptualization of alternative perspectives considerably more difficult. This inattention to "responsible intellectual existence" on the part of evangelicals both reinforces and is reinforced by the problematic rhetorical practices examined in this book.

Third, evangelicals need to *cultivate a greater appreciation for humility as an overarching attitude*. "Intellectuals," states self-identified evangelical intellectual James Sire, "play with ideas, pun with their terminology, laugh at them. This may seem an odd characteristic to attribute to intellectuals. But if thinking persons do not have the distance from ideas that is necessary for humor, if they cannot laugh about what they think, they stand in grave danger of being ideologues. The ideologue's devotion to one central idea excludes any ability to see its potential flaws or any reasonable objections to it. The ideologue is a plague on intellectual life."[38]

Sire's point about ideas applies equally well to evangelicals' understandings of what their faith means, how to apply it to life's experiences, and how to use it to engage in public discourse and political activism. The notion of "humility" that Sire and I have in mind here goes beyond responses to particular situations, instead encompassing a broader attitudinal framework for life.

Theoretically speaking, Kenneth Burke described this sort of broad framework in terms of "comedy" and the "comic frame." In *Attitudes toward History*, Burke explicitly warned against the dangers of what he called the "tragic frame" for understanding and interpreting events and motives. "Tragedy," in Burke's view, stems from a natural tendency on the part of human beings to convert into immutable realities the metaphoric possibilities that give rise to perspective. Interpretations of reality, to put it another way, are regarded as realities not to be questioned.

In this book, Burke refers to this process in a number of different ways. "Bureaucratization of the imaginative," for instance, occurs when "[a]n imaginative possibility is . . . embodied in the realities of a social texture."[39] With such a process, however, comes the inevitable need for revision since, according to Burke, "human beings are not a perfect fit for *any* historic texture" and "because a given order must, in stressing certain emphases, neglect others."[40] As a perspective rigidifies, therefore, it becomes increasingly unable to adapt to the recalcitrance posed to it by the physical and social worlds, while at the same time becoming increasingly regarded by its adherents as not open to question. This rigidification of perspective and the temptation to adhere to reductionistic representations of reality—problems discussed more explicitly in chapter 6—are manifestations of the tragic frame. Such a frame generally promotes not cooperation, but victimage.[41]

Because Burke recognized the ultimate consequences of the tragic frame (particularly with the advent of nuclear weapons), he advocated "comedy" as a corrective to tragedy. He embraced the "comic frame" as an approach to symbols and to perspective because it maximizes flexibility and varied action in perspectives. It "enable[s] people *to be observers of themselves, while acting*," encouraging not "*passiveness*, but *maximum consciousness*."[42] The comic frame shifts the essence of hierarchical transgression from "crime" to "stupidity," in keeping with Burke's assertion that "[t]he progress of humane enlightenment can go no further than in picturing people not as *vicious*, but as *mistaken*."[43] In "lowering the stakes," as it were, the comic frame more easily allows for critique of a given perspective as well as the specific metaphors, attitudes, and motives falling under that perspective. What is called for, then, is for people and communities to hold their convictions, their understandings of reality, their interpretations of the acts and motives of others in a more tentative, self-reflective manner that exhibits an honest acknowledgment of human limitations.

Burke's theoretical admonitions fit well with the more context-specific admonitions of sociologist Robert Wuthnow. In Wuthnow's view, Christians need to remember their own fallenness in order to represent faithfully the truth they hold dear. "Throughout its history," he observes, "Christianity has recognized the dark side of human nature sufficiently that the need for a rule of law has been commonly acknowledged. One hoped for the salutary effects of personal salvation but knew that even professed Christians are subject to the same temptations as everyone else and that laws must be instituted to guard against these temptations."[44]

Such a view of humility, according to Wuthnow, stands in stark contrast to the increasingly common "brand of Christianity" that "attaches little significance to the reality of evil" in their lives, that "naively asserts the possibility of Christians leading happy and morally victorious lives," and that "more or less exempts Christians from having to abide by the same sorts of laws as everyone else."[45] Operation Rescue, in my judgment, exemplifies this errant brand of Christianity. As seen throughout this book, the rhetoric of Operation Rescue encourages for Christians just this sort of thinking about the Christian faith: unreflective confidence in the righteousness of what they are doing, unwillingness or inability to engage in significant dialogue with those who disagree, single-minded devotion to the perfectionist task of remaking the nation and perhaps even the world in their image. This is a vision of tragedy, not comedy. This is a vision of hubris, not humility. "Christians can be civil," Wuthnow declares, "but only if they recognize that their best values are subject to corruption."[46] As a whole, Operation Rescue activists were blinded to this recognition by symbolic tools of their own making, which helps to explain how their rhetoric has played a significant role in fostering incivility and even violence.

Humility is needed in greater measure in the evangelical Christian community, then, to help evangelicals to avoid the blindness that so afflicted the thinking of Operation Rescue activists, and to put their public engagement and political activism within a broader and more proper context. This sort of humility also needs to become a more central attitude behind all public discourse in a pluralistic, democratic polity, as implied particularly in the analyses of Hunter.[47] "Civil society can withstand greater diversity," observes Wuthnow, "as long as groups with different values and lifestyles are willing to engage each other in dialogue . . . being willing to give up some control over one's own claims to know the truth, subjecting them to self-evaluation and to the critical commentary of others."[48] The willingness to do this, particularly for those identifying themselves as Christians, should stem from the recognition that "[n]one of us sees with divine wisdom, but only through a glass darkly."[49]

The failure of evangelicals to bring this sort of contribution to the public sphere is considerably ironic, since in many ways the beliefs and values of their faith tradition uniquely suit them for this task. The Christian religion, as philosopher and religious studies scholar Winfried Corduan points out, gives a uniquely prominent role to the themes of human finitude and fallenness (while also preserving the profound value and dignity of human beings), redemption, and reconciliation with God and with others.[50] Claiming that the classic tradition of hymns captures particularly well what he has termed "evangelicalism at its best," Noll describes the distinctive aspects of the "relatively cohesive religious vision" in this diverse array of religious music. In this vision, he states, "[t]he holiness of God provided occasion for worship, but even more a standard that revealed human sinfulness, human guilt, and human need for a savior. At the heart of the evangelical hymnody was Jesus Christ, whose love offered to sinners mercy, forgiveness, and reconciliation with God. In this Savior redeemed sinners found new life in the Holy Spirit, as well as encouragement in that same Spirit to endure the brokenness, relieve the pain, and bind up the wounds of the world that the great evangelical hymn writers almost always depicted in strikingly realistic terms."[51] In addition, this vision emphasizes "a vision of human need inspired by the love of Jesus and devoted not to extrinsic social or political causes, but to the good of the ones being served,"[52] and it emphasizes the strength and value for evangelicals of continually and realistically coming to terms with their own shortcomings and failings. Though evangelicals "have acted at our best only inconsistently," observes Noll, "there is nothing in that fact contradicting evangelical conviction. In fact, for evangelicals to confess how far short they have fallen of the divine beauty that they claim to honor is a very important first step toward realizing evangelicalism at its best."[53] So for evangelicals, then, emphasizing the attitude of humility—in how they conceptualize their faith and how to live according to it—is not a compromise of their faith but actually a profound affirmation of it.

Fourth, evangelicals need to *be more fully cognizant of the fundamental power of rhetoric in its generative, perspective-shaping capacities.* While the evangelical Christian community certainly would do well to improve its rhetorical skills in the traditional areas of argumentation and persuasion, as discussed above, it also needs to understand and appreciate the more fundamental power of language and symbols to influence human beings (as profoundly "symbol-using" beings) in more subtle and more profound ways, as discussed in chapter 2. Evangelicals need to know how even matters of truth, theology, and "common-sense" are profoundly *rhetorical* in nature, as scholars like David Cunningham point out.[54] Evangelicals also need to recognize rhetoric and communication, as media scholar Quentin Schultze has, as profoundly human—even religious—activities that can "cocreate culture" and help to "establish communities of justice and peace."[55]

Finally, and most critically, evangelicals need to *use rhetoric strategically to cultivate more nuanced perspectives on Christian faith, Christian practice, and public engagement.* A key aspect of this task, to my mind, involves careful attention to the relationship between rhetoric and representation, as discussed in chapter 6. It also involves the task of conceptualizing metaphors and representative themes that strike the proper balance between simplicity and complexity, and that enable a wide range of motivational resources of the evangelical faith tradition to be usefully drawn upon in thinking about what the faith means, how to live accordingly to it authentically, and how to act upon it in public engagement and political activism. In so doing, evangelicals should be able to make sense of their faith in a way that preserves both humility and conviction, and in a way consistent with another insightful explanation Noll has provided about evangelicalism "at its best." "Evangelicalism at its best," he explains, "is an offensive religion. It claims that human beings cannot be reconciled to God, understand the ultimate purposes of the world, or live a truly virtuous life unless they confess their sin before the living God and receive new life in Christ through the power of the Holy Spirit. Such particularity has always been offensive, and in the multicultural, postmodern world in which we live it is more offensive than ever. But when evangelicalism is at its best, that declaration of a particular salvation is its one and only offense."[56]

One useful approach to this task might involve thinking about and promoting alternate organizing metaphors to serve as what Burke called "representative anecdotes" for evangelicals and evangelical faith. Chapter 6 shows the sheer inadequacy of metaphors like "holy warrior," which, unfortunately, have been pervasive not only in the rhetoric of Operation Rescue but also in the rhetoric of the Christian Right more generally. But what about the metaphor of "stewards" to refer to evangelicals, as Levan and Schultze have suggested? What about the metaphor of "witness" to refer to evangelicals? What about the metaphor of "romantic journey" to refer to the Christian life, as suggested by evangelicals Brent Curtis and John Eldredge?[57] These metaphors strike me as definitive possibilities to pursue in the task of using symbolic resources to balance humility and complexity in the evangelical faith, as well as to provide a broader understanding of the meaning and application of the evangelical faith that is both workable and sufficiently nuanced to avoid the problems described in this book.

While I have focused a fair degree of attention in this concluding chapter on the rhetorical practices of American conservative evangelical and fundamentalist Christians, the lessons of Operation Rescue to be gleaned from the analyses of this book do not apply merely to them. The analyses of this book indicate that the problems of Operation Rescue (more specifically) and politically minded conservative evangelicals (more generally) are in large part a reflection of how they talked and continue to talk about their religious faith: in large part, to put it another way, a reflection of their rhetorical practices. By attending to and reforming their rhetorical practices, evangelicals can make great progress in living out their vision and presenting their vision to the world in more humane and edifying ways.

But these rhetorical problems are also quite germane to public discourse and political activism more generally, and they are quite germane to all those who seek to make their voices heard on public and political matters. The rhetorical problems that have afflicted Operation Rescue and evangelical Christians have also been a problem for many—if not most—other public and political advocates, as writers like Hunter and Guinness have insightfully pointed out. If all public and political advocates were to attend to the negative example of Operation Rescue and reform their rhetorical practices, then great progress could be made toward mitigating the distress of the contemporary "culture war," and great progress could be made toward what Hunter in *Before the Shooting Begins* calls "substantive democracy," in which the significant moral differences inherent in a pluralistic society could be handled in ways that both maximize the appreciation for human dignity and respect, and minimize the temptations to engage in coercion or violence. Ultimately, then, the lessons of Operation Rescue are not just for evangelical Christians. They are for all of us.

Notes

1. Cal Thomas and Ed Dobson, *Blinded by Might: Can the Religious Right Save America?* (Grand Rapids, Mich.: Zondervan, 1999), 117–18.
2. Jim Wallis, *Who Speaks for God? An Alternative to the Religious Right—A New Politics of Compassion, Community, and Civility* (New York: Delacorte Press, 1996), 23.
3. While this idea is strongly implied in *God's Name in Vain*, Carter has developed it more explicitly in his earlier book, *Civility*. See Stephen L. Carter, *God's Name in Vain: The Wrongs and Rights of Religion in Politics* (New York: Basic Books, 2000); *Civility: Manners, Morals, and the Etiquette of Democracy* (New York: Basic Books, 1998).
4. See James Risen and Judy L. Thomas, *Wrath of Angels: The American Abortion War* (New York: Basic Books, 1998), 377; Sara Diamond, *Not by Politics Alone: The Enduring Influence of the Christian Right* (New York: Guilford Press, 1998), 132.
5. Kenneth Burke, *A Grammar of Motives* (1945; reprint, Berkeley: University of California Press, 1969), 504.
6. Kenneth Burke, "Terministic Screens," in *Language as Symbolic Action: Essays on Life, Literature, and Method* (Berkeley: University of California Press, 1966), 53ff. See also the discussion in Burke, *A Grammar of Motives*, 135–37.
7. Burke, "Terministic Screens," 54.
8. Ibid.
9. Christopher Levan, *Living in the Maybe: A Steward Confronts the Spirit of Fundamentalism* (Grand Rapids, Mich.: Eerdmans, 1998), 25–26.
10. Ibid., 36.
11. Ibid., 141.
12. See Dallas A. Blanchard, *The Anti-Abortion Movement and the Rise of the Religious Right: From Polite to Fiery Protest* (New York: Twayne Publishers, 1994), 46; Eric Hoffer, *The True Believer: Thoughts on the Nature of Mass Movements* (1951; reprint, New York: Harper and Row, 1989).
13. See G. K. Chesterton, *Orthodoxy: The Romance of Faith* (1908; reprint, New York: Image Books, 1990), 20.
14. Mark A. Noll, *American Evangelical Christianity: An Introduction* (Malden, Mass.: Blackwell Publishers, 2001), 217, 223.
15. Ibid., 233.
16. Ibid., 214.
17. Richard John Neuhaus, *The Naked Public Square: Religion and Democracy in America*, 2nd ed. (Grand Rapids, Mich.: Eerdmans, 1986), 195.
18. Os Guinness, *The American Hour: A Time of Reckoning and the Once and Future Role of Faith* (New York: Free Press, 1993), 179.
19. Ibid., 171.
20. Ibid., 163, 165, 167.
21. Ibid., 177.
22. Risen and Thomas, *Wrath of Angels*, 366.
23. Robert S. Cathcart, "Movements: Confrontation as Rhetorical Form," *Southern Speech Communication Journal* 43 (1978): 233–47.
24. Robert S. Cathcart, "Defining Social Movements by Their Rhetorical Form," *Central States Speech Journal* 31 (1980): 267.

25. Charles J. Stewart, Craig Allen Smith, and Robert E. Denton, Jr., *Persuasion and Social Movements*, 4th ed. (Prospect Heights, Ill.: Waveland Press, 2001), 18.

26. Celeste Michelle Condit, *Decoding Abortion Rhetoric: Communicating Social Change* (Urbana: University of Illinois Press, 1990); Suzanne Staggenborg, *The Pro-Choice Movement: Organization and Activism in the Abortion Conflict* (New York: Oxford University Press, 1991).

27. Kenneth Burke, "Literature as Equipment for Living," in *The Philosophy of Literary Form: Studies in Symbolic Action*, 3rd ed. (Berkeley: University of California Press, 1973), 293–304.

28. J. Christopher Soper, *Evangelical Christianity in the United States and Great Britain: Religious Beliefs, Political Choices* (New York: New York University Press, 1994), 43–44.

29. Noll, *American Evangelical Christianity*, 13.

30. Thomas and Dobson, *Blinded by Might*, 59–60.

31. Christian A. Smith, *American Evangelicalism: Embattled and Thriving* (Chicago: University of Chicago Press, 1998), 150, 179ff.

32. Christian A. Smith, *Christian America? What Evangelicals Really Want* (Berkeley: University of California Press, 2000), 193, 195.

33. While I am in a sense "bracketing" here the question of whether or not the involvement of religious voices in public dialogue is positive and helpful, I acknowledge that it is a disputed question, particularly in political philosophy. For a helpful and concise representation of this debate, see Robert Audi and Nicholas Wolterstorff, *Religion in the Public Square: The Place of Religious Convictions in Political Debate* (Lanham, Md.: Roman and Littlefield Publishers, 1997). For a positive argument in this respect, see Paul J. Weithman, *Religion and the Obligations of Citizenship* (Cambridge: Cambridge University Press, 2002).

34. James Davison Hunter, *Culture Wars: The Struggle to Define America* (New York: Basic Books, 1991), 322.

35. See, for instance, Blanchard, *The Anti-Abortion Movement and the Rise of the Religious Right*.

36. See, for instance, Mark A. Noll, *The Scandal of the Evangelical Mind* (Grand Rapids, Mich.: Eerdmans, 1994); David F. Wells, *No Place for Truth: Or, Whatever Happened to Evangelical Theology?* (Grand Rapids, Mich.: Eerdmans, 1993).

37. Noll, *Scandal of the Evangelical Mind*, 27.

38. James W. Sire, *Habits of the Mind: Intellectual Life as a Christian Calling* (Downers Grove, Ill.: InterVarsity Press, 2000), 81.

39. Kenneth Burke, *Attitudes toward History*, 3rd ed. (Berkeley: University of California Press, 1984), 225.

40. Ibid., 225–26.

41. For a brief discussion of victimage, see, for instance, Burke, *The Rhetoric of Religion: Studies in Logology* (1961; reprint, Berkeley: University of California Press, 1970), 4–5.

42. Burke, *Attitudes toward History*, 171.

43. Ibid., 41.

44. Robert Wuthnow, *Christianity and Civil Society: The Contemporary Debate* (Valley Forge, Pa.: Trinity Press International, 1996), 69.

45. Ibid.

46. Ibid., 70.

47. Hunter, *Culture Wars*; see also *Before the Shooting Begins: Searching for Democracy in America's Culture War* (New York: Free Press, 1994).
48. Wuthnow, *Christianity and Civil Society*, 97.
49. Ibid., 67.
50. See Winfried Corduan, *A Tapestry of Faiths: The Common Threads between Christianity and World Religions* (Downers Grove, Ill.: InterVarsity Press, 2002).
51. Noll, *American Evangelical Christianity*, 267.
52. Ibid., 276.
53. Ibid., 277.
54. See David S. Cunningham, *Faithful Persuasion: In Aid of a Rhetoric of Christian Theology* (Notre Dame, Ind.: University of Notre Dame Press, 1991).
55. Quentin J. Schultze, *Communicating for Life: Christian Stewardship in Community and Media* (Grand Rapids, Mich.: Baker Book House, 2000), 14–15.
56. Noll, *American Evangelical Christianity*, 272.
57. Brent Curtis and John Eldredge, *The Sacred Romance: Drawing Closer to the Heart of God* (Nashville, Tenn.: Thomas Nelson Publishers, 1997).

Index

abortion history, 74–92
Aggies (Texas A&M University), 33
American Medical Association (AMA), 80–81
anti-intellectualism, 53–56, 61–65
Appleton, Joan, 187–89
Arena, John, 119
Aristotle, 27–28
assault, 27, 30, 64, 80–81, 151, 153, 158, 184
Atlanta protests. *See* protests

Baby Jane Doe, 92, 124, 136
Baby John Doe, 13, 92, 124
Baker, Ann, 147–48, 154
Barthes, Roland, 144
Benham, Flip, 8, 11 140, 208
Berger, Peter L., 29, 39
Blanchard, Dallas, 42, 97, 204
Black, Edwin, 162
Black Panthers, 195
Blamires, Harry, 53
bloodguiltiness, 99–100, 105, 166
Branham, Robert James, 43, 108
Britton, John Bayard, 112. *See also* Hill, Paul J.
Burke, Kenneth, 6, 24, 26, 29, 31–34, 36, 61, 67, 78, 88, 114–17, 145, 201, 202, 209, 213–14, 216
  identification, 32–34, 78, 123–26, 131
  perspective, 31–32, 117
  representation, 115–19
  scene, 119

Cable News Network (CNN), 8, 140, 183
Caesar, 84
calcified rigidity, 132–33
Carter, Stephen L., 2–4, 18, 172–73, 199–200, 211, 218
Cathcart, Robert S., 208
Catholics, 5, 7, 107, 123
Cicero, 28
civil disobedience, 8, 60, 61, 68, 81, 84, 105, 147, 150, 155, 181, 190, 208
civil rights movement, 5, 7, 16, 30, 146–48, 155, 181, 183, 195
clinics, abortion, 5, 7, 10–12, 119, 121, 142, 146, 148, 152–55, 158, 160, 165, 169, 180–90, 194, 208
College Hill United Methodist, 150. *See also* Gardner, George T.
Condit, Celeste M., 43, 75–79, 87, 144–45, 170, 209
conversion, 107–9
Crowley, Sharon, 32
Curtis, Brent, 217, 220
Cunningham, David, 37, 216

Darrow, Charles, 42
Darsey, James, 163, 172–77
Darwinism, 50
Daughton, Suzanne, 118
delegitimizing discourse, 145–54
Denton, Robert E. Jr., 31, 40, 208
Deuteronomy
  21:1–9   99, 103, 104
Disciples of Christ, 51, 56

222

Disney World protest, 11. *See also* protests
Dobson, Ed, 2–4, 44, 199–200, 205, 210
Dobson, James 108
Dolan, Frederick M., 173
Donahue, Phil, 141
Dumm, Thomas L., 173
Duncan, Hugh Dalziel, 195–96

Edelman, Murray, 16, 28
Eldredge, John, 217, 220
Erickson, Millard, 55
ethics, 175, 202
  Judeo-Christian, 88, 102, 129
  situational, 87
evangelicalism, 46–48
evolution, 52
Exley, Richard, 159–60, 163–65, 167–68
Ezekiel
  33   63

FACE Act. *See* Freedom of Access to Clinic Entrances Act
Falwell, Jerry, 45, 57–58, 108, 149
  See also Moral Majority
federal crime. *See* Freedom of Access to Clinic Entrances Act
Fee, Gordon D., 36, 46
feminist, 9, 35, 81
fetal
  ashes, 167
  images, 102, 170
Fetal Indication and Termination of Pregnancy (FITOP), 167. *See also* Tiller, George
fetus(es), 81, 82, 83, 94, 141, 170. *See also* fetal
feudal images, 150–51
Finkbine, Sherry, 144
Fosdick, Harry Emerson, 51
Founding Fathers, 58, 60, 65
frames
  competing, 188–89
  rejection, 61
Freedom of Access to Clinic Entrances Act, 10, 12, 17, 180–82, 184–85, 187–92, 194–95, 207

May 12, 1993, Senate hearing, 184–96
Freedom of Choice Act, 183
Friedman, Yosef, 108
fundamentalism, 3–5, 9, 11, 12, 42–45, 48–68
  and anti-intellectualism, 61–65
  and modernism 51–52
  and separatism 52–53

Gardner, George, T., 150. *See also* College Hill United Methodist
Garrison, William Lloyd, 173
Gearhart, Sally Miller, 35
generative function of rhetoric, 26, 28–29, 31, 37, 78, 115, 141, 143, 145
Gideon Project, 43
Gilchrist, Jane, 150
Ginsburg, Faye, 5, 43
Glessner, Thomas A., 78–80, 82
Goldhagen, Daniel Jonah, 64
Gospel(s), 106–7, 125
Graham, Billy, 47, 52
Great Awakening, 46–48
Green, Keith, 108, 111
Green, Melody, 108
Gregg, Senator, 30, 39, 193
Griffin, Michael, 20, 115, 128, 130. *See also* Gunn, David
Guinness, Os, 2, 4, 18, 44, 199, 205–6, 211, 217
Gunn, David, 20, 115, 128, 130–31, 140, 154, 180, 182–83, 185–86, 200. *See also* Griffin, Michael
Guyton, Van, 105

Harding, Susan Friend, 176
Harkin, Sen. Tom, 184–85
Harley, Gloria, 123
Hart, Roderick, 4
Hatch, Nathan O., 55–56, 58
Hatch, Orrin, 184, 190
Hebraism, 161
Hebrew scripture, 173
Hebrews, 168, 170
hegemony, 14, 44–45, 53, 56–59, 61, 65, 67–68, 118, 201

history. *See* abortion, history
Hill, Paul J., 112, 128–33, 180. *See also* Britton, John Bayard
Hoffer, Eric, 148, 203
holy war, 116, 120, 121, 123, 126, 128–30, 201
Hunter, James Davison 13, 16, 38, 46, 113, 143, 160–62, 172, 174–76, 200, 211, 214, 217

Identification. *See* Burke
invitation/temptation, 34–35
Isaiah
    1:12–15   99, 103
    1:16–17   100, 104
Israel, 50, 63, 86, 103–4
    "new" myth, 57–58, 88
    See also Judah
Israelites, 103, 129. *See also* Jews
Ivie, Robert L., 117–18

James
    1:27   84
Jarman, Peggy, 153
jeremiad, 102, 111
Jewish, 79, 107
Jews, 8, 87, 89–90, 107, 130, 175
Judah, 100, 103–4
judgment, God's, 75, 87, 103

Kassebaum, Sen. Nancy, 184, 190, 192
Keen, Sam, 145
Kelly, Judge Patrick, 9–10, 153, 158
King, Andrew, 24
King, Martin Luther, Jr., 7, 30, 146–47, 155, 190
2 Kings
    24:2–4   100
Knight, Bob, 150–51
Koop, C. Everett, 42, 59
Kopp, James, 128
Kuhn, Thomas, 29
Ku Klux Klan, 149–50

law, 65. *See also* Freedom of Access to Clinic Entrances Act

Divine, 85
Higher, 88, 102
Mosaic, 103
Lee, Jesse, 109
Levan, Christopher, 204, 217
Levin, Yehuda, 108
Leviticus
    20:1–5   84
Lewis, Curtis Lee, 51. *See also* fundamentalism
Little, Daniel J., 105
Lowery, Joseph, 147
Luckmann, Thomas, 29, 39
Luke
    9:23   125, 137
Luker, Kristin, 75–76, 81–83

Machen, J. Gresham, 51
Mahoney, Patrick J., 153, 159, 168, 170–71
Malcolm X, 30
Mark
    8:34   125, 137
Marsden, George M., 13, 48–52, 58
Matheny, Marilyn, 121, 125
Matthew
    5:13   111
    25:31–46   125, 137
    10:38   125, 137
    16:24   125, 137
McCloskey, Donald N., 77
McFarland, Steven T., 180–81
McMillan, Beverly, 105
medical, 80, 82, 140, 147, 149, 151, 184–85
Merritt, W. Davis (Buzz), 153–54
metaphor, 29, 79, 117–18, 123, 127, 145, 170, 201, 213, 216–17
Michelman, Kate, 147–48, 152, 185
Moral Majority, 45, 57, 67. *See also* Falwell, Jerry
Morella, Rep. Constance, 183
Mugavero, Tony, 107

National Organization for Women (NOW), 11, 152, 153
Nazi(s), 8, 25, 87, 89–90, 91, 131

Neuhaus, Richard John, 2, 4, 18–19, 52, 199–200, 205, 211
Newson, Debra, 125–26
Nikas, Nikolas T., 187–88
Noll, Mark A., 48–49, 53–55, 58–59, 173, 205, 211, 213, 216–17
Noonan, John. T., 79

O'Keefe, John, 7
Operation Rescue National, 10
Operation Rescue West, 12
Orwell, George, 74, 92

Patterson, George, 180
Paul, St., 106
Pell, Senator Claiborne deBorda, 184–85
Perelman, Chaim, 28, 32
1 Peter
   1:17   199
Philippians
   1   106
Phillips, Wendell, 173
Plato, 25, 27
Pliny, 81
poverty, 39, 117
   rhetorical, 161
pregnancy, 81, 82, 90, 125, 149, 151, 184, 191
premillenial dispensationalism, 49–50
Protests
   Disney World, 11
   Falls Church, Virginia, 187
   Minneapolis–St. Paul, 127
   Siege of Atlanta, 8, 9, 74, 141, 143, 146, 154, 182
   Summer of Love, 86, 95, 159, 160, 163
   Summer of Mercy, 7, 9–12, 99, 141–143, 146–47, 151, 153–54. *See also* Wichita, Kansas
Proverbs
   24:11   96
Psalm
   82:3–4   84
   106   102
public vocabulary, 143–45

Quindlen, Anna, 148, 153
Quintilian, 28

Racketeer Influenced and Corrupt Organizations (RICO) law, 10, 12, 181
radical, 56, 127, 159–61, 163, 172–74, 177–78, 185, 188, 209
reductionism, 131–32
Reno, Janet, 184–85, 191–93
repentance, 99, 123, 126, 174
rhetoric
   Darseyan Radical. *See* Darsey, James
   definition of, 31–36
   as evangelism, 24–38
   imposes, 35
   of militarization, 118
   of pro-choice movement, 16, 24
rhetorical theory, 14, 26–28, 35
Risen, James, 5, 127, 137
rights. *See* civil rights movement
Robertson, Pat, 57–58
Rodriguez, Pablo, 186–87
Roe v. Wade, 14, 75–76, 78–79, 83–86, 88, 96, 101, 144, 164, 167

Sandeen Ernest R., 49
Satan, 16, 87, 165–66
Satanic, 87, 121
Scheffer, Francis A., 14, 42, 45, 59–68, 77
Scopes Trial, 51–52
Secular, 39, 47, 53, 55,
   Humanism, 59–62, 175
separatism, 52–53
Shaneyfelt, Myrna J., 120
Siege of Atlanta, 8–9, 74, 141, 143, 146, 154, 182. *See also* protest
Sire, James, 212
Smeal, Eleanor, 140, 183
Smith, Christian, 210
Sobel, Carol, 149
Soper, J. Christopher, 46–47, 69, 97, 109, 210
Sophists, 25–27
Staggenborg, Suzanne, 208
Stanley, Charles, 9–10
Stuart, Douglas, 36

Summer of Love, 86, 95, 159, 160, 163. *See also* protest
Summer of Mercy campaign, 7, 9–12, 99, 141–43, 146–47, 151, 153–54. *See also* Wichita, Kansas
Federal response to, 9–10, 153, 158
Supreme Court, 10, 12, 75–76, 84–85, 147, 181, 183, 194. *See also* Roe V. Wade

Taber, Brenda, 119–21
Ten Boom, Corrie, 8, 89–90
terrorism, 154–55, 183, 185, 196
terroristic, 149, 153–54, 183, 185
Terry, Randall, 5–9, 11, 14, 24, 39, 45, 68, 74, 77, 84–85, 87–92, 96, 98–100, 102, 105–7, 111, 122, 141, 147–48, 150–51, 156–57, 169
Thomas, Cal, 2–4, 44, 199–200, 205, 210
Tiller, George, 20, 140, 153, 163–64, 167
See also Fetal Indication and Termination of Pregnancy (FITOP)
Todd, Jesse E., Jr., 151

Tomczak, Larry, 109
Toulmin, Stephen, 28
Trocmé, André, 8
Tucci, Keith, 11, 106

Vaughn, Bishop Austin, 107

Wacker, Grant, 45, 51
Wallis, Jim, 199, 200
Weber, Timothy P., 42, 50, 101
Wells, David F., 54, 61, 91, 107,
Weslin, Norman, 165–66
White, Hayden, 77
Wichita, Kansas, 148, 150–51, 164. *See also* George Tiller
abortion clinics, 142, 152, 153, 158
Summer of Mercy campaign, 7, 9–12, 99, 141–43, 146–47, 151, 154.
Summer of Love campaign, 95, 159, 163
Wichitans, 159
World War I, 202
World War II. *See* Nazi(s)
Wuthnow, Robert, 214